Fanatic

Why We Love the Things We Love

Joe Ungemah

OXFORD
UNIVERSITY PRESS

OXFORD
UNIVERSITY PRESS

Oxford University Press is a department of the University of Oxford.
It furthers the University's objective of excellence in research, scholarship,
and education by publishing worldwide. Oxford is a registered trade mark of
Oxford University Press in the UK and in certain other countries.

Published in the United States of America by Oxford University Press
198 Madison Avenue, New York, NY 10016, United States of America.

Library of Congress Cataloging-in-Publication Data
Names: Ungemah, Joe, 1976– author.
Title: Fanatic : why we love the things we love / Joe Ungemah.
Description: New York, NY : Oxford University Press, [2024] |
Includes bibliographical references and index.
Identifiers: LCCN 2024023091 (print) | LCCN 2024023092 (ebook) |
ISBN 9780197783863 (hardback) | ISBN 9780197783887 (epub)
Subjects: LCSH: Fanaticism.
Classification: LCC BF575.F16 U54 2024 (print) | LCC BF575.F16 (ebook) |
DDC 152.4—dc23/eng/20240624
LC record available at https://lccn.loc.gov/2024023091
LC ebook record available at https://lccn.loc.gov/2024023092

DOI: 10.1093/9780197783894.001.0001

Printed by Sheridan Books, Inc., United States of America

Contents

Acknowledgments

This book could not have been written without the support of all the amazing individuals I interviewed and profiled. I learned so much from my fellow psychologists and was inspired by the work they do every day to improve the lives of others. I am grateful to Justine Mastin, Anastasia Press, Jordan Kocon, Stacy Remke, Richard Fryer, Zachary Hansen, Suzanne Chabaud, Renea Reinardy, Mark Aoyagi, and Helen Williams for their time and energy to ensure I got the psychology right. I am also highly indebted to Marj, Kris, Carly, Michael, Ben, Felix, Dave, Scott, Barbara, Kate, Mark, and Chris, who shared their stories openly and helped bring what "fanatic" means to life. These stories were complemented by the expertise of Amir Berenjian, Chuck Olsen, Thong Nguyen, and Helen Dorey, who helped show the potential for fanaticism to shape culture and society. A note of gratitude goes out to Elton Hassel, Marie Ungemah, Keri Ungemah, Sarita Kundrod, and Jeff Lin, for connecting me to both fanatics and experts, as well as Dominic Iannazzo and Julia Floberg, for assisting me in gaining some real-world fanatic experience. Lastly, I thank Dana Bliss, Abby Gross, Kenzi Judge, Lorelei Whitney, and Gail Lyman, for reviewing various chapters and helping me make this book better.

Acknowledgments

Introduction

What Is a Fanatic?

Did you hear about the Californian man who went to Disneyland every day consecutively for 2,995 days? Apparently, his favorite ride was the Matterhorn Bobsleds and he ate regularly at the Pizza Port in Tomorrowland.[1] Speaking about food, did you hear about the guy from Wisconsin who has been eating at least one Big Mac per day for the last 50 years? With over 32,000 burgers consumed, he only missed 8 days of scarfing down his favorite handheld meal.[2] That is not nearly as impressive as the woman from Australia who can simultaneously rotate 200 hula hoops[3] or the Mexican mountain climber who just claimed the fastest ascent for the top three mountains with supplementary oxygen, climbing Mt. Everest, K2, and Kangchenjunga in just under two years.[4] And so it goes with the *Guinness Book of World Records*, which is masterful at chronicling the human experience from the amazing to the outlandish. Behind each record is an individual who found fascination doing something new, often to the point of exhaustion, and gained notoriety along the way.

Being a fanatic seldom results in a world record, and I would argue that we are all fanatic about something. From the food we eat to the media we consume or the hobbies we enjoy, there is plenty of fascination to go around. This book is dedicated to exploring the why behind fanaticism, taking a hard look at the social, physical, cognitive, and emotive drivers that pull us closer to a particular product, experience, or social cause. Definitions of who gets called a "fanatic" consistently point to a high degree of interest, obsession, or passion toward a given topic, but diverge in the connotation applied to this label. Some definitions point to fanatics as having excessive devotion or extreme views

---

[1] Disneyland's Record-Breaking Regular Shares His Wisdom from Nearly 3,000 Park Visits in a Row by A.J. Willingham, CNN, April 10, 2023.

[2] Wisconsin Man Celebrates Scarfing Down Big Macs Almost Every Day for 50 Years by Antonio Planas, NBC, May 20, 2022.

[3] Marawa the Amazing: How One Woman with 200 Hula Hoops Became a Teen Girl Guru by Jane Howard, Guardian, February 21, 2019.

[4] Mountaineer Viridiana Alvarez Chavez of Mexico Snags Guinness World Records Title by Stacey Lastoe, CNN, August 25, 2020.

Fanatic. Joe Ungemah, Oxford University Press. © Oxford University Press 2024. DOI: 10.1093/9780197783894.003.0001

about topics like religion or politics.[5] I prefer a more balanced view, closer to that offered by the second definition from the *Collins Dictionary*, which emphasizes a person's enthusiasm toward activities or ways of life without the judgment.[6] Throughout this book, we will meet fanatics who take interest in a wide range of pursuits, from devotion to science fiction to doing good in the community, engaging in extreme sports, seeking thrills, and collecting bottles. Common across all the people profiled is the notion that fanaticism brings us a great deal of psychological wellness and joy, as well as acts as a core foundation for our own self-concepts.

From an outside perspective, some of these pursuits might seem rather strange, which is captured by the *Cambridge Dictionary*'s definition, wherein others are likely to judge a fanatic's behavior as unreasonable.[7] This definition, too, is problematic, as people sharing the same fanaticism understand what drives them toward their topic and therefore, judgment about what is reasonable seems to be more of an in-group, out-group issue. Moreover, living in a world without variation in passions would be simply bland, more akin to the dystopian worlds of George Orwell's *Nineteen Eighty-Four* or the movie *Brazil*, places that I prefer not to visit. Fanaticism provides an opportunity for individuals to go deep on a topic, which can enrich our culture and potentially lead to the creation of new things. At the very least, fanaticism provides an opportunity for conversation that allows us to have more meaningful relationships. Just inquiring about another person's passion opens a world that is more personal, as these topics are core to self-concept and often shared with close friends. One of the key aims of this book is to find out what others are fanatic about and to observe what this knowledge does to the quality of relationships. Knowing that some these passions can be hard to relate to, an extra dose of curiosity might be needed, and the ability to keep personal judgment at bay.

This is not to say that fanaticism is universally beneficial. Just like any other personal characteristic, going too deep on a topic may result in maladaptive behavior and negative consequences to healthy living. Knowing the difference between collecting and hoarding, or between commitment and addiction, hinges on a deeper understanding of the traits and motivations of fanatics. Using psychology as a guide, this book unpacks the underpinnings of a range

---

[5] Merriam-Webster. Fanatic definition. https://www.merriam-webster.com/dictionary/fanatic (accessed April 19, 2023).

[6] Collins Dictionary. Fanatic definition. https://www.collinsdictionary.com/us/dictionary/english/fanatic (accessed April 19, 2023).

[7] Cambridge Dictionary. Fanatic definition. https://dictionary.cambridge.org/dictionary/english/fanatic (accessed April 19 2023).

of fanaticisms, discovering that many of the motivations are held in common by fanatics despite very different outlets. Psychological concepts like identity, camaraderie, nostalgia, mastery, and flow appear multiple times and, therefore, provide a basic rubric for how potential areas of fanaticism capture and retain our attention. Moreover, for any given type of fanaticism, a complex and interacting web forms around the topic, which can even tap other forms of fanaticism. The more complex the web and intersectionality, the greater the stickiness of that particular pursuit.

Through the stories captured in this book, I have learned that the mechanics of fanaticism are not straightforward. For example, the motivations for pursuing a passion can be based on either embellishing a positive or alleviating a negative. For the latter, we will meet fanatics and practitioners who were drawn to their area of fanaticism out of a desire for preventing others from experiencing the type of trauma or anxiety that they personally endured. These types of fanatics did not initially choose what they wanted to do, but found their passion as a means to gain personal meaning and grow. In stark contrast, other types of fanatics in this book are not looking to the past for their inspiration, but are focused intently on the future, driven to innovate or introduce the masses to technology that they hope will make for a better world. Yet most surprising to me were the fanatics drawn to their specific topics for tangential or indirect reasons. I discovered that a specific interest in art or food may have nothing to do with its consumption, but rather in its creation or offering. Knowing that someone is a chocoholic doesn't mean very much, as the fanaticism might be rooted in the craft of making desserts, judging products and writing reviews, traveling to remote growers, or countless other derivatives. Only a conversation with the fanatic can unpack the meaning behind their behavior.

The stories captured in this book are as specific as the types of fanaticism demonstrated. Each person had a moment in time when the stars aligned, whether moving to a new city, meeting the love of their life, or having some extra office space to fill, that created the opportunity for a fanaticism to surface. That specific pursuit fulfilled a combination of motivations for the fanatic, whether social, physical, cognitive, or emotive in origin. These four categories appear multiple times in this book and are not chosen at random, but are established by applied psychology to help understand the factors for why someone moves toward or away from a specific pursuit,[8] which in turn

---

[8] Edgerton, N., and Palmer, S. (2005). SPACE: A psychological model for use within cognitive behavioural coaching, therapy and stress management. Coaching Psychologist, 2, 25–31.

can help shape behavior.[9] In addition to these drivers, the stickiness of a fanaticism appears to be influenced by a handful of personality traits. Individuals who are open to and seek out new experiences appear to gravitate toward fanaticism, while traits like decisiveness and resilience help to keep them there. At times, the gravity of the fanaticism can be too much and jeopardize living a healthy life. To better understand when that line has been crossed, I interviewed a range of applied psychologists who, despite working in divergent fields, work similarly with clients to raise awareness of problematic behavior, explore its root causes, and set in motion new ways of living.

In writing this book, I discovered a second group of practitioners who do not focus on the problematic versions of fanaticism, but instead use it as a means to build relationships with their clients, create safe spaces to unpack difficult personal challenges, and try out something new. There is so much to learn from these practitioners, specifically in their openness to explore another person's fanaticism with genuine interest and empathy. Taking their lead, I sought out a personal experience broadly aligned with each type of fanaticism captured in this book. From volunteering as an ultramarathon pacer to digging up old privies in the hope of finding an antique bottle, I gained an appreciation for a broad range of interests. Along the way, I was able to connect with my interviewees on a much deeper level, even if very few of these fascinations will ever be sticky enough to be repeated.

If you are a fellow practitioner in applied psychology, I hope this book provides additional perspective for how to unpack human behavior and help you discover why individuals are willing to move toward a particular area of fascination, whether it is a product, experience, or social cause. It might also mitigate the negative connotations that often accompany fanaticism, by demonstrating how it acts as both a source of happiness and a central feature of personal identity. Instead, if you happen to be an academic, researcher, or student of psychology or related discipline, I hope the discussion sparks a research topic or two, as there is much yet to discover about fanaticism, from expanding on the motivations unearthed in this book to unpacking the countless ways it is exhibited in everyday life. Understanding the intersectionality between fanaticisms and the line between positive and negative versions of it have the potential to elevate what applied psychologists can do. Lastly, for those readers who are just fanatical about psychology, I hope the stories in this book broaden your outlook and appreciation of the human condition. To this end, I have come to realize that the fanatics out there are the ones who make the world a brighter place, which of course includes all of us.

---

[9] Weiss, R., Edgerton, N., and Palmer, S. (2017). The SPACE coaching model: An integrative tool for coach therapists. Coaching Today, October, 12–17.

PART 1
THE SOCIAL

1
Galactic Connections

Walking through a city on game day, it is easy to spot the fanatics all around us. There they are dressed up in their team's colors, in jerseys with the numbers of their favorite players on the back or wrapped in striped scarves representing the local club. On game day, it is perfectly acceptable to wear a block of cheese on your head in support of the Packers or to carry a Vuvuzela in preparation of making as much noise as possible during a penalty kick. Some fans go farther, wearing very little beyond body paint, even if it is the middle of winter. Against all the different types of fanaticism out there, sports reign supreme, with Gallup estimating that over 60% of the American population characterize themselves as sports fans, a number that has been holding steady since 2000.[1] Although regional variation exists for exactly what sport we are talking about when answering that question, globally most people are obsessed with football (the type played with your feet). Nielsen estimates that a staggering 40% or more of the world adult population takes an interest in football, with the UAE topping the list, with 80% of the population either interested or very interested in the sport.[2]

Sports are not alone in creating a high level of buzz in popular culture, with a handful of music groups and movie franchises achieving similar levels of notoriety. In 2022, the rock band Queen achieved a milestone by selling seven million copies of their *Greatest Hits* album in the United Kingdom, which equates to one in four households rocking out to "We Are the Champions." Looking instead at Hollywood, a poll conducted in 2019 by *Hollywood Reporter* and *Morning Consult* found that 63% of Americans considered themselves fans of the Marvel universe, with the Star Wars epic coming in a close second at 60%.[3] Particularly revealing about this poll is that popular appeal does not necessarily translate to deeper levels of fanaticism. Although the Marvel films are based on the comics, only 37% of the respondents enjoyed the printed version, while 13% admitted to having dressed up as one of the characters. As a potential way of getting more involved in their fandom,

---

[1] As Industry Grows, Percentage of US Sports Fans Steady by Jeffrey Jones, Gallup, June 17, 2015.
[2] Fan Favorite: The Global Popularity of Football Is Rising, Nielsen, June 2018.
[3] Among Fandoms, Marvel May Reign Supreme, Poll Finds, Hollywood Reporter, July 17, 2019.

Fanatic. Joe Ungemah, Oxford University Press. © Oxford University Press 2024. DOI: 10.1093/9780197783894.003.0002

Comic-Con is an annual convention that pays homage to the greatest comics, science fiction, and fantasy sagas ever imagined, but had only reached 21% of respondents' awareness of its existence. Even if they were aware, general interest in attending a convention like Comic-Con was low at 32%. This difference in involvement, from enjoying *Avengers: Endgame* to dressing up as Loki or from watching the FIFA World Cup at home to traveling to see a match in Qatar, is driven as much by social connection as by a compelling narrative or rivalry. Yet there is more to the social benefits resulting from a fanaticism based on film or music, as compared to the more stereotypical sports fanaticism, that are worth exploring and will be discussed soon.

My personal experience with fandom and conventions runs deep. I attended my first convention as an 11-year-old, feeling that I was instantly teleported into parallel social universe. I remember distinctly being dropped off in the wood-paneled station wagon that was the pride and joy of my parents and loathed by everyone else in the family. We entered the Regency Hotel through its prominent gold covered, geometric entry built in homage to 1970s modernism. My brother and I made our way with trepidation to the registration table, grabbed a program, and poured over the StarCon conference events. The choices ran the gauntlet of the cult classics, from *Battlestar Galactica* (the one featuring gold necklaces and capes) to the *Man from U.N.C.L.E.* Only in this universe did 1960s spy chic exist on equal footing to spandex wearing science fiction. Being a primarily Star Trek convention, it didn't take us long to spot a few Vulcans, Klingons, and Andorians as we meandered our way down to the exhibit hall. After perusing endless tables of Trek memorabilia, I was pleased with my purchase of a gray tribble (straight out of "The Trouble with Tribbles") that came complete with an internal squeaker. I vowed that at the next conference, I would save up for a replica phaser, communicator, or tricorder.

My memory isn't great on what else we did that day, beyond attending a preview of a hotly awaited franchise reboot. *Star Trek: The Next Generation* was due to air later that year in September and promised to put the Star Trek franchise firmly back on the map of terrestrial TV. The fans were anxious to see what the new show had to offer, and a lot was at risk for their fandom. The show that they had lovingly followed for decades after its cancelation in 1969 was to receive a massive makeover, with a brand new crew and a phenomenal budget of over $1 million per episode. When the trailer started, the Trekkies went mental, especially over the way the *Enterprise* would jump to warp speed. The show itself didn't disappoint. Two years later, I found myself at the same convention, but this time, the crowd overwhelmingly welcomed the cast of the *Next Generation* and Star Trek fandom got a new lease on life. For my part, I scored one of those replica communicators I was enamored with.

What is it about a show like *Star Trek* that creates its own ecosystem of fandom? To find out, I attended three days of immersive science fiction and anime at GalaxyCon. Upon entering the exhibit hall, I found myself on familiar ground. Still there were the fans dressed as their favorite characters, from the three Commander Rikers in line to get an autograph with Jonathon Frakes (one even carrying a trombone) to the Groots and Gamoras there to meet actors from *Guardians of the Galaxy*. On sale was the regular assortment of novelty t-shirts, comics, memorabilia, and replica props, with a notable shift from mass-produced items to hand-crafted art. Autograph tables made up the other side of the hall, with autograph prices ranging from $20 for lesser-known animators to $100 for William Shatner's signature (cash only please, no credit cards). For an extra fee, fans could purchase VIP passes, with expedited autograph line, or private photo ops with the stars. Packages for multiple characters could cost over $200, yet the obvious commercialization of the experience was overshadowed by the visible enjoyment of the fans meeting their heroes.

What has changed since my last convention was the breadth and range of fandom on display. Comics and anime had a huge presence at GalaxyCon, in some ways overtaking superheroes, science fiction, and the cult classics. Nowadays, it is somehow possible to have George Tikae headline alongside John Cusack, who is better known for his off-beat comedies, and Demolition Ax & Smash from the WWF. What held the event in common was its dedication to the world of fandom, with its motto "Everyone's Welcome! Everyone's a fan of something, and that unites us all!" They implore guests to "meet celebrity and creative guests from comics, movies, TV, science fiction, fantasy, anime, cartoons, video, games, wrestling and more!" and to partake in "video gaming tournaments, costume contests, comedy shows, late night karaoke, burlesque, dance parties, and workshops of all kinds."[4]

A noticeable shift from my StarCon days was the appreciation and admiration conference goers had for each other. Cosplay has become more important than ever and appears to be a primary draw alongside the headlining acts. Every few minutes, I heard audible cheers of guests running into a character from their specific preferred fandom. As GalaxyCon explains, "Lots of people dress up as their favorite characters, and people come from all over to see and be seen . . . Cosplayers often get treated like stars by other attendees due to the amount of workmanship that goes into these costumes." GalaxyCon is first to

[4] GalaxyCon Minneapolis Program, November 8, 2019.

admit that you don't need to wear a costume to prove that you are a devoted fan. A tattoo, car decal, or t-shirt is all that is needed to signal fandom.

For Marj, it is a com badge that she has dutifully worn on her coat for decades. Marj was a Trekkie from the beginning, even before the term "Trekkie" was even used. Not owning a TV herself, she visited her neighbors to catch the live broadcast of the original *Star Trek* series, first aired in 1966. She was smitten by the vision painted by creator Gene Roddenberry; a crew of explorers who lived life with compassion and humor. For her, the characters demonstrated the potential of the human spirit and a future not bogged down by the cultural strife that existed in the late 1960s and early 1970s. In the show, people were treated with respect and dignity, together sharing in adventure and exploration. When I spoke with Marj, she reflected on the fact that *Star Trek* was able to tackle social issues that were difficult to discuss in any other format and often did so with humor. Marj connected with how realistically the characters were portrayed, with their full set of desires, strengths, and faults, unlike other television shows of the time.

After three seasons, *Star Trek* was canceled, but its imprint on society and Marj was still in its infancy. Marj kept her fanship going by collecting Star Trek magazines (which she still has in all their original brown wrappers), reading hundreds of books set in the Trek universe, and rewatching those original 79 episodes dozens of times. Working as an operating room (OR) nurse, Marj increasingly turned to *Star Trek* for escapism and a moment of calm during her day. The connection to *Star Trek* reached a new height when an accident left her son severely disabled; the series became a bridge between them, where each could take part and enjoy in the same activity. Marj read the books to her son and later brought him to conventions and the cinema to see the *Trek* movies. She made the movies an event, inviting friends along with her son and printing t-shirts for the entire group. Her favorite was a picture of Kirk on it with the caption "Inter-galactic Stud" printed beneath.

The t-shirt caption says it all; Marj felt most connected to the Captain of the *Enterprise*, James Tiberius Kirk, played by William Shatner. When I asked why Kirk, Marj responded, "How could it be anyone else? He was a wonderful character, handsome, and with good morals. And he was the Captain!" Marj had the opportunity to meet William Shatner at her third science fiction convention, this one held in Seattle. During his talk as a headliner, Shatner quipped about the apples in Pike Market, which set the stage for Marj's encounter. Marj worked months painting a portrait of Captain Kirk, holding an apple, and had made a print to give to Shatner that day. Instead of the normal quick 2 minutes reserved for fans at the autograph table, Shatner pulled Marj aside to thank her for the print and engaged her in a rather lengthy conversation. She came to realize that there was a lot in common between the character of James T. Kirk and William Shatner. Marj described him as a truly "interesting and kind man." That interaction forever changed her fanship with Star Trek. Marj was not only a fan of Kirk but also of Shatner, and these were two separate things.

Working as an OR nurse, Marj dutifully wore a Star Trek com badge on her garb throughout her career. Many of the patients recognized the insignia and broke into conversation about the show, momentarily taking their mind off of their physical injuries. Even for those who were in the dark about what it was, the badge provided an opportunity for Marj to share a bit about herself with her patients. After retirement, Marj continued the practice of wearing the com badge, just to remind people that Trekkies are "still out there." Not everyone in Marj's social circle shared in her fanship, yet they all appreciated that Star Trek was a core part of who she was and who she is today. Marj has seen all the reboots and is excited about news of a future TV series. To her, the reboots have brought the excitement of *Trek* to a whole new audience, without losing the positivity and humor of the original series. *Trek* is so much more than a show for Marj, it is the promise of a positive future, full of possibilities for what humanity can accomplish. In Marj's words, "It makes my heart happy. It is the hope for humanity and the future that we all want."

Although Marj has relationships to other Trekkies, her connection to Star Trek is best described as fanship, a term I used specifically when telling her story. Acting as a core component of fan identify, fanship is defined as the person's psychological connection to the topic of their interest, which in Marj's case is Star Trek. People enjoying fanship gain personal well-being from feeling part of a distinct and positive group. In contrast, the other component of fan identify is fandom, which is a person's psychological connection to others who share in their interests. Although related, fandom is a separate construct than fanship and leads to some very different behaviors.[5] For example, fans reacted very differently to Michael Jackson's death depending on whether they were connected primarily through fanship or fandom. Fanship resulted in fans seeking out his music and a quest to learn more about his life, while fandom was expressed by fans turning to each other to collectively mourn their loss.

When a person becomes a fan, irrespective of whether their identify is driven more by fanship or fandom, they can become immersed in a culture that includes a range of artifacts. Fans regularly take on fan speak (new

---

[5] Ray, A., et al. (2017). Psychological needs predict fanship and fandom in anime fans. Phoenix Papers, 3, 56–68.

language), alter their dress code (costuming), partake in fan fiction or filking (music), consume fanzines, and attend organized events. In the sporting world, wearing your team's jersey, trading player statistics, and singing the team's fight song all tick the boxes of a subculture, as does playing fantasy football and tailgating. Although looking and feeling very different, science fiction might rival sports in its depth and breadth of cultural artifacts, which play a part across a range of fanaticisms. The seeds for science fiction fanaticism were sown in the 1920s, when Hugo Gernsback launched the *Amazing Stories* magazine in 1926. Without a mechanism for fans to connect with each other, the editor suggested that readers provide their names and addresses when contributing to the discussions column. Connections between science fiction fans blossomed, followed by the emergence of fanzines, like Raymond A. Palmer's *Comet* fanzine first published in 1930, and opportunities to attend conventions, like the 1936 meeting of the Futurians in Philadelphia.

Star Trek is a special case of science fiction fan culture, as the depth of its followership has transcended decades and generations like no other franchise (although Star Wars is arguably getting close). It is hard to imagine how fragile its foundation was, as a fierce letter-writing campaign by fans kept the show from being canceled after its first series. Although it did get renewed for two additional seasons, the popularity of the show didn't really take off until syndication. With an expanding fan base, Star Trek conventions first popped up in 1972, adding a mechanism for the consumption of fanzines, manuals, and novels dedicated to the Star Trek universe. In its first 25 years, over $500 million of merchandise was sold and over four million Star Trek novels were purchased in 1991 alone. With major motion pictures released throughout the 1980s, followed by *The Next Generation* and other TV franchises in the 1990s, Star Trek became a juggernaut that shows no signs of slowing down. But more than that, it is a cultural movement that scholars have compared to a form of living religion.[6] Through its utopian view of the future, faith is placed in humans and science to unite the universe and solve its great mysteries. *Star Trek* is about the potential of the human spirit. In the words of a fan first seeing the series in 1966, "We noticed people of various races, genders and planetary origins working together. Here was a future it did not hurt to imagine."

It is easy to see why Marj felt compelled to engage in *Star Trek* and use it as both an escape and ideal to aspire toward. The specific path that Marj took in her fanship is actually the norm, where a fan is first attracted to a show, then begins building connections with a specific character and sometimes, with the actor or actress. During GalaxyCon, I attended a panel titled "This Year

---

[6] Jindra, M. (1994). Star Trek fandom as a religious phenomenon. Sociology of Religion, 55, 27–51.

in Feelings" to learn more about the personal connections that fans have with their favorite characters. Justine Mastin was on the panel and provided an inside look at the connection between fanship and emotional wellness. Justine's profile describes her as a "Narrative Therapist, Yoga Teacher, Podcaster, Author and Superhero."[7] Her practice, Blue Box Counseling, is a calling card to potential clients interested in science fiction, through its subtle reference to the Tardis from *Doctor Who*.

In many respects, the relationship fans have with the target of their fanship is like any other relationship. Even though they are fictional characteristics, the feelings of kinship and empathy are real, it's just that the characters cannot reciprocate. In Justine's words, "Black Widow can't love you back." As viewers, we know a lot about the back stories of characters, to a depth that is often unparalleled in reality, and that makes connection to these characters easy and natural.

Justine uses the common language of science fiction fanship to make connections with her clients in her counseling practice. Establishing trust between client and therapist is a prerequisite for clients feeling free to open up and share their deepest concerns and desires. Knowing that they share a common fanship with Justine allows an instant conversation point and a universe of characters and stories to anchor a conversation about the real word. Justine refers to her practice as "therapeutic fanfiction" and uses well proven techniques in narrative therapy to externalize the problems a client is having and to explore what is happening on a deeper and objective level. She also uses play techniques, encouraging patients to consider "what if" scenarios in a fictional universe, to highlight implications of such actions in the real world. It is a take on fan fiction, just applied to a more practical endpoint beyond pure entertainment.

One of Justine's favorite universes for therapy is Lord of the Rings, as it is loaded with characters, struggles, and connections. Using the trilogy as the backdrop in a therapy session, she might ask what Frodo would do when faced with temptation, what burden the client is carrying that is similar to the ring, or who is the Samwise Gamgee that could be on hand to help and support. Justine describes fanship as a type of spirituality, where fans are able to make sense of their lives and use the stories to get through a rough patch. They will often attach themselves to a character that resonates with them on a deeper level, because of a similarity in personality (like how confident or outgoing they are), make-up (including characteristics like gender, sexual orientation, or age), back story (such as a split family), current struggles, or a

---

[7] GalaxyCon Minneapolis Program, November 8, 2019.

combination of them all. As a therapist, understanding why a specific character is preferred can unearth a lot about what is happening for a specific client and can draw attention to who is the client's core self (that part of us that guides decision-making).

This process of attachment and the basis for narrative therapy relies on "parasocial relations," where fans find themselves drawn to a particular character, which often morphs into a broader interest in the actor and other roles that they might have portrayed. At times, a conflict emerges between the character portrayed on film and the actor or actress in real life, which on first blush would appear to put therapy at risk. It is unusual for actors or actresses to be fans of a franchise before becoming part of it. As a notable exception, Whoopi Goldberg is known to have been a fan of the original *Star Trek* series when she asked Gene Roddenberry to create a character for her on the *Next Generation*. The show's creators responded favorably and built her a bar (Ten-Forward) and with it, the character Guinan was born.[8]

More typically, actors and actresses consider it just a job and sit at conventions rather bemused at just how much energy and excitement is directed toward them. The discord between job and fanship is best illustrated by a sketch by William Shatner on *Saturday Night Live* (*SNL*) aired on December 20, 1986, when he pleaded with fans at a convention, "Having received all your letters over the years, and I've spoken to many of you, and some of you have traveled . . . y'know . . . hundreds of miles to be here, I'd just like to say . . . get a life, will you, people?! I mean, for crying out loud, it's just a TV show!" Rather than being put off by the sketch, Marj recognizes that being at the center of a deep fanship can put pressure on actors and actresses that goes beyond typical appreciation. She prefers to think of Shatner as having had a particularly bad day when he was on *SNL* and feels that the sketch does not reflect who he is. She loves him anyways.

As can be imagined, therapeutic fanfiction requires a lot of extracurricular activity in knowing a range of science fiction universes. The good news is that Justine is a self-described nerd and has a particular interest Buffy, Twin Peaks, Harry Potter, Lord of the Rings, the new *Doctor Who*, and *Supernatural*. Because of her client base, she needs to override her own preferences and become somewhat expert on the Marvel Universe and the works of Hayao Miyazaki. Justine is constantly on the lookout for how fanship can be used to enhance well-being. For example, she has combined it with another of her passions, yoga, offering sessions where traditional poses are reinterpreted

---

[8] When She Was Down, "The Next Gen" Beamed Her Up by Ian Spelling, Chicago Tribune, July 30, 1993.

against a fictional narrative read out by the instructor. The narrative enhances the overall experience, giving participants the reasons for their movement.

When a show is canceled or a main character dies off, fans experience loss and deal with it in a variety of ways. One particular fan at GalaxyCon described how she went into her room to mourn the loss of her favorite character for days, minimizing contact with family and friends until the sting wore off. Justine sympathizes by pointing out that normal grieving occurs with loss in fanship, but society doesn't take it seriously. There is no shame in being connected to a fictional character and it is important to show some self-compassion. Justine went through it when Buffy died in Season 5; her hero was dead and she felt that she just lost a dear friend. Some fans do turn toward each other to talk about their loss, in an effort to process and understand what just happened. Others go back and watch reruns to experience the "happy times" again. Justine points out that fans often make up their own endings to a tragic event, typically referred to as a fan fix. Unlike real life, fans can bring characters back to life, keep a story going, or simply right the wrong of a poorly written script.

On the whole, Justine believes that fanship provides an enrichment to well-being, providing a mechanism for people to understand their lives and a narrative to talk through difficult or emotion-filled issues. Gone too far, fanship can become a problem if the fictional universe overcomes real life, causing clients to miss work or give up on personal relationships. Other times, toxic forms of fanship can arise, where fans become possessive of their favorite franchise and engage in bickering around facts or what the true narrative is. Justine sees these as signs that a client might have been bullied in the past or has experienced some other form of attachment injury. The client likely has found a safe place in fanship and feels threatened by anyone who might take away their solace. But short of these typical signs of trauma or addiction, fanship can enrich a person's life and provides a shorthand for people to connect on common interests.

In comparison to the average GalaxyCon attendee, Kris is a relative latecomer to the world of science fiction. Growing up, she was not surrounded by Star Trek or Star Wars, but instead immersed herself in fine art and music. She took up the bass guitar at 14 years old, played in a band, and considered pursuing a career in graphic design. You would best describe her as alternative. The first step into her self-described nerdom occurred with an initial interest in comics, which then evolved into a half-hearted openness to watch shows that she was convinced she wouldn't like. Upon watching her first Star Wars movie in her late twenties, Kris experienced a self-described awakening that spiraled into her coleading the Minnesota Force fan club and spending her free time volunteering at charitable events. Kris was given the gift of a "second childhood," filled with exploring all the shows and movies she missed out on growing up, including *Star Trek*, *Dr. Who*, *Firefly*, and the Marvel and DC Comics universes.

Kris attended her first convention in 2014 and was overcome by the experience of being surrounded by others who shared the same passion. Just like her, they loved making costumes and wanted an excuse to show them off on other days beyond Halloween. Walking around the convention halls, Kris found it easy to strike up a conversation with complete strangers about the costumes they were wearing, as visible icons of a shared identity, no different than a sports fan wearing the jersey of a favorite team. The more obscure the character, the better for both the person in costume and the observer who caught the reference. At conventions, Kris was free to talk to strangers about shows and characters, but also compare notes as fellow costumers. Only in these settings did it seem appropriate to ask, "so, how do you make such realistic side-buns." According to Kris, the modern convention is about "creating and being part of fandom," which is noticeably different than fanship and the conventions I personally experienced two decades ago, which focused more on collectibles and celebrities. These elements are still there, just dialed back in favor of more active fan participation.

At the 2016 convention, where Kris was searching for ways to expand her fandom beyond the conventions and through conversation, she learned about the Minnesota Force, where she could put her costuming skills to a good and practical use. The Minnesota Force is a local fan club dedicated to Star Wars that is described as all inclusive and made up of makers, dice rollers, book readers, collectors, artists, and illustrators. A big part of the club is attending charitable events in costume. The Minnesota Force is similar to the international Star Wars fan club, the 501st Legion, which is known as "Vader's First" and promotes the tagline "Bad Guys Doing Good."[9] One critical distinction between it and the more casual Minnesota Force is the strict costuming requirements of the 501st, as Lucasfilm will engage the group for movie premiere's and to locate extras for its films and TV shows. As of late December 2019, the 501st had over 13,500 active members and over 28,500 approved costumes.

Kris was hooked on the Minnesota Force after her first couple of social meetings. She remembers fondly attending a rescreening of the 1978 Star Wars Holiday Television Special, which has gained notoriety for being that

[9] Minnesota Force. Website. https://www.minnesotaforce.wordpress.com (accessed May 18, 2023); 501st Legion. Website. https://www.501st.com (accessed May 18, 2023).

special type of bad that is good in a cult-classic type of way, like a slow-moving train wreck. Her first premier event was for *Rogue 1*, where Kris reveled in her role as a pseudocelebrity. From there, she attended events for the Make a Wish Foundation, Children's Hospital, and a series of nonprofit charity fun runs. Having the ability to make sick children forget their surroundings gives her a lift that she hadn't experienced before, similar to other fanatics we will meet in later chapters who are intent on helping or bringing happiness to others. Volunteering filled a void that Kris didn't realize that she had in her life, "I feel really, really good with seeing people lose their minds over the characters." And Kris does play a range of characters, including General Hux, Poe Dameron, Kylo Ren, Admiral Ackbar, a Twi'lek Jedi, and of course, Princess Leia. Kris has branched out from the Star Wars universe and is also a member of Minnesota Superheroes United, allowing her even more opportunity to connect and volunteer in the community. She is fanatical about Batman, Captain America, Falcon, Catwoman, Scarlet Witch, and Black Widow.

Kris could not have predicted the social support that her newly made friends would provide her. In 2017, Kris's mom was suddenly diagnosed with cancer and after a swift decline, passed away later that year. She was the center of Kris's universe, and watching her fade away put Kris into an emotional spin. When her mother was going through the roughest patch in hospital, Kris's volunteer work provided a sense of normality to cling onto. She asked her mom directly whether she was okay with her leaving the bedside, knowing that her mom was suffering. Her mom encouraged her to go and "make people happy and tell me how it went." Her mom recognized that Kris needed a community and that her friends would be there after she was gone. Kris initially joined a fan club, but came away with much more, "Never would I think I would get a family out of it." The Minnesota Force was her "type of therapy," giving something to look forward to and a goal to work toward. Parallels to Kris's experience will be found in the next chapter, with a deeper dive on how fanaticism can provide a mechanism to cope with loss and trauma. Specific to Kris, she was comforted in the knowledge that her mom would approve of what she was doing; giving back to the community and having fun while doing it.

When Kris thinks about the word "community," her Force friends are who she thinks of and not her coworkers or fellow city dwellers. It is a group of people, connected in part by nerdom, but more from social connection and meaningful interaction. For the most part, Kris has escaped the toxicity that can sometimes arise with fans, when they compete for who has made the best costume or knows the most about a given show. The volunteering element of Kris's fandom has likely protected her from encountering too many of these types of people, who tend to loiter in anonymous online forums. Meeting with fellow fans in real life at charitable events like those held at the local Children's Hospital, where a choice is made beforehand about who will play Princess Leia, creates a prosocial environment where everyone benefits. One key distinction about Kris's fanaticism is that she is connected more through fandom than fanship. Despite her affinity for Star Wars and specific Marvel and DC superheroes, she is attached to the opportunity to connect and create with others, using the backdrop of the Star Wars as the canvas for her art. With its far-ranging worlds and almost infinite cast of characters, it is a big universe to play in and no doubt will provide Kris a creative outlet for years to come.

Like Kris, active members of any fandom are reported to gain the psychological benefits of a genuine community. The psychological sense of community has been defined by psychologists as a perception of similarity and interdependence between group members, a willingness to give or help others within the group, and the safety gained from being part of a dependable and stable group.[10] Four dimensions are typically cited as critical for any group to be considered a community.[11] First, individuals must gain a feeling of belonging from group membership. Defining what it means to be part of the group, especially in relation to nonmembers, heightens a sense that the group is unique and meaningful. Second, members must feel that they have some voice and influence over the group if it is to be considered a community, put in balance by the social norms that come with being part of the group.

The next criteria for community involves the fulfillment of psychological needs. Group members must gain some type of pleasure or reward from being part of the community. Interestingly, the pattern of motivations drawing members to their community differs significantly depending on the type of group they have joined. Fans might be motivated by a need for heightened self-esteem and a sense of family, feelings of escapism and aesthetic enjoyment, desires for entertainment and tangible rewards, or a combination of them all. Comparison studies across a range of fandoms discovered that sports fans were found to be highly motivated by a desire for entertainment.[12] In contrast, those who accompany sports fans to games, but who do not consider themselves true fans, are driven by motivations for affiliation and therefore, see sports as a means to an end. These motivations are different than anime fans, who are driven by the needs of escapism, belonging, and self-esteem,

---

[10] Obst, P., Zinkiewicz, L., and Smith, S. (2002a). Sense of community in science fiction fandom, part 1: Understanding sense of community in an international community of interest. Journal of Community Psychology, 30, 87–103.

[11] McMillan, D., and Chablis, D. (1986). Sense of community: A definition and theory. Journal of Community Psychology, 14, 6–23.

[12] Schroy, C. (2016). Different motivations as predictors of psychological connection to fan interest and fan groups in anime, furry, and fantasy sport fandoms. Phoenix Papers, 2, 148–167.

among others. Moreover, what motivates group members in their fandom does not relate to what motivates their fanship. As an extreme example of this, anime fans have been found to be sexually attracted to the art (their fanship), but not necessarily to each other (their fandom).[13]

Lastly, members must share an emotional connection if the group is to be considered a community. Shared history goes a long way to building up these bonds, as are multiple opportunities for deep interactions. The four dimensions of belonging, influence, fulfillment, and connection are not mutually exclusive, but rather build on each other to strengthen the psychological sense of community. For example, opportunities for connection can reinforce that the group is unique and special, leading to the fulfillment of social status. Taken together, a sense of community has been shown to benefit members' psychological well-being, from improving self-esteem to promoting social integration, trust in others, and personal satisfaction. It has also proven helpful in combatting social isolation and feelings of distress, loneliness, and alienation.[14]

Surprisingly, even very brief encounters between community members can have a marked impact on well-being. For example, brief encounters with a coffee shop barista living in the same community have been shown to heighten feelings of belonging. Seeing another fan wearing an icon of their fandom, like Marj's Star Trek communicator pin or another Princess Leia costume for Kris, creates instant recognition and a sense of common identity (one of the drivers of community). Even if nothing is said to each other, this form of weak interaction is valuable to strengthening a sense of community and paving the way to emotional well-being. Better yet, the icon provides an opportunity for a conversation and a deeper conversation around their common fandom.

The benefits of fandom appear to have an overwhelming positive impact on fans and their communities, yet there is an alternative version of fandom with a darker side, which is best explained by looking outside of science fiction and fantasy. When fandoms become entirely self-serving, they have the potential to spiral away into intolerance and rejection of anyone who is not part of the in-group. Such is the case of football hooligans, who might have had an affinity for their clubs at one time, but are characterized more by an attraction to aggression and causing social mayhem. Although recognizing that "hooliganism" is a coverall term, Eric Dunning describes hooligans by their

[13] Ray, A., et al. (2017). Psychological needs predict fanship and fandom in anime fans. Phoenix Papers, 3, 56–68.

[14] Wan, D., Hackathorn, J., and Sherman, M. (2017). Testing the team identification-social psychological health model: Mediational relationships among team identification, sport fandom, sense of belonging, and meaning in life. Group Dynamics: Theory, Research, and Practice, 21, 94–107.

affinity for verbal and physical violence, vandalizing property, and wielding weapons with the intent to harm others, both at sporting events and in the vicinity.[15] Moreover, such actions are not limited to game day, but can occur any time where allegiance to football teams provides an excuse for aggression. Dunning reviewed the prevalence of hooliganism from 1908 onward, discovering over a hundred incidents of football-related violence during that time, occurring in 37 countries. Notably, this list included the Heizel tragedy from the 1985 European Cup Final, where Liverpool hooligans charged the Italian fans, leading to the collapse of the stands and a loss of 39 lives. Sadly that is not the record holder for bodily harm, as a match between Peru and Argentina eclipses Heizel by racking up over 5,000 fan injuries and approximately 300 deaths.

The leadup to such tragedy is driven through the same psychological processes inherent to any other type of community, but they are based on different foundations. Through six years of intensive and international field work, Ramon Spaaij found that hooligan identities are overly indexed on pleasurable emotional arousal, hard masculinity, territorial identifications, reputation management, a sense of solidarity, and representations of sovereignty and autonomy.[16] Hooligans construct a large part of their identity on the differences between the self and others, engaging in confrontation to prove superiority. One of the hooligans interviewed described his experience as exuberance, "The kick of fighting your rivals is overwhelming. You cannot really understand it unless you're in it. It gives you a sense of power, a sense of control. It's an absolute high. It's something that I don't often find in normal life." Interacting with their personal motivation to engage in violent acts is the environment that they often find themselves within. The presence of alcohol, geographical proximity to rivals, sociopolitical factors like unemployment, the size of the stadium, and the segregation of fan bases can all set in motion the potential for violence and tragedy.

The reputations gained through violence follow the hooligans both on and off the street, with social codes established around who should be the target, where confrontation takes place, and when. In the words of another hooligan profiled by Spaaij, "They go too far sometimes. I mean, what's the point in attacking innocent people who have nothing to do with football hooliganism? There's no honor in that." Rivals with large reputations for violence have been known to walk by each other on the street, with no more than a glance of

---

[15] Dunning, E. (2000). Towards a sociological understanding of football hooliganism as a world phenomenon. European Journal on Criminal Policy and Research, 8, 141–162.

[16] Spaaij, R. (2008). Men like us, boys like them: Violence, masculinity, and collective identity in football hooliganism. Journal of Sport and Social Issues, 32, 369–392.

recognition, if the time and place are not right. In the words of a hooligan profiled by Spaaij, "Of course, we run into each other all the time. Usually I just nod and walk on. Honestly, there is no point in confronting him on the streets, is there? I mean, where would that end? He knows where I live, and I know where he lives."

For members of the same hooligan group, feelings of belonging and solidarity run deep and provide much more of the glue than the allegiance to a sports team. In the words of one hooligan, "For many of us, friendship, belonging, and adventure are just as important as fighting, if not more important. I mean, if it was only about violence you could just beat up anybody in the streets. Hooliganism is much more than that." The bond that hooligans can feel toward each other can be as strong, if not stronger, than family. In a study by Knijnik and Newson on Western Sydney's ultras, the authors discuss how identity fusion overwhelms a personal sense of self through immersion with the group.[17] Fused individuals react automatically to threats to the group, whether they come from the media, police, football authorities, or rivals, and often turn to violence and retribution when the stakes are high.

The underlying identity of hooligans, with an us-vs.-them mentality, cannot be more different from the typical fandoms based on science fiction or fantasy. Although conflict may exist within the Marvel universe or may be played out in the Star Wars saga, this does not translate to aggression in the real world. Trekkies may not particularly like Star Wars as a franchise, but fights breaking out at Comic Con over the issue do not make the headlines. Rather, the science fiction fandoms provide an alternative reality for like-minded individuals to find each other and share in their collective passions. It is strange to think that science fiction fans might feel the same sense of belonging, voice, fulfillment, and emotional connection as hooligans, but the impact on the larger community is strikingly different. Kris, Justine, and Marj use science fiction and fantasy as a bridge. It has the power to disarm others, take their mind off current troubles, and provide a deeper level of connection. For hooliganism, the opposite is true if you are part of the out-group. Game day brings excitement and confrontation that capitalizes on established social divisions. A hooligan's form of fanaticism is based on competition, power, and authority, which is the antithesis of the stories told in science fiction, which often do not look favorably on bullies. The Empire failed and Harry vanquished Lord Voldemort.

Beyond the core messages inherent to much of the science fiction literary cannon, its global appeal allows its fandom to outpace more traditional

[17] Knijnik, J., and Newson, M. (2021). "Tribalism," identity fusion and football fandom in Australia: The case of Western Sydney. Soccer and Society, 22, 248–265.

communities based on where someone studies, lives, or works. In a study where science fiction fans were explicitly asked about the affinity they feel for their interest group in comparison to the physical community in which they lived, their psychological sense of community was higher for science fiction across every single measure.[18] This was evident in my conversation with Kris, who felt closer to her Force friends than to her neighbors. In the research, fans experienced feelings of belonging, enjoyed cooperative behavior, gained friendship and support, and felt empowered to shape what the group was about. One element that did set science fiction fandom apart was members' conscious identification with their community. Potentially because of the stigmatization of being called a nerd and the social exclusion resulting from it, science fiction fans are not shy about grabbing onto their shared identity.

Science fiction fans are not the only ones who relish the identity of being alternative. Strangely, a fair amount of research on fandom has been conducted on the "furry" community, which is made up of individuals who have an interest in anthropomorphism and zoomorphism (giving human traits to animals and vice versa). Community members express their interest through artwork, role playing, wearing costumes (called fursuits), and interacting through fursonas (an anthropomorphized animal avatar). When asked to compare their furry and their personal identities, most say that their furry identity exaggerates aspects of their personal identity.[19] If community members described themselves as fairly extroverted in their personal lives, their furry identifies pushed their self-confidence and outgoing nature to a whole new level (exaggerations of personality are not limited to furries and have been replicated with other types of fandom). Like many other fandoms, furries experience significant stigmatization, with 47% of furries believing that they are viewed negatively and 45% reporting that they hide their furry interests from people at work, school, or home.[20] It is no wonder that furries feel that they can be more themselves when they put on their furry identity.

In the past, communities were typically associated with a physical location. Interest groups, like science fiction fandoms, have challenged the notion that physical presence is key driver of enduring communities, shifting the focus to the quality and character of the relationships held between members. Science fiction fans may also be a special case for early adoption in this regard, with

[18] Obst, P., Zinkiewicz, L., and Smith, S. (2002b). Sense of community in science fiction fandom, part 2: Comparing neighborhood and interest group sense of community. Journal of Community Psychology, 30, 105–117.

[19] Reysen, S., et al. (2015). A social identity perspective of personality differences between fan and non-fan identifies. World Journal of Social Science Research, 2, 91–103.

[20] Schroy, C. (2016). Different motivations as predictors of psychological connection to fan interest and fan groups in anime, furry, and fantasy sport fandoms. Phoenix Papers, 2, 148–167.

25% of members reporting to communicate over the internet rather than face-to-face as early as 2002.[21] Current-day technology has the potential to push interest groups even further, as access to limitless libraries of content and the ability to connect members instantly allow for a whole new level of cultural immersion. Media channels such as Twitter are used simultaneously when fans are watching the same show, while on-demand videos allow any fan to become a trivia expert.[22] Fans can also dip in and out of multiple fan cultures with ease, using purpose-built portals to navigate the universe of different fandoms. As a sign of the times, furries are particularly adept at online interaction, with 95% of this community creating and communicating via their fursonas.[23]

I'm not sure it was the first time that I have attended a conference panel with speakers dressed in costume, but it was definitely a first for me to have Cat Boy as a moderator. Anastasia Press and Jordan Kocon were representing CARE Counseling (Childhood Through Adulthood Relational and Emotional Counseling) and spoke about the benefits of fandom on mental well-being. They were there to "celebrate their inner nerds, showing up to talk about mental health."[24] And they were not alone. Over the course of two sessions, close to 100 GalaxyCon fans took time out of seeing celebrities and perusing the trade hall, to talk about the impact fandom has on their personal well-being. If nothing else, just having a formalized panel on mental health is a big change for the convention scene. Unlike those I attended two decades ago, there is a recognition that science fiction and other fandoms are a major part of a person's life and therefore, can have an inordinate impact on mental health. Conventions have the potential to rally fans around topics that are deeply personal for the greater good, especially considering that many of the fan base have felt excluded or bullied in the past due to their interests.

I was able to interview both Anastasia and Jordan after the convention to dig deeper into how fandom is used in therapy. Anastasia specializes in trauma and is involved in building training curriculum for her fellow therapists. Her longest-running fandom involves video games and anime, but has broadened out as she has gotten older. We talked about one of her more recent fanships, the science fiction show *The OA*, which ended after two intense series. *The OA*

[21] Obst, P., Zinkiewicz, L., and Smith, S. (2002a). Sense of community in science fiction fandom, part 1: Understanding sense of community in an international community of interest. Journal of Community Psychology, 30, 87–103.

[22] Highfield, T., Harrington, S., and Bruns, A. (2013). Twitter as a technology for audiencing and fandom: The #Eurovision phenomenon. Information, Communication and Society, 16, 315–339.

[23] Reysen, S., et al. (2015). A social identity perspective of personality differences between fan and non-fan identifies. World Journal of Social Science Research, 2, 91–103.

[24] GalaxyCon Minneapolis Program, November 8, 2019.

spoke to her on a deeper level, with its combination of slick cinematography, art, and spirituality. As a therapist, Anastasia specifically liked how much gray space was created in the plot line and characteristics; so much of the show was open to interpretation and allowed the viewer to have an opinion about what was real. The characters themselves were all damaged in some way, which created an opportunity to empathize with their struggles and a desire for the therapist in her to see the characters ultimately prevail.

Anastasia's fandom of *The OA* led her to read posts on Reddit, where she noticed some themes consistent with what she knows as a mental health practitioner. The fans engaging in the show used a similar vocabulary, even poaching some terms from psychology to describe how characters were dealing with trauma or interacting with each other. This is similar to other forms of fanaticism profiled in this book, where communities adopt "phatic communication," a term used to describe a shorthand or technical information understood within the community, but that is less understandable for outsiders. Such communication can build barriers between the in- and out-group, yet works to solidify social connections and feelings that the group is special. We'll see this topic come up again in regard to high-risk sports. The fans of *The OA* were making the show what they wanted it to be, using that gray space to fill in and personalize the plot line, then sharing it out with the community. Anastasia points out that humans are naturally social beings and constantly looking out for shared experience. Shows like *The OA*, with their loose interpretations and broad range of characters, allow for a rich universe for fans to explore together. This type of connection is different from what Kris experiences with fellow Star Wars costumers and volunteer superheroes, being both more cerebral and less dependent on physical location, yet it would be hard to argue that the resulting community is any weaker.

Anastasia notes that the time invested in thinking about characters in a TV series, taking part in collaborative gaming, or role playing with cosplay all have the tendency to amplify social skills. When considering that science fiction fans can sometimes feel like social outcasts, building up confidence to successfully engage with others and express their true selves can only be a good thing, especially for the younger or more introverted members of the community. Fandom provides an opportunity to connect and, for those individuals whose experience with traditional social groups haven't worked out, "fandom provides space where other parts of society have let them down." The science fiction community may be the first place where members feel that they are part of something and they are ok.

Fans are typically drawn to shows that in some way mirror or illuminate their inner world, even when not evident at the surface level. In Anastasia's words when talking about gaming fandoms, there is a "certain type of person drawn to being a barbarian." For many of Anastasia's clients, their attraction to a particular show or character is a result of experiencing significant trauma in the past. Anastasia explains that due to the nature of how trauma affects the formation of memories, with gaps in time or incomplete information about the run-up to the event, individuals can turn to fanship to make sense of it all. The fictional stories and characters build a narrative that might be otherwise absent from their real-life experience, allowing them to gain objectivity and break the situation apart. Anastasia also notes that, by talking it out, clients gain empathy for themselves, with more compassion and less blame for the trauma they endured.

"Of all the billions of experiences we have, there are a handful of events that are chosen to explain our lives," says Anastasia. Often, the traumatic ones make the cut, despite the fact that they can be incomplete and have enduring consequences on self-esteem and feelings of self-worth. Through therapy and using fanship as a lens to understand trauma, clients have the potential to re-write the narrative or even put some memories to rest. Fanship is not tethered to reality, and thus provides space for exploration of different perspectives and experimentation for alternative conclusions. In this way, fanship provides the opportunity for posttraumatic growth, where clients can find meaning and power in a traumatic experience. In comics, there are plenty of examples where this plays out, for example, when a young Bruce Wayne witnesses the death of his parents, resolves to fight crime, and becomes the caped crusader of Gotham City.

Anastasia is on the lookout for specific characters that a client gravitates toward, as they have the potential to enhance their personality either consciously or unconsciously. She recommends being curious and asking questions: "Why did you choose that particular character? What does it tell you about yourself?" For example, is the character dealing with loss or challenging their identity in some way? Anastasia herself, for example, is attracted to role of Dungeon Master in Dungeons and Dragons, as a means of building her own assertiveness and learning "how to take up more space."

When asked by her clients whether it is ok if a chosen character has a dark side, Anastasia doesn't cast a choice in character as universally bad, but as a signal that there might be a topic worth exploring. She asks herself as a therapist, "What does this person like about their dark side? What purpose does it have?" For example, people who have experienced trauma might fall prey to repetition compulsion, where they replay the event repeatedly and can put themselves in perilous situations where the trauma is likely to recur. The client repeats themselves in the vain hope of fixing the original trauma by somehow getting it right the second or third time around. The trauma itself might not be a "big T" type of event, involving violence or harm, but rather might represent a more everyday variety (like a breakup or argument), but is impactful for the client nonetheless. Anastasia is also on the lookout for when fanship turns into a form of obsession. Just like any other type of addiction, immersing oneself in fanship can consume a client's social, emotional, or physical well-being. When this arises, she questions why the fanship has become so alluring and opens up a conversation about what void exists in the real world that is being filled by the fanship.

Jordan uses his fanship in a highly applied way, bringing his affinity for Dungeons and Dragons directly into his clinical practice. He uses the framework of the game as a way to explore the narrative underlying his clients' lives and, through conversation, tests out how different interpersonal conflicts might be resolved. The game provides the space and freedom for clients to try something new, without real-world consequences, similar to the freedom provided by virtual reality as discussed in a later chapter. Through therapy, clients both build up the confidence to deal with the source of their conflict and work out the kinks in how best to approach it, with the net result of reducing anxiety and improving their well-being.

Jordan's own fascination with gaming goes back to elementary school, when he crowded around the family's Nintendo 64 to play *Legend of Zelda*. He was drawn to both the cognitive challenge presented by the puzzles in the game and the feeling of doing something dangerous. Playing the hero gave him a boost in confidence and self-image, something that crossed over to his discovery of Dungeons and Dragons, which shares the same frame as an adventure game with heroes and villains. Yet, unlike the Nintendo game platform, which was universally loved by his peers, Jordan encountered a social stigma to role playing that caught him entirely off-guard.

Dungeon and Dragons premiered in 1974 and arguably was the first roleplaying game of its kind, complete with adventures involving a wide range of characters representing mythical races and occupations, guided by the storytelling of a designated Dungeon Master. A few tragic incidents in the early 1980s associated the game with psychological illness and self-harm, a misconstrued relationship that was fueled by fundamentalist religious groups who feared that the game was corrupting the youth. A campaign against the game, called Bothered About Dungeons and Dragons (BADD) described the game in 1983 as "a fantasy role-playing game which uses demonology, witchcraft, voodoo, murder, rape, blasphemy, suicide, assassination, insanity, sex perversion, homosexuality, prostitution, satanic type rituals, gambling, barbarism, cannibalism, sadism, desecration, demon summoning, necromantics, divination and other teachings."[25] It couldn't get much worse for the image of early role players and when *60 Minutes* dedicated an episode to the social harms of Dungeons and Dragons, the stigma was cemented into the public consciousness.

It took 30 years and countless studies exploring the causal links between Dungeons and Dragons and mental health for the moral panic to disappear. Yet, when Jordan first began playing the game with a classmate during his 6th grade lunch hour, unease about the game was palpable and not just among his teachers and friends' parents. Jordan's soccer buddies thought the game was odd and began questioning why he was spending time immersed in a fictitious world rather than playing ball. Trying to talk up the game among his friends made matters worse. Feeling that he was becoming a social outcast, Jordan decided to abandon Dungeons and Dragons.

Both society and Jordan moved on. In his late teens, Jordan returned to role playing, finding it an ideal way to keep connected with old friends who were attending college across the country. Coming together during summer or winter breaks, the friends would pick back up on the game, share some food, and reconnect like nothing had changed. One such game lasted 2 years, and came to a rather abrupt end when the Dungeon Master declared, "one of your characters is going to die today." The group got into a panic. Was 2 years of effort really coming down to this? Would the tragedy be fair or at least entertaining? What would happen to that player after their character died off; would they still have a place in the game? Jordan confessed that it is hard not to take the killing of your character personally.

The jump to using Dungeons and Dragons in therapy was more happenstance than a well-thought-out plan. Jordan was in therapy with an online gaming fanatic, when he made a connection between the client's character and one he had encountered in Dungeons and Dragons. Drawing on the client's interest in gaming, Jordan suggested that they try something new by using the structure of Dungeons and Dragons to gain perspective and experiment with some new behaviors, in the safety of a make-believe environment. The experiment was a success not only for the client but also for Jordan, giving him the confidence to try out the technique with other willing clients.

In the 2 years following that first therapy session, Jordan learned that the approach is not for everyone, but should be reserved for those who embrace playfulness and can suspend their disbelief, a prerequisite for engaging in a sometimes far-flung story line. Although it appeals more strongly to teens, the game's effectiveness as a form of treatment does require a certain amount

---

[25] The Great 1980s Dungeons & Dragons Panic by Peter Allison, BBC Magazine, April 11, 2014.

of wisdom about how to navigate the social environment. Jordan's connection with his client also plays a major role, as the player must empower Jordan to play the Dungeon Master and trust that he is not acting to embarrass or prey on the client's emotions.

Together, Jordan and his clients create a story. First, Jordan helps guide a choice in character that is appropriate for both the situation and his client's experience with the game. Novices are advised to choose a character that mirrors their reality, to simplify the gameplay. More advanced players are encouraged to try on a persona that allows them to probe more deeply into their assumptions and ingrained behaviors. Next, Jordan will develop a story arc that will bring the client's real-world challenges to the forefront. For novices, he will position the game as a role-playing technique that will allow them to talk about and confront relationships with their parents, siblings, friends, or coworkers in a safe environment. Jordan will then introduce his role as Dungeon Master and will insert himself in the game, sometimes as a companion character and sometimes as an antagonist, depending on the specific aims of the session. He will then use mechanisms in the game to move the plot forward, such as throwing in divine objects as loot for the characters to fight over.

The brilliance of the game is in how it provides the scaffolding for the story and gameplay, without becoming prescriptive. Story arcs are familiar, puzzles provide challenge, and the dice introduce both chance and personal risk for the players. Over those first two years, Jordan polished his approach, improving how he chose stories and puzzles, but also knowing when to pull back when the session gets too emotionally raw. Yet, the most significant challenge for Jordan is how to keep the momentum going between therapy sessions. Unlike his college friends, whose gameplay is limited only by physical exhaustion and the amount of pizza on hand, his clients are limited to less than an hour a week to both cram in the game and talk about its implications for the real world. This limitation aside, Jordan is convinced of the benefits of gaming in therapy. His clients are provided both an opportunity to practice life skills that they would normally avoid in a safe environment and the ability to try again if things do not go as planned. If they are willing, they can go further by trying on a different persona, potentially dialing up how forceful or forthcoming they are or dialing back their impulsiveness. They can think through different courses of actions and see how chance plays a key part in relationships. Most importantly, they learn to be less critical and treat themselves with compassion.

Whether used directly in therapy or as a vehicle for social connection, the genre of science fiction provides a rich tapestry for building or restoring personal relationships. The type of fanaticism that its devotees show toward these alternative universes is one of emotional attachment and connection. Yet, the direction of a fan's relationship to the genre varies greatly among their peers. Some fans are drawn to a specific character or story arc. They might feel empathy for what the character is going through, admiration for their traits, or freedom to think about their own lives from a different vantage point. Marj showed this type of fanship for Captain James T. Kirk, extending it beyond the show to include William Shatner. Like many other Trekkies out there, Marj's relationship to Star Trek and its characters provided hope in humankind and enjoyment from decades of adventure. In comparison, Kris's connection to Star Wars is best described as fandom, with her affinity directed toward other costumers and role players immersed in a galaxy far, far away. Kris enjoys sharing tips and tricks about building screen-ready costumes, and participating in fundraising events and hospital visits to put a smile on a kid's face.

Fanship and fandom are different in how relationships are experienced, but equal in their potential to improve emotional well-being. The relationships fans share with characters are similar to those experienced in real life, complete with feelings of loss when a show is canceled or character is killed off. Meanwhile, the connections shared between fans go deeper and faster through the use of shared social norms and instantaneous common interests. Justine, Anastasia, and Jordan use both fanship and fandom in their practices, as a means to accelerate the personal connection to the client, create an opening to explore difficult issues or conflicts, make a narrative that connects significant life events, and experiment with new behaviors in a psychologically safe environment.

Like any other type of fanaticism, immersing oneself too much in science fiction can tip over into a negative, for example, if a fan misses work to binge a new series or alternatively, when fascination with a character turns into outright obsession. Such process addictions will appear again in this book, specifically on topics like gaming and exercise. Yet on balance, the benefits far outweigh the risks, with science fiction providing an unique catalyst for healthy and fulfilling personal relationships, especially with its lack of aggression toward an out-group. With the genre freed from the basement and making gains as a form of popular culture, fans are able to relish their fanaticism with less fear of being characterized as nerds or outcasts. Jordan's experience of being shunned by his soccer friends is less likely now than it was before the relaunch of the Marvel and DC Comics universes. In making the jump to the mainstream, let's just hope that the genre doesn't lose its magic along the way, keeps its disdain for hooligans, and continues to provide that rich tapestry that lends itself so well to social connection. Fandom based on science fiction and fantasy lends itself well to a social type of fanaticism, but is by no means the only way that people find meaningful connection with others. As will be explored next, it can be during our darkest moments when tragedy and loss catapult us into a social form of fanaticism that is instead based on love and compassion.

2

Lemons to Lemonade

Nothing signifies summer more than the smell of sunscreen lotion. That smell of coconuts, bananas, and lime instantly brings me back to my summer school holidays, sometimes spent on the beach building sandcastles and jumping waves, other times spent hanging out at the pool and eating popsicles. It was a magical time, with never-ending sunsets and weekdays that blended into weekends. Summers existed for biking around the neighborhood, mowing lawns to earn pocket money, and staying up late to watch the latest block-buster. I can remember the anticipation I had those last few days of school, waiting for the freedom and fun to begin. Yet for Carly Fischer and her family, the summer school holiday no longer holds such meaning, but rather marks the tragic anniversary of the loss of her younger brother, Nic, an event that forever changed the family dynamic and the course of their collective lives.

It was a perfect summer day in Parkes New South Wales, Australia, three days after the Christmas holiday. One week before, Carly's parents, Judy and Tony, threw a class party for 25 kids, celebrating their graduation from primary school and the beginning of high school. Nic was excited for the change and was fully enjoying the summer break. Out in the backyard with Nic were his four cousins, ages 13, 10, 8, and 4, spending the day in and around the pool, which played a prominent role in Nic's short life. Nic loved water and was a confident swimmer. His mother, Judy, described him as "fun-loving, full of mischief and very competitive in all the sports he played," which included water-skiing, football, and snow skiing.[1] On that particular day, Nic began playing a game very common among kids—the long-breath game. Paired up against one of his cousins, Nic was competing to see who could hold their breath longest under water before coming up for air. It was a normal game with no roughhousing, just like the one I played dozens of times before when I was a kid. But on the third round, Nic simply just didn't come up for air again.

It is hard to contemplate how childhood fun can turn into tragedy. In Judy's words, "We were sitting beside the pool at the time and he just didn't surface

[1] Shallow Water Blackout Prevention. Website. https://www.shallowwaterblackoutprevention.org/memorials/nic-fisher (accessed January 6, 2022).

Fanatic. Joe Ungemah, Oxford University Press. © Oxford University Press 2024. DOI: 10.1093/9780197783894.003.0003

after one of the 'turns' . . . not a sound, in chest deep water . . . who would believe he was actually drowning." Upon realizing that Nic failed to resurface,
the adults moved quickly to resuscitate his breathing. The response of the ambulance was quite swift, arriving within 6 minutes of the call, but Nic was already too far gone and his death was ruled as a drowning. Carly summed it
up that her "perfect family was broken in a day." Nic's accident represents the
convergence of both trauma and grief in the same episode. There was no early
warning that a day at the backyard pool would turn out any different than
countless times before. Yet for Nic's family, the trauma experienced would forever shape their lives, going beyond the grief of losing a loved one to more
usual means.

The current thinking by psychologists diverges from popular conceptions
of grief by asserting that no two individuals will experience grief in exactly the
same way. A series of neatly staged phases across a set timeline has given way
to thinking about grief as oscillations of emotions and memories. According
to Robyn Howarth, most people do experience "a period of sorrow, numbness,
and even guilt or anger, followed by a gradual fading of these feelings as the
griever accepts the loss and moves forward."[2] They might experience feelings
of sadness, physical symptoms like insomnia, and cognitive difficulties like
a lack of concentration. Through bereavement, the grieving individual gradually accepts the new reality of living without the physical presence of their
loved one. Reconciliation between their old and new reality requires a significant amount of cognitive work by the griever. Initially, they have to accept
the reality and pain associated with death and learn how to navigate daily life
without the other individual. Eventually, they will begin reframing their personal identity and finding renewed meaning in life and sometimes they will
grow in unanticipated and remarkable ways.

How a person dies plays an important part in grief. For example, if a death
resulted from a violent encounter or natural disaster, a stress reaction might
be triggered by the trauma. Survivors will likely experience feelings of fear,
helplessness, and horror, which in turn can create increased arousal and prevent people from sleeping or concentrating. Hypervigilance and bouts of
anger are also known to occur. The combination of grief and trauma has been
termed "complicated grief" or more recently "prolonged grief disorder" by
psychologists, with the symptoms of loss (i.e., longing and loneliness) and traumatic distress (i.e., numbness and helplessness) coming together in a distinct

---

[2] Howarth, R. (2011). Concepts and controversies in grief and loss. Journal of Mental Health Counseling,
33, 4–10.

pattern that is separate from either depression or anxiety.[3] Complicated grief can be triggered by a sudden death, the quality of relationship with the deceased, and/or through personal predispositions in how grief is processed. Individuals experiencing clinically significant symptoms of complicated grief endure intrusive and distressing thoughts, memories, and images about the trauma that lead to physiological reactions and distress similar to the original occurrence. According to Howarth, complicated grievers can "get 'stuck' in the course of their grief, concentrating on the traumatic aspects of the death and unable to proceed through the normal bereavement process."[4] When stuck, these individuals typically experience intrusive fantasies, pangs of severe emotion, strong yearnings, excessive avoidance of people and places associated with the deceased, lack of sleep, and maladaptive changes in work, social, or recreational undertakings.

Even more complex are individuals who experience ambiguous loss, where the death itself remains unclear and without resolution.[5] One type of ambiguous loss is physical, where a loved one might be missing physically, but is kept psychologically alive because the death or whereabouts of the individual are unknown. Examples of this type of loss include pilots missing in action during war or kidnapped children where the case has gone cold. The second type of ambiguous loss is the mirror opposite, where the physical body is present, but psychologically the person is lost due to impairment, such as people suffering with dementia or surviving within a coma. In these cases, grievers commonly become immobilized in their decision-making, experience conflict with each other due to different interpretations about the situation, and feel isolated, as society in general has difficulty in recognizing and responding to nondeath losses. In a paper written to clergy to help them to counsel on the topic, Pauline Boss advises that "grief is frozen, life is put on hold, and people are traumatized."[6] She believes the trauma is akin to posttraumatic stress disorder (PTSD), in that the pain is far beyond normal human expectations, yet unlike PTSD, it remains in the present for years if not a lifetime. Moving beyond the trauma, let alone growing from it, can seem insurmountable.

From families losing loved-ones due to COVID-19, the social unrest following the death of George Floyd, and more recently, the upswing in violent crime and mass shootings plaguing American cities, the early 2020s saw its fair

[3] Neria, Y., and Litz, B. (2004). Bereavement by traumatic means: The complex synergy of trauma and grief. Journal of Loss Trauma, 9, 73–87.

[4] Howarth, R. (2011). Concepts and controversies in grief and loss. Journal of Mental Health Counseling, 33, 4–10.

[5] Boss, P., and Yeats, J. (2014). Ambiguous loss: A complicated type of grief when loved ones disappear. Cruse Bereavement Care, 33, 63–70.

[6] Boss, P. (2010). The trauma and complicated grief of ambiguous loss. Pastoral Psychology, 59, 137–145.

share of both trauma and grief. It seems highly appropriate that I find myself meeting Stacy Remke at a coffee shop on Lake Street, a stretch of road that was the epicenter of one of the largest riots in US history, second only to the riots following the beating of Rodney King in LA. In total, the Minneapolis riots caused at least 2 deaths, 604 arrests, and $500 million in damages across 1,500 properties.[7] Stacy has immense experience in grief counseling, with field experience working in palliative care, teaching at the University of Minnesota, and authoring *The Insider's Guide to Grief*.[8] I was keen to talk to Stacy to unpack the relationship between trauma and grief, and to learn how some individuals can transcend tragedy to a state of posttraumatic growth.

Stacy starts out our conversation by recounting the first time she experienced personal loss, with the death of her grandfather. As a 10-year-old, Stacy distinctly remembers how unprepared the adults were in the days following her grandfather's death, as they struggled to deal with the funeral, notify friends and family, and clean up all the odds and ends of life. She also noticed a pattern of "stoicism in the community," where no tears were shed in a church filled with people. As the only person visibly upset, she remembers that the adults commented that she was "so sweet to cry." Even at a young age, Stacy recognized a need for society to learn how to show and accept grief. Her fascination with grief grew into a career, initially working with families experiencing the unimaginable loss of children with terminal diseases. Stacy guided them through the grief process, by helping them reorganize their lives, reaffirm the love that they had for their child, and recognize the impact that the child had on the lives of others. As her experience grew, Stacy helped establish one of the first children's palliative care programs of its scale and kind in the United States. She now focuses more broadly on developing grief literacy at the community level, strongly believing that by attuning to grief, especially with its relationship to trauma, our society has the potential to heal long and open wounds.

When I asked her about the connection between grief and trauma, Stacy began at the societal level and talked about how a broader recognition of grief in the context of historical trauma is finally occurring. Recognition is growing about how specific populations experience a recurring pattern of trauma and loss, as well as the effect this has both on the population and the larger society. Stacy emphasizes that there is a difference between big "T" trauma and little "t" trauma, the latter characterized by intersections between income, racial,

---

[7] For Riot-Damaged Twin Cities Businesses, Rebuilding Begins with Donations, Pressure on Government by Jeffrey Meitrodt, Star Tribune, June 14, 2020.

[8] Remke, Stacy. (2013). Insider's Guide to Grief. St. Paul: Lowertown Press.

or gender imbalances and the resulting lived experience, where frequent and often violent situations erupt around an individual, though it might be hard to pinpoint a single traumatic event. When experiencing trauma, Stacy explains, the loss might result in what Tashel Bordere describes as "suffocated grief," where deep and unrelenting emotional pain that is not recognized and that is lacking an appropriate outlet can take a turn into behavioral outbursts that feed the cycle of punishment rather than support.[9] Stacy has personally experienced instances of trauma leading to complicated grief through her practice and interaction with students. She has encountered individuals who were able to successfully confront their stress responses, but sometimes could not fully identify the grief that was buried deep within them.

For those individuals who are not stuck in the grieving process, bereavement can progress to renewed personal meaning for the griever. According to Gillies and Neimeyer, finding meaning helps the bereaved to adapt to a changed world across the social, behavioral, psychological, and physiological domains.[10] They do this through three separate processes, specifically making sense of the death, finding benefit in the experience, and undergoing identity change. The amount of distress experienced depends on how consistent the death is with the griever's preloss meaning structures, what psychologists call a person's "assumptive world." We all have assumptions about how benevolent, predictable, and controllable the world is, which comes into focus with challenging life events. Although deaths that make sense for the griever (i.e., the death of a grandparent after a long and fulfilling life) may be distressing, they will not be as disruptive to the griever as losses that make an individual reexamine their specific take on the meaning of life. In fact, when the death follows expectations, those preexisting mental structures are reinforced.

The pathway is very different when the death breaks expectations, causing cognitive dissonance between the death and a griever's assumptive world, which in turn initiates the needs of making sense of the death, finding benefits, and changing identity. This is especially true for individuals experiencing a traumatic loss. Not only are their assumptive worlds broken but also there is no buffer to the shattering of their social world. In a matter of moments, a person's cognitive schema about the meaning of life, their sense of identity, and their self-worth is flipped on its head. With no warning or preparation for what is to come, a griever can be led to believe that the world is meaningless,

---

[9] Take Note: Dr. Tashel Bordere on Suffocated Grief by Lindsey Whissel Fenton, WPSU, July 17, 2020.

[10] Gillies, J., and Niemeyer, R. (2006). Loss, grief, and the search for significance: Toward a model of meaning reconstruction in bereavement. Journal of Constructivist Psychology, 19, 31–65.

that they are unworthy of good things, or similar thoughts, which in each case can be hugely distressing.

Not everyone makes it through the grieving process, even the uncomplicated variety, into a healthy psychological state. In a longitudinal study of hundreds of elderly bereaved spouses, researchers George Bonanno, Camille Wortman, and Randolph Nesse identified five distinct trajectories for bereavement.[11] Some of the bereaved landed in a state of chronic depression, experiencing significant depression prior to and after the loss that persisted for at least 18 months. Others had chronic grief, where distress was low before the loss, but was significantly higher after the loss. For the distressed-improved population, the significant distress before the loss dropped to normal levels after the death of their loved one. For common grief, low distress before the loss heightened to a peak at 6 months after the loss before returning to normal at 18 months. Lastly, the resilient group showed persistent low levels of distress prior to, during, and after the loss. The takeaway message from this research is that for two of the bereavement groups, outcomes will land on either chronic depression or grief, which psychologists believe is influenced by the grievers' ability to rewrite their self-narratives, integrate the loss, and find renewed meaning in life.

To combat distress immediately after death, a griever does two things at once. First, they do the "grief work" that attacks the separation with the lost loved-one, rotating through bouts of crying, yearning, and remembering. When talking about the grief work, Stacy references Stroebe and Schut's dual processing model of grief that involves oscillations between loss and life orientations and the resulting range of emotions, with everything from sadness and depression to joy and learning.[12] "The emotional pain of loss can be likened to a wave: crashing, and then ebbing . . . when they come crashing, those waves can threaten to knock us over." The waves can last months or years after the loss, but with potentially lower peaks and higher valleys than those experienced directly after death. "Grief is very messy—it will shake and surprise you," relates Stacy, who points out that many grievers initially doubt themselves. They think, "How can I feel this bad—I must be doing something wrong." Stacy emphasizes that this is not the case, "It is human nature. Pain and suffering are signals that something is wrong. It feels big in the moment, but that feeling will pass." Stacy is quick to point out that hard emotions like sadness are frequently the norm, but other individuals may demonstrate

[11] Bonanno, G., Wortman, C., and Nesse, R. (2004). Prospective patterns of resilience and maladjustment during widowhood. Psychology and Aging, 19, 260–271.
[12] Stroebe, M., and Schut, H. (1999). The dual process model of coping with bereavement: Rationale and description. Death Studies, 23, 197–224.

instrumental grief, where the griever will get busy or take on intellectual tasks as their primary strategy for grieving. Instrumental grievers may establish memorials for their loved ones or clean closets right away. It is their way of coping and is an equally valid strategy to grieve. Stacy's ability to show empathy and openness to emotion, in whatever shape it takes, is what I admire most about her. As will be discussed shortly, she holds this trait in common with those who have grown through their own versions of trauma and loss.

At the same time as doing the grief work, the bereaved are working to restore and build a life without the physical presence of their loved one. It is in this other domain that the reconstruction of meaning occurs, where a new reality with a different assumptive world and identity is formed. For some, this work becomes the foundation for posttraumatic growth. It begins by an attempt to make sense of the loss, which can be particularly difficult when the event is unanticipated or random, which is more likely with higher levels of trauma. According to Gillies and Neimeyer, "To protect ourselves from the pain and restore the order, security, and predictability we felt in our lives, we strive to find reasons for what has happened."[13] Typically, about 70% of individuals will have made sense of the loss after 6 months, yet there is strong variability depending on the nature of death. For example, parents of children who died of SIDS have been reported to significantly struggle with making sense of their loss.

For Carly and her family, Nic's death fell into the category of hard to comprehend. How could a healthy child like Nic, who was a confident and capable swimmer, succumb to drowning in chest-deep water? Why could nothing be done for Nic with such a swift response by both the adults supervising the kids and the paramedics when they arrived? Judy and Tony desperately sought answers during the following years, coming across a woman named Sharon Washbourne, who had lost her own nephew, Jack, in a similar backyard accident.[14] Jack was swimming laps in the pool and was concentrating so hard on achieving his personal target that he ignored his body's urge to breathe and lost consciousness. On his next breadth, he took on water instead of air and quickly drowned. The most frightening part is that there were no outward signs of trouble—no splashing and no distress. Like Nic, Jack was being supervised that day, by adults who were equally powerless to prevent "shallow water blackout" or "hypoxic blackout." The condition occurs when a swimmer takes a quick succession of breaths repetitively, causing an imbalance between

---

[13] Gillies, J., and Niemeyer, R. (2006). Loss, grief, and the search for significance: Toward a model of meaning reconstruction in bereavement. Journal of Constructivist Psychology, 19, 31–65.

[14] The Game that Took Jack's Life: Boy's "Hypoxic Blackout" Death by Angela Thompson, Sydney Morning Herald, February 15, 2013.

the amount of oxygen and carbon dioxide running through their body. When combined with exhaustion or physical exertion, already low levels of oxygen deplete quickly and cause an individual to blackout. The swimmer runs out of time to initiate a breath and when they go unconscious, the body forces a breath underwater, causing drowning and death within seconds. Unlike typical drowning, shallow water blackout victims succumb to brain damage three times faster, due to the brain having already been deprived of oxygen.

Strangely it is often the most accomplished and confident swimmers that succumb to shallow water blackout. It has affected a long list of competitive swimmers, spear fishermen, Navy SEALS, snorkelers, and free divers. By training harder, these physically fit individuals push the body to its limits. According to Shallow Water Blackout Prevention, there are four rules that can help safeguard against it, specifically, never to push the body to hyperventilation, never to ignore the urge to breathe, never to swim alone, and never to play breath-holding games.[15] One of major difficulties of addressing shallow water blackout is its confusion with more typical forms of drowning. It is approximated that 140,000 deaths occur worldwide from drowning and up to 20% of these are attributable to shallow water blackout, but it is only now that the distinction is more widely recognized by health agencies and swimming associations.

Carly and her parents found the group formed by Sharon Washbourne to raise awareness about shallow water blackout and, by joining it, began the process of understanding and accepting the events leading to their loss. Carly talked about the impact of Nic's death on them, "Mum and Dad are not the same as they were prior to Nic dying. There are permanent changes in the family dynamic. All that grief meant that we could not all be fully present" in the ups and downs of normal family life. Unlike a rare disease where physical decline progresses over a longer time, Nic's sudden death did not provide any type of preparatory grief, causing the family to experience complex and overlapping emotions all at once. Beyond grief, there were feelings relating to trauma of helplessness and remorse about not being able to resuscitate Nic, as well as guilt by the siblings for not being poolside on that specific day. Beyond all, sadness that such a vibrant life was taken so unnecessarily played a major role.

It might sound strange at first, especially in light of the overwhelming negative emotions that Carly and her family experienced, but finding meaning in death is a key component of rebuilding one's life following tragedy. Finding

---

[15] Shallow Water Blackout Prevention. Website. https://www.shallowwaterblackoutprevention.org (accessed January 6, 2022).

meaning resolves the existential crisis left in place by the loss of a loved one and can restore perceptions of a predictable world. According to Gillies and Neimeyer, identifying benefits requires either a positive reappraisal of the event and its aftermath or a glossing over of the negatives, to help the grieved adapt to the loss.[16] Either way, finding benefits allows an individual to build new meaning structures, using some of the raw material provided by the loss. Benefits can range from a changed outlook on life, better interpersonal relationships, or freedom to try a new lifestyle. This transition is not immediate, but requires months or years to materialize, and as such, grievers should be patient and allow the process to unfold naturally. For Judy and Tony, sense making transitioned into benefit finding, due to the illusive nature of shallow water blackout.

Over the following two decades, Carly and her family worked to "keep Nic's memory alive" by doing some good in the world. The type of fanaticism that has arisen from Nic's passing is driven by a combination of social connection and the creation of meaning out of the unfathomable. First and foremost, they work to raise awareness about the risks of shallow water blackout. Nic's profile can be found on the Shallow Water Blackout Prevention website and the family speaks openly about Nic, believing that if each conversation "can even save one life, then it is worth it."[17] Judy and Tony also serve as chapter leaders for The Compassionate Friends NSW, a peer support community offering friendship to families who have lost children. When a tragedy like Nic's occurs within 200 km of Parkes, Judy and Tony will travel to visit the family face-to-face and offer the special type of support and understanding that comes only from families who have experienced the loss of a child. They are also quick to offer support for families across Australia via phone or video. Carly and her family recognize that parents experience an inordinate amount of grief when they lose a child. Not only do they grieve for their own loss but also they often bear the burden of grief for the other children in the family.

Alongside healthcare providers, support groups like the one Carly's family belongs to can help grieving parents by acknowledging the roles they played in the life of their child, identifying tangible memories and remembrance activities for them to carry forward, and validating the positive impact that the child had on the world.[18] Judy and Tony adjust the level of support they provide

---

[16] Gillies, J., and Neimeyer, R. (2006). Loss, grief, and the search for significance: Toward a model of meaning reconstruction in bereavement. Journal of Constructivist Psychology, 19, 31–65.

[17] Shallow Water Blackout Prevention. Website. https://www.shallowwaterblackoutprevention.org/memorials (accessed January 6, 2022).

[18] Kochen, E., et al. (2020). When a child dies: A systematic review of well-defined parent-focused bereavement interventions and their alignment with grief and loss theories. BMC Palliative Care, 19, 1–22.

depending on what the family desires, but connecting with peers like Carly's parents "helps them ease the pain of loss and is highly rewarding," states Carly. The work is hard. Not only do Carly and her parents see people experiencing the worst days of their lives but the interactions can subconsciously trigger the pain and sadness of Nic's passing. As emphasized by current psychological thinking, grief is never truly done, but oscillates with peaks and valleys across a lifetime. To their credit, Carly and her family power through their own feelings, knowing that their resilience and dedication can help families when their need is the greatest.

Beyond benefit finding, Nic's passing created meaning for Carly by reshaping her identity. Nic's passing forever shaped her perspective on the world and professional career. Carly works as a psychologist, meeting with clients both clinically and as an occupational psychologist, driven by a fascination with the human condition, to understand her own story and those of others through a scientific lens. Like Justine Mastin, whom we met in the last chapter, Carly's personal experience has transcended to her profession and shapes how she connects with her clients as a practitioner. Carly's personal experience with trauma reinforced a need to "stay connected to the world and strive to be truly nonjudgmental" in her work and when supporting others going through grief. She has learned that trauma can happen to anyone, at any time. Carly works with her clients to understand this fact, supporting them to let go of personal judgment and free them from the burden that they have endured. When the time is right, she can help them realize that trauma can provide an opportunity for personal growth, even if the trauma itself is never forgotten.

The transformation that Carly underwent to accept and grow from the grief and trauma she endured is consistent with what psychologists call posttraumatic growth. According to Richard Tedeschi and Lawrence Calhoun, posttraumatic growth is "the experience of positive change that occurs as a result of the struggle with highly challenging life crises."[19] The types of challenges they are referring to break apart a person's assumptive world, as discussed previously. People who endure such challenges can gain an increased appreciation for life and feel that they are more resilient, independent, and confident as well as more aware of life's fragility. They likely will identify new possibilities for their lives and may explore taking new and different paths than the ones taken to date. Posttraumatic growth also results in transformation in social relationships, with individuals demonstrating greater empathy for others and

---

[19] Tedeschi, R., and Calhoun, L. (2004). Posttraumatic growth: Conceptual foundations and empirical evidence. Psychological Inquiry, 15, 1–18.

establishing deeper social relationships. They often feel a need to talk about traumatic events and, by doing so, tease out which relationships are strong enough to bear the burden of heavy and complicated topics. Intimacy, compassion, and vulnerability are discovered anew.

Stacy Remke points out that not everyone navigates through tragedy into posttraumatic growth. Some may instead reconstruct themselves with maladaptive behaviors, like falling into substance abuse. If they do make it through to experiencing posttraumatic growth, they are often described as "sadder, but wiser" or, in Stacy's words, "a heart that breaks open that is bigger and stronger." From a theoretical vantage point, Tedeschi and Calhoun suggest that posttraumatic growth and distress are separate but related constructs, triggered from the same event, but taking independent paths to a resolution. Although some level of distress will occur following trauma, they agree that posttraumatic growth is not guaranteed. This is because the trauma itself is not the cause for the growth, but rather an individual's struggle with it. As mentioned before, the bereaved do both the grief work and sense-making at the same time. Those who engage more deeply in sense-making are more likely to come through the loss with posttraumatic growth.[20] The psychological research also indicates that individual disposition might play a part. For example, traits like optimism, extroversion, and openness to experience appear related to growth, as do some elements in the social environment.[21] If a griever is surrounded by a strong network of family and friends, they are likely to grow following the loss. In turn, the griever might be motivated to give back to their community, sparing someone else from experiencing the same type of loss.

To this end, Carly is doing her part to build supportive environments by plugging a gap often overlooked in family tragedy, specifically the experience of siblings. Carly hopes that through her own personal experience, she can provide the social support necessary to tip the balance toward posttraumatic growth. When a family tragedy occurs, siblings are often the "forgotten mourners," who disappear into the background. Yet, they experience a range of emotions that can be as intense as those the parents experience. Like Carly, they can feel guilt that they survived when a sibling perished or powerless that they were unable to prevent the tragedy from occurring. Over time and left unaddressed, the thoughts and feelings of siblings can prevent them from becoming well-balanced, functioning adults. Carly believes that siblings often

[20] Tolstikova, K., Fleming, S., and Chartier, B. (2005). Grief, complicated grief, and trauma: The role of the search for meaning, impaired self-reference, and death anxiety. Illness, Crisis and Loss, 13, 293–313.

[21] Prati, G., and Pietrantoni, L. (2009). Optimism, social support, and coping strategies as factors contributing to posttraumatic growth: A meta-analysis. Journal of Loss and Trauma, 14, 364–388.

lack the tools to effectively evaluate their experience and, therefore, need to be given the space to discuss their loss and explore the thoughts and feelings that go alongside of it without judgment. The first step is recognizing that parents and siblings experience grief that presents itself in distinct ways. In addition, there is a cumulative effect with the likely change in the amount and type of attention siblings receive from their now-grieving parents.

In my interview with Stacy, she echoed many of Carly's observations about grief and loss. "This is a process. You can do things to support the process, but grief itself cannot be alleviated. People need to go through it." She emphasizes that even if a loss is expected and an individual engages in preparatory grief, the turmoil following death is no less intense. "When someone you care about, and organize your days around, and count on dies, it is like tearing apart of the world—your world. The pain of loss is great and feels shattering. Whether you anticipated the death, or were surprised by it, doesn't matter." When Stacy consults with the bereaved, she talks about grief with the analogy of tulip bulbs waiting patiently underground for Spring. Under the snow and ice, the tulips are gaining strength, building roots, and readying themselves to bloom. So too will the bereaved emerge from the loss, but it will require significant effort, and when the time is right, they will navigate through the grief and make meaning from life once again. Stacy talks about the strain on the body, early on in grief, "The sad feelings, or the tears, or the fatigue would hit me. Or I caught a cold. Or something else seemed to get in the way of me feeling back to normal. It was 'always something.' And basically, it was all grief."

In addition to the physical drain, grief often manifests in our memories. Stacy states, "You may find you have memories of your person—sweet ones or upsetting ones—just pop into your head, often at the most surprising times. These can be distressing just in how unexpected they can be, and how much emotion they can carry with them." Over time, guilt, about words left unsaid or actions not taken, may take over. Stacy stresses that we need to show compassion for ourselves in these moments and give ourselves a break when we feel "foggy in the brain," attempting to remember names, tasks, or directions. These are symptoms of the brain working overtime, using its cognitive resources to work through grief. Eventually, the bereaved will come to a point where they will need to reconcile the artifacts left behind. In Stacy's words, "One of weirder aspects of grief is the fact that things outlive their people. As we come to terms with the loss of our beloved, we still see the artifacts of their life all around us. There are their clothes, their books, their furniture and knick-knacks, leftovers in the fridge. The scraps of handwriting, and the unfinished projects awaiting completion on the kitchen counter: life interrupted mid-stream."

The grief work is expected to be quite disturbing to the bereaved, and others can help. People close to the bereaved might be grieving themselves with the same loss and as such, provide a reminder that they are not alone. Yet Stacy points out that family and friends will grieve in their own unique way, which might clash in style or timing. This is where the support offered by Carly and her family comes in. They can provide the type of understanding and support of lived experience. However, not being close to the loss will mean that they will likely be out of step of with where the bereaved are at in the grieving process and will need direction from the bereaved about what is needed and how they can help. As an alternative, the bereaved can turn to trained therapists, who play a vital role by listening deeply and without judgment, as well as by helping individuals work their way through complicated grief, involving heightened trauma.

When therapists are used, it is essential that they stay attuned to where their patients are both in the grief work and in the sense-making process, with no assumptions about how the story will end. In a paper written to clinicians, Tedeschi and Calhoun remind practitioners that posttraumatic growth "is neither universal nor inevitable. Although a majority of individuals experiencing a wide array of highly challenging life circumstances experience posttraumatic growth, there are also a significant number of people who experience little or no growth in their struggle with trauma."[22] One key determinant is whether an individual will have the cognitive capacity to grow, without the intrusion of additional stress following the trauma. Individuals experiencing PTSD, as defined by particularly acute and frequent intrusion, avoidance, and arousal symptoms, can find growth unattainable. Additionally, individuals who find themselves in a cycle of repeated trauma might not have the internal or external resources to fully grieve or find meaning before the next loss occurs.

As mentioned in my conversation with Stacy, the public consciousness has changed over the last decade in recognizing that certain segments of society are in a frequent and recurring pattern of loss and trauma. In this vein, Robyn Douglas led a field study involving over 500 children and adolescents receiving outpatient care for trauma and bereavement to confirm whether ethnicity and income predicted traumatic stress and maladaptive grief reactions.[23] The authors believed that polyvictimization (experiencing multiple forms of

[22] Tedeschi, R., and Calhoun, L. (2004). Posttraumatic growth: A new perspective on psychotraumatology. Psychiatric Times, 21, 58–60.
[23] Douglas, R., et al. (2021). Racial, ethnic, and neighborhood income disparities in childhood posttraumatic stress and grief: Exploring indirect effects through trauma exposure and bereavement. Journal of Trauma Stress, 34, 1–14.

trauma), deaths of multiple loved ones, and exposure to violent death created a scenario where certain segments of the population did not recover from grief and trauma in the same way. Neighborhood income disadvantage, as defined by a poorer environmental conditions, higher crime rates, and increased barriers to access for mental health services, was purposely called out as a distinct factor from ethnicity.

The research sadly confirmed what is already known, that certain segments of society are carrying a greater burden. For the Black youth who participated in the study, the prevalence of polyvictimization and the exposure to violent deaths were associated with higher stress and maladaptive grief reactions. These patients showed symptoms of reliving the trauma, life avoidance, lasting changes in cognition and mood, and hyperarousal, such as heightened vigilance to anticipate the next traumatic event. Latino youth fared better with lower levels of stress, which the authors surmised might be due to the types of social and familial support provided in the community. The study confirmed a growing body of research that shows particular segments of society get caught into an unpredictable, uncontrollable, and malevolent world where trauma is the norm due to a broader system of oppression, which in turn results in little to no room for recovery or posttraumatic growth. Instead, these youth are constantly "on-point," readying themselves for the next traumatic event.

This is the world that Michael Combs successfully escaped and has helped thousands more youth like him avoid. Michael grew up in Colorado Springs, a city just shy of 100 miles south of its much more established sibling, Denver. As a kid of the eighties, I remember traveling to the Springs and visiting the local tourist traps like Seven Falls, the Cave of the Winds, and the Garden of the Gods. I remember fondly the part in the tour when the lights were turned out in the cave, just to experience what a pure blackout feels like. My family didn't stop there—we also pulled the car over to see the replicas of cliff dwellings and a ghost town that offered visitors a taste of the old west. The educational benefits might have been marginal, but as a 10-year-old, these were great places to go. I never saw the side of Colorado Springs that Michael came from, but his version offered few opportunities for youth and limited intellectual stimulation. The largest employer at the time was a call center for MCI, while the Air Force Academy cast the largest shadow of what being an adult meant. Michael and his brother had little understanding of what a "career" was or how to get one, and both were on an alternative path to what Michael described simply as "street activities."

One day, Michael was called to his high school principal's office, which for him was a pretty common occurrence. He started packing his backpack even before he knew for certain that the school announcement was for him.

Instead of being reprimanded or being sent home, Michael was surprised to find himself redirected to the school counselor on that specific day. Michael spoke fondly of the counselor, who was known to informally look out for the students, beyond what was required by the job. Michael's school was primarily attended by Black and brown students, yet only a few visible minorities made up the school staff. These specific staff members provided a cushion of empathy and support for students like Michael, and on this day they opened up a pathway that would profoundly change the trajectory of not only Michael's life but his brother's too. Instead of facing a life on the street, jail, or worse, Michael found himself at an inflection point.

The counselor asked Michael if he would attend a presentation by INROADS, the well-established nonprofit organization that "creates pathways to careers for ethnically diverse high school and college students across the country," as part of the organization's mission to "to identify, accelerate and elevate underrepresented talent throughout their careers."[24] Michael remembers sitting in a room with three well-dressed African American men, who talked to him about what life was like in corporate America. Some of the content might not have sunk in completely, but what Michael did recognize was that this was an opportunity outside of a bleaker future and he readily applied for the program.

As an INROADS participant, Michael interviewed with Electronic Data Systems (EDS) for an internship position. Because he didn't have much experience with computers, the opportunity to work at EDS was foreign to Michael, especially as they offered him a spot on third shift, which operated late at night. If Michael accepted the internship, he knew that he would be kissing away his last summer vacation as a high school student. Overhearing that Michael was vacillating on the opportunity, his grandma intervened and spoke directly to him, "Opportunities like this do not come to people like us. You don't say no. You prove yourself to make first shift." Michael took the internship, worked evenings from 10 PM until 7 AM, attended the INROADS development programs on weekends, and entered college with money in the bank. In time, he made first shift, just as his grandma had predicted.

A big part of the INROADS philosophy is that alumni give back when they are in a position to do so. Michael never knew what it was like to be CIO, CFO, or CEO, let alone whether he would want to become one. But through the program, he was exposed to a much larger world of possibility and knew that in time he would make his impact, just like the three recruiters who visited Michael's high school. He stayed with EDS every summer during college and,

[24] INROADS. Website. https://www.inroads.org (accessed November 25, 2021).

upon graduating, took a full-time position with the company and was placed in its leadership program. Before long, Michael found himself on a plane bound for Australia to take on an international assignment, which served as a second inflection point in his working life. Michael was sitting in a conference room during his second week on the job and noticed that he was the only person of color in the room. Still getting his bearings as an American living in Australia, he casually asked the group where all the Indigenous people were in the company. The group responded with embarrassed laughter. His boss in a matter-fact way explained that there were no Indigenous people in the company and that he shouldn't really expect to encounter them in the workplace. This troubled Michael a great deal and later, he confronted his boss with an idea—to replicate his experience with INROADS at EDS in Australia.

With his boss's support, Michael approached the University of Melbourne to advertise his program. When he walked into his first recruiting event, he found a handful of interested students and successfully recruited one very committed EDS intern. Although Michael wanted a bigger program, great things often start small, and EDS was thrilled with the progress made. The country manager requested five more interns for the following year, and Michael's program was named the company's diversity initiative of the year. With the foundations in place, it was time for Michael's next leadership rotation, and he was transferred by the company to London. Upon returning to Australia a year later, this time to Sydney, he was shocked and saddened to learn that his internship program had floundered and was subsequently mothballed. Without his personal energy and commitment, no further interns were recruited, despite the best intentions of the company's leaders.

Michael's disappointment pushed him in a new direction and to commit fully to his desire to give back to society. His path to fanaticism for doing good was complete. He quit his job at EDS and took the plunge on establishing CareerTrackers, the first Aboriginal and Torres Strait Islander professional development program of its kind. The first year saw 18 participants on the program, a modest start for a program that as of 2021 hosts over 1,000 participants across Australia, supported by a network of over 200 companies hosting interns, 27 of which have committed to a 10-year strategic partnership.[25] Among its success stories, CareerTrackers students complete university at higher rates than their non-Indigenous peers and 95% of alumni are placed in full-time employment within 3 months of graduation, making on average $62,000 in their first year, which is more than double the average income for Indigenous Australians. Michael expanded the concept to other

---

[25] CareerTrackers. Website. https://www.CareerTrackers.org.au (accessed November 28, 2021).

underrepresented groups, from Māori students in New Zealand to asylum-seekers in Australia and the forgotten populations living in Papua New Guinea. Underlying his fanaticism is Michael's motivation to pay back the help he received when he was at an infliction point in his youth, "I know how it feels not to have opportunity and I don't want anyone to feel that." Michael's fanaticism is driven by social justice and a deep belief that relationships are built on reciprocity and fairness. Without the outreach of INROADS and the opportunity provided by EDS, Michael believes he could have easily ended up in jail. That reality "sits inside you." He considered it his "responsibility to help others avoid that path—to ignite the good in them for their benefit and their families." Michael's fanaticism is about turning the negatives of hardship and inequality into a force for change. It doesn't hurt that through Michael's work, he encounters some truly exceptional organizations and people. He is thankful every day to "get to work and collaborate with some really smart people."

I met Michael when CareerTrackers was in its infancy. Michael was blanketing employers in Sydney for potential internship sponsors for a new class of participants. For my part, I was a regional manager for a company specializing in recruitment and development. I remember the meeting distinctly, as Michael's passion for what he was doing was infectious, as were the personal stories of the two former interns that he brought with him that day. Although we did not have the right opportunities for meaningful internships, a few of the psychologists I worked with volunteered with me to build out and lead the interns through a personal development program. Using a series of assessments as our guide, including tools to evaluate personality and motivation, we provided coaching to the interns. Through the assessments, they gained self-awareness about potential career paths and workplaces where they would thrive, while the experience itself provided real-world practice with the types of assessments they would encounter when applying for a job. We also included some basics around interview skills. As Michael emphasizes, the barriers experienced by the interns are formidable and gaining experience to demystify, build confidence, and learn employer expectations can enable them to truly show what they can do.

One case clearly underlines this point: An intern from that year was interested in architecture, yet the barriers to a potential career were formidable. As a member of CareerTrackers, an internship interview was arranged with a prominent firm in Sydney, yet getting him to that meeting was pitted with obstacles and new experiences. Growing up in a rural and isolated corner of Queensland, the intern had never traveled to Brisbane or its airport. He had never flown in a plane, nor caught a taxi, nor even entered a professional office building. Moreover, the intern did not own clothes that would be appropriate for an interview and had little experience in what a meeting like that would be like. If employed, he would be the second person in his entire extended family to hold a job. Michael understood these challenges and was committed to set the intern up for a positive and rewarding experience. Our component was only a small part of the intern's preparation, by providing him with some knowledge and experience about the interview, yet I felt a tremendous amount of pride in furthering the attainment of his dream to work as an architect. During my interview with Michael for this book, which was over a decade later, I asked about this specific intern and was delighted to hear that he had a fantastic experience working in Sydney, eventually became the architect that he dreamed he could be, and has gained some international accolades for his work.

To get reacquainted with the obstacles that CareerTrackers participants experience on a daily basis, I decided to provide a set of one-to-one career coaching sessions for a group of high school students living in my current city. The four students were members of a program similar to CareerTrackers built for families experiencing financial hardship, involving an internship opportunity alongside normal course work and leadership development. The internships were offered by a breadth of area companies, from healthcare to financial services, and the students were encouraged to try out a variety of workplaces during their participation in the program. Similar to the students that I encountered in Australia, the participants lacked exposure to a wide range of professions and based their potential academic and career options on a limited sample of family and friends. If they knew of an uncle or family friend doing well, they gravitated to that profession without considering whether it was a good choice for them personally. What was strikingly about this particular set of students was the hard-working nature of their families. Across the four students, their caregivers were either small business owners or worked multiple jobs, while the students themselves worked outside of school hours, contributing what they could to their families. As such, the challenge for me was to recognize the reality that these students routinely experienced, but provide a wider perspective on what their career options could be like with additional education or apprenticeship.

It had been a while since I had done one-to-one coaching, and I was nervous about how well the approach and tools would be received by the students. The assessments that I used were commercial grade and meant for more experienced employees, however I chose them for the breadth of personality and motivational variables included. In addition, I decided that the students would experience these tools in the near future and, therefore, experiencing what an assessment feels like would be a good activity on its own. The trade-off was that students at this age generally lack the self-insight into their psychological drivers to complete the tools in a consistent way, and this was what I found when I reviewed their assessment results. All but one student was extremely low on how consistently they responded to the assessments, meaning that I would have to rely much more on our conversation to understand their potential fit to different careers and workplaces.

I sat down with each student for a 1-hour coaching session, beginning with an open conversation about their internship experience, interests in school, and whether they had any extracurricular activities. From there, we went through the assessment results, looking for connections between their personal experience and future possibilities. My first student, H., demonstrated a strong interest in caring for the needs for others, driven in part by observing his mother, who worked in cosmetology, and his aunt, who worked as an interpreter for the deaf. We discussed at length how he could take the need to help people and turn that into a career as varied as working in emergency services to clinical or medical applications. As potential blockades to this plan, H.'s natural inclination was to a maintain a limited social network and to hold back when speaking about his own interests. Taken together, these tendencies could result in H. not exploring all potential avenues or failing to advocate for himself when a good opportunity presented itself.

K. had a very different profile from H. and had very clear expectations about his future career. His uncle had a successful roofing company, hiring a number of crews for work across the upper Midwest during the summer and projects further south during the winter. K.'s plan was to graduate high school then join his uncle and learn the business, so as to eventually own his own construction company. Working with this personal insight, K. and I talked about three distinct capabilities in running a construction company, specifically the trade (i.e., roofing), the business (i.e., commercial aspects like accounting), and contracting. Although K. had great insight that he needed to learn these capabilities, he was less clear on how these components could come together. K.'s initial thinking was to finish high school and then begin roofing full time with his uncle before potentially returning to school to learn business. I was able to challenge this thinking by emphasizing the momentum that he has built both in school and with the internship program and how he could use these existing relationships to find a suitable business degree. We talked about how he could still work as a roofer during the summers, to make money and learn the trade, and attend school either part-time or during the off-season to make good on the momentum already built up.

M. was in a different place than either H. or K., in that she was caught between two very different potential career paths. On one hand, she was interested in medicine and pursuing a career in the health profession, but on the other, she expressed interest in becoming a real estate agent. Like H. and K., this latter preference was based on who she knew personally and a perception that they were doing well in life. From a personality vantage point, M. showed the dynamism to make either a possibility, with energy, tenacity, and competitiveness in her profile, as well as a strong orientation toward careers that are more social in nature. We talked about how best to evaluate these two options as she started to consider what she would need to do for college and beyond. My last student was the youngest of the four and did not come into the session with any clear ideas about future careers. For X., we spent the hour discussing his profile and building self-awareness, such that he could start asking the bigger questions about the types of jobs that could motivate him the most.

Common across these four students were a few characteristics that are worth mentioning. All four showed an unique combination of strong emotional control, high tolerance toward criticism, and low general anxiety. Either through lived experience or by pure chance, these students had the potential to weather challenges and learn from them. Yet, they also showed hesitancy in how they interacted with others, from being lower on trust to demonstrating a lack of social confidence in expressing their opinions and needs. Advocating for themselves and building social relationships was a common need, which thankfully was being addressed through their internship program and the community created with their peers in the program and sponsors.

For my part, I truly enjoyed getting to know these students and taking the opportunity to speculate on what their potential futures could hold. Unlike working with adults, the conversations required much more effort, both to build up self-awareness and to key into core themes. Yet, the students' honesty and openness more than made up for the effort invested. Knowing that this was probably one of the first career conversations that they had had, I held back on providing any strong recommendations, fearing that they would take this advice literally and potentially close down strong alternatives. This was especially true for this group both because of their age and the limited breadth of their relationships, where the experiences of close family members shaped their concept of work. Through my limited time working with the students, I was reminded of the impact that I could have on broadening perspective and asking the big questions. Just like the architect from CareerTrackers that I had met when living in Australia, these students experienced societal and historical barriers on a daily basis. By gaining exposure and support around the world of work, their options could expand exponentially and they could take control over their own futures, to pursue the work that is the best fit for them personally. As with CareerTrackers, I was content being a small part of the community standing behind these students as they explored their possibilities and am thankful for people like Michael who bring such communities together.

In many ways, Michael was not the clear choice for establishing a program like CareerTrackers. He was an outsider to Australia, had limited exposure to the country's history, and was not part of the culture he was helping. On the other hand, it might have been because he was the outsider that he could ask the obvious question, "Where are all the Indigenous workers?," and feel able to do something about it. Michael used his vulnerability as a strength. In the early years, he looked around for validation that he was on to something good, using his hypervigilance to push the program faster and further. He reminded himself that the lack of equity he had experienced growing up in Colorado Springs provided a foundation for understanding the needs and obstacles faced by the interns on his program. He built trust with the community that what he was doing was authentic. With every new corporate sponsor, Michael was able to build CareerTrackers into a de facto component of each organization's hiring. In Michael's words, "we ingrained programs into the corporate machine."

The first class of CareerTrackers participants are now well established in their careers and Michael finds himself taken aback by how much the participants use the content from the program. Michael spoke about an encounter he had with a program alum, where the two met at the train station prior to heading out for a meeting with a new potential sponsor. The alum drilled Michael about the state of his appearance, suggesting that he was dressed too casually and was letting himself down on looking professional. This anecdote works also to pinpoint where CareerTrackers is within its evolution. Michael stepped down as CEO in February 2020, believing it was time for the organization to be led by an Indigenous Australian. Michael remains as a strategic advisor to the board, but keeps his influence at arm's length. He likens the transition to being an empty-nester, with kids moving out of the house to go to college. Although he is enjoying the quiet life for now, Michael knows that his fanaticism will return, "it is quite addicting—the job is never done." He is still driven by social justice and knowing just how long the journey is for society to live up to its own ideals, there will be plenty of opportunity for Michael to get back involved and again be "an agitator for change."

Carly and Michael started their lives worlds apart, but independently found a common type of fanaticism based on trauma and turning it into something meaningful. Like Kris from the Minnesota Force, whom we met in the last chapter, their type of fanaticism is social in nature, finding kinship with others in the pursuit of compassion and love. Neither Carly nor Michael initially chose to do what they do, but were able to find meaning and grow. Carly does more work these days as part of the support network than as a clinician, but in either case, she continues to give back to the world, turning a very unfortunate event into a reason to do good. She continues to talk about shallow water blackout, educating anyone who will listen about the risks of pushing the body too far while underwater. She talks at conferences and advocates about sibling grief and the need to recognize the forgotten mourners of family tragedy. Lastly, she continues to support victims of trauma both as a psychologist and compassionate friend for those living in her community.

Similar to Carly, Michael is working on the prevention of trauma, but the type of trauma he is addressing is of a historical and wide significance. Using his own experience growing up with limited options, Michael is constantly on the outlook for societal inequality and finding ways to alleviate some of the deep obstacles preventing others from living the life that they desire. Like what Stacy Remke talked about, he is driven to break the cycle of repeated trauma, as characterized by polyvictimization, exposure to violence, and living under stressful conditions that place young people in a state of hypervigilance, rather than allowing them to thrive socially and professionally. Through his work with CareerTrackers, Michael has touched the lives of thousands of young people, putting them on a track to pursue professions aligned more to their passions than the socioeconomic status that they might represent. Just like with INROADS, the impact of Michael's work will likely be exponential, as each alumni gives back to the next generation of scholars and thereby promotes an ever-growing network of opportunities.

We are all better as a society for the fanaticism and acts of kindness by people like Carly and Michael, who give so much of themselves to prevent others from experiencing their anxiety and pain. They give to us without a need for recognition or a drive to stroke their own egos; their altruism is genuine, as they have discovered a way to give through loss. They are also resilient, a trait that is shared with other fanatics profiled later in this book, notably those driven by change and innovation. "Sadder but wiser" or "a broken heart that is bigger and stronger" might be fair ways of describing fanatics like Carly and Michael who have experienced trauma (and potentially grief), created meaning from it, and reinvented themselves in a way that benefits us all. Yet, the reality is that such fanaticism originates from a world that has been broken, either with unfulfilled promises or personal tragedy. Like the tulips under the snow, personal growth emerges slowly, but with energy and dedication, the love felt for others in loss can be carried forward into a new reality.

On the anniversary of Nic's death, Carly remembers her brother with the following Facebook post, "20 years of missing you. 20 million moments we wish you were here. 20 thousand times I've felt your presence when I needed it. It feels like yesterday and a lifetime ago all at once since you've been around. You've missed so much. The heart is just ever so much heavier today. If only you were here. Love you my little brother."

PART 2
THE PHYSICAL

3
Ultra Physical

Underlying the fanatic behavior shared by Marj, Kris, Carly, and Michael are deep social connections formed with others to either share the joy of a fictional universe or navigate significant loss and trauma. Other types of fanaticism do not share such a dependency on the social world to drive fanatic behavior, but instead are characterized by personal introspection and an isolation from others. My first foray into this alternative type of fanaticism took place on a sunny, late afternoon in the town of Buena Vista, which lies around 20 miles south of Leadville, Colorado. As I walk into the aptly named combination coffee and mountaineering shop, The Trailhead, I am thrilled to see my longtime friend Ben, who has graciously provided a glimpse into the burgeoning sport of ultramarathons. To me, Ben seems to epitomize what an ultramarathoner should be. His eyes are bright with energy, his complexion tanned from a summer of outdoor running, his body thin and muscular, and his face much more bearded than I remembered. Although he is starting to gray, I am in no doubt that Ben is probably at the top of his physical game. There is something very rugged and natural about trail running and from what it looks like, it leaves its mark on its participants. Beyond his physicality, Ben's demeanor is well tuned to the sport. Like many ultramarathoners, Ben is open to experience, keen to lend a hand, and humble. His connection to the sport is personal and not driven by outdoing the other participants. The goal for the far majority of ultramarathons is to finish; to drive down the temptation to quit and push yourself over the finish line to earn a buckle.

The Leadville 100 is the second-oldest race of its kind. It was born out of economic catastrophe, when the Climax Mine closed in 1982. With the loss of 3,250 jobs, Leadville took the unenvious position of the city with the highest unemployment rate in the nation. Leadville would have preferred to be known for its designation as a National Historic Landmark District, a once thriving silver mine, and the highest incorporated city in North America, with an altitude close to 2 miles above sea-level. Its past involved an eclectic list of characters, including Molly Brown, Jesse James, Wyatt Earp, and Doc Holliday. Looking for an opportunity to reinvent the town and boost visitor numbers, Ken and Merilee Chlouber established the "Race Across the Sky,"

Fanatic. Joe Ungemah, Oxford University Press. © Oxford University Press 2024. DOI: 10.1093/9780197783894.003.0004

a run that would take participants up and over Colorado's toughest mountains. The inaugural race in 1983 had only 45 runners, in comparison to the near 1,000 participants consistently experienced twenty years later. In a letter to participants, Ken and Merilee write that their core motivation was family: "What could we do for Leadville and what could we do for you. And you, from your heart responded. Leadville became home."[1] The mission of the race has not changed, "to make a positive difference in Leadville and each and every one of you (runners)." Every year, Ken provides a motivational talk to participants, emphasizing his key message: "You're better than you think you are, and can do more than you think you can."

The notoriety of the Leadville 100 was elevated in the early 1990s, when the race was visited by members of the secluded Tarahumara tribe from Mexico. Known as the Running People, the tribesmen spent their lives trail running, learning how to relax into a run in a way few other elite athletes can imitate.[2] In 1993, a pack of five Tarahumara took three of the top five spots at Leadville. The first non-Tarahumara finished a full hour (equivalent to six miles) behind, which is even more impressive considering that the tribesmen did not train for the race and ran in makeshift sandals made of leftover tires. ESPN got word of their achievement, and soon the Leadville 100 hit prime time, with the *New York Times*, *Sports Illustrated*, *Runner's World*, and *Le Monde* following the Tarahumara triumph. Attention got amped up further when Ann Trason entered the race. Touted as an epic battle of the sexes, the 1994 event saw Ann blow past the field early in the race, holding the lead until the final 10 miles, when a single tribesman named Juan Herrera sprinted by, with his woolen poncho flaring out behind him. Ann finished second, setting the women's record for a 100-mile race at 18:06:24, which by 2024 has yet to be broken. For their part, the Tarahumara finished strong, taking 3rd, 4th, 5th, 7th, 10th, and 11th places. Despite their amazing finish, the tribesmen found the circus of the event too much and decided never to set foot in Leadville again.

The first ultramarathon was born out of a very different type of endurance race, when in 1959, the avid horseman Wendell Robie bragged about his amazing horse to a group of companions gathered around a campfire in Robinson Flat, located close to Lake Tahoe.[3] To prove the point that his horse was as good as any horse from the past century, he organized a ride from Tahoe to Auburn over mountains and canyons for a few select friends. Other

---

[1] Leadville Trail 100 Run. Athlete Guide. https://www.leadvilleraceseries.com/wp-content/uploads/2019/08/Leadville-Athlete-Guide-100-RUN-Read-Only.pdf (accessed August 17, 2019).

[2] McDougall, C. (2009). Born to Run. New York: Vintage Books.

[3] A Horse Race Without a Horse: How Modern Trail Ultramarathoning Was Invented by Karen Given, Only a Game, June 28, 2019.

riders got jealous after hearing about their excursion and encouraged Wendell to do another, and thus the Western States 100 trail ride (now the Tevis Cup) was born. One of the horses entered in the 1971 ride, named Rebel, was ridden by a stocky 205-pound man named Gordon Ainsleigh. Gordy took an unconventional approach to the downhill sections of the race; he chose to run alongside his horse rather than walk. The strategy was highly effective, as he passed many of the other riders who were taking it slow.

In a string of bad luck, Gordy lost Rebel to a failed romantic relationship and then lost his replacement horse when it went lame just before the 1973 ride. Attempting to lift his spirits, Drucilla Barber, the secretary of the Western States Trail Foundation, approached Gordy with an unconventional proposition; how would he like to compete in the 1974 ride, but without a horse? Taking it half-seriously, Gordy brushed off the idea, convincing himself to that he would find a horse by race time. But he didn't; and at the age of 27, Gordy found himself entered into a really long and dangerous horse race without a horse. The morning of the race, Gordy got himself to the start line, said to his friends, "Well, I guess I'll be going," to which they replied, "Well good luck, Gordy," as he disappeared into the darkness. Gordy recapped that moment, "It was like nobody knew it was happening. One of my favorite words is auspicious—this is very inauspicious. It was amazing."

At the 40-mile mark, things were looking dire for Gordy. It was 107 degrees Fahrenheit and on the climb up Devil's Thumb (which rises 1,600 feet in 1.6 miles), Gordy was ready to quit. At that moment, Gordy's friends provided some much-needed support and specifically, gave him some salt. As this was the first race of its kind, Gordy was running without water or aid stations. Despite the fact that he spread 10 quarts of Gatorade out across the trail, it simply was not enough. Within 30 minutes of taking some salt tablets, Gordy was back on his feet and ready to complete the race, which we did with a forward roll over the finish line. Through complete happenstance, Gordy had become the first ultramarathoner.

The following year, a man named Ron Kelley heard about Gordy and decided to attempt the same feat, but fell short of finishing by 2 miles. The 1976 race similarly only had one runner, a man named Ken Shirk, who was nicknamed Cowman. The problem with Cowman was that he liked to talk. Gordy also liked to talk, so when the two them got into talking at one of the aid stations, the delay cost Cowman the race, as he disqualified himself from the 24-hour cutoff. It was not until 1977 that the race became official, with sponsorship and advertising in *Runner's World*. Fourteen runners competed, with one participant breaking the 24-hour mark and two more completing the race in under 30 hours. Gordy himself competed again in 1978, with 62 other runners. The sport has grown exponentially from those early years. In 2018 alone, there were 115,000 ultramarathoners competing in more than 2,000 races.

Technically, an ultramarathon can be defined as having any distance above the standard 26.2-mile (42.2 km) marathon. Distance-limited races come in some standard formats at 50 km, 50 miles, 100 km, or 100 miles. They can also be time-limited, with common formats including 6-hour, 12-hour, 24-hour, and 48-hour formats. Easily the most ridiculously long race in the world is the Sri Chinmoy Self-Transcendence race, which is a 3,100-mile race carried out over 52 days.[4] Runners are allowed to run between 6 AM and midnight to accomplish a minimum of 59.6 miles per day. As of 2019, only 43 people have completed the Transcendence, the fastest in 40 days, 9 hours, and 6 minutes. The crazy part about the Transcendence is that runners complete the race around a single block in New York City. Runners head down the sidewalk on 84th Avenue, go past a playground and alongside Grand Central Parkway, around Thomas Edison High School, and circle back on 168 Street to 84th again. They do this loop again and again 5,649 times, and the only break in the monotony comes when the runners are allowed to change their running direction the following day.

There does appear to be an upper limit to what the human body can endure. In a study of the Race Across the USA, where runners travel from California to Washington, DC, in 140 days, scientists discovered that finishers successfully dialed back their energy use to a level of about 2.5 times the body's resting metabolic rate (approximately 4,000 calories a day for the average person).[5] Above this level and the human body cannot digest, absorb, and process enough food to allow for the higher energy expenditure. Higher levels of exertion can occur for shorter events, for example, a marathon runner uses 15.6 times their metabolic rate, but as the distance increases to levels like the Transcendence, the pace has to slow way down. The speed limit for ultramarathons is not set by the heart, lungs, or muscles, but instead by the gut.

As mentioned, ultramarathon running has grown exponentially since the 1970s and now appeals to a much wider and more diverse population, which is also why average running performance has not improved over the decades.[6] On average, ultramarathoners are 44.5 years old, predominately male, and married, and hold a bachelor's degree or higher. Over the course

[4] Sri Chinmoy Self-Transcendence: The 3,100-mile Race Around New York by Justin Goulding, BBC Sport, June 21, 2019.
[5] Ultimate Limit of Human Endurance Found by James Gallagher, BBC News, June 6, 2019.
[6] Knechtle, B., and Nikolaidis, P. (2018). Physiology and pathophysiology in ultramarathon running. Frontiers in Physiology, 9, 634.

of their lives, these runners have had a stable body weight. Unsurprisingly, they are healthier than the general population, having experienced less serious illnesses and missed fewer days of work. Yet unfortunately for them and especially bad considering where they like to run, ultramarathoners do tend to experience more allergies and a higher rate of exercise-induced asthma. Their first participation in an ultramarathon usually occurs around 36 years old, with 7 years of competitive long-distance running under their belt. Unlike almost every other sport, peak performance happens much later in life for its athletes. The fastest men competing in 100-mile races are 37 years old, while women are slightly older at 39 years old. Pretty much everything I just described applies to Ben; in a sport that is anything but average, Ben fits the description of how and when a person finds themselves as a part of the ultramarathon community.

The path Ben took to reach this particular Leadville 100 ultramarathon is as rugged as the race itself. Ben self-describes as an unnatural athlete and someone who would not typically be tagged as a runner. His legs are shorter than they should be, and his speed and coordination are so-so. Ben's talents on the surface are in a very different discipline; Ben holds a PhD in music and is a concert pianist. His hands flow across the piano in a way that many of us who are amateur musicians only wish they could. It's just that his superhuman musical coordination didn't translate to throwing or kicking a ball. Yet, what did endure was a combination of intense focus and perseverance. To prepare for a major recital, Ben would invest 9 months of dedicated practice, hours a day, to perfect his playing. Over and over, he would work to master the expression of each note to voice the right emotion. This is not so different from the long hours dedicated to building up stamina prior to an ultramarathon. Nonrunners often ask how a runner gets over the boredom of pounding the pavement for hours on end, akin to how nonmusicians speculate about practicing the same piece of music for the better part of a year. As Ben puts it, "Talent only gets you so far. The rest is discipline."

I spoke with Richard Fryer, a registered psychologist specializing in performance sport to better understand the motivations behind athletes like Ben. After initially studying electrical engineering and working in the corporate sector, Richard decided to follow his passion and work full-time with athletes. Richard's journey started when he watched Steve Redgrave compete in the 2000 Olympic Games held in Sydney and decided that he would try his hand at rowing. With a retooling of his professional background as a psychologist, he soon realized that he made a better coach than athlete. Over the next decade, Richard designed the psychology educational program for British rowing coaches, moved to Australia, and began assembling a portfolio of clients. He made the full-time switch to sport performance in 2020 and by 2023 was the National Psychology Lead for Archery Australia and Senior Consultant with the Australian Institute of Sport. He works across a wide range of sports, from water polo and archery to skeleton and athletics, and is particularly proud that 30 of his clients competed in the Tokyo Olympics and Paralympics.

Early in our conversation about performance, Richard pointed out that is very hard to recognize whether an athlete has achieved the higher limits of their capability, as the context of sport is dynamic and doesn't permit any true "do-overs." He encourages his clients to focus on their personal goals and aspirations, instead of just the outcomes of a game or match. Overly focusing on outcomes can often make "things happen, like an increase in anxiety or a fear of failure." Richard is quick to clarify that he is not proposing abandoning outcomes as a measure of performance, but rather to put them in perspective of how the full story unfolds. Positive outcomes act as reinforcements, especially if accomplished under pressure, and very practically ensure continued funding for the sport. When working with Olympic athletes, Richard has seen a wide range of mindsets, from those who are just happy to "have the shirt, but have little belief that they have a chance at medaling," to experienced athletes who know what to expect as they prepare for the Games. For this latter group, they know that the Olympic journey takes discipline to hone skill and ensure consistently high performance. To make this jump, Richard says that they will have to ask themselves, "Do I want it enough and will I pay the price, knowing what it will take?"

When put underneath the psychological microscope, ultramarathoners in particular are highly intrinsically motivated people. Instead of putting emphasis on the competition, they draw their energy from the adventure of the ultramarathon itself; pushing the limits on what the human body can do and reveling in that experience.[7] Later in this book, we will encounter the psychological driver "benign masochism," a term used to describe an athlete's quest to push the body to its limits and gain great pleasure from managing this feat. Like their high-risk sporting peers, ultramarathoners take interest in and enjoy preparing the race strategy, managing their bodies during the race, discovering how far they can go, and sharing the experience with their cocompetitors. This last point requires a little extra explanation. Although the act of running an ultramarathon is an incredibly solo activity, with the runner focused a great deal on their own mental and physical endurance, the spectacle of the run and its accomplishment is witnessed by a host of other runners

---

[7] Roebuck, G., et al. (2018). The psychology of ultramarathon runners: A systemic review. Psychology of Sport and Exercise, 37, 43–58.

and support crews. Sharing in such a momentous challenge and overcoming it together makes the ultramarathon community a tight-knit bunch, a characteristic that will come up again when we meet skydiving fanatics.

I initially sought out an interview with Richard for his professional expertise and was unaware until about halfway through our conversation that he had firsthand experience of running ultramarathons and the grit needed to accomplish such a feat. After completing his first marathon in 2018, he decided to compete in the Tarawera 50K race in New Zealand, which he described in equal measure as both "organized pain and suffering" and a "transcendent experience." He had paced one of his ultramarathon friends during the overnight and most grueling part of the run. Describing these experiences, Richard underscores not only the power of the ultramarathon community but also the role that uncertainty plays in an athlete's motivation to stick with the sport. When it comes to performance, a guaranteed outcome is not nearly as motivating as the unknown,[8] which is why techniques that involve athletes envisioning themselves on the podium can inadvertently backfire.[9] An athlete's anxiety about winning spurs action and higher levels of performance, especially when the challenge is viewed within their capability to overcome.

Richard is always listening for the word "hope" when he works with his clients, knowing that hope is the antithesis to strategy and effective preparation. To turn anxiety into performance requires athletes to address both their "implementation intentions" and the likely barriers that they will need to overcome. He looks for ways to simulate the expected challenges and will put his clients into physical and mental distress, "By questioning what can go wrong, we can make their worry productive." Along the way, he works to improve the athlete's ability to focus on the present moment and trust their judgment when experiencing discomfort to push into higher levels of performance. Richard's goal is to ensure a "consistency in behavior when the pressure is on," which can only be accomplished through commitment and discipline.

The amount of preparation dedicated to ultramarathons can cross over into neuroticism, with the risk of missing the point of ultramarathon running. Garry Curry, who had completed the Leadville 100 on 23 separate occasions by 2019, provides advice to first time runners: "Recognize how lucky we all are to be able to be part of such a grand adventure. Take a second sometime this weekend and look around at these magnificent mountains and be inspired by

[8] Abuhamdeh, S., and Csikszentmihalyi, M. (2015). Enjoying the possibility of defeat: Outcome uncertainty, suspense, and intrinsic motivation. Motivation and Emotion, 39, 1–10.

[9] Mattie, P., and Monroe-Chandler, K. (2012). Examining the relationship between mental toughness and imagery use. Journal of Applied Sport Psychology, 24, 144–156.

the indomitable spirit that's on display."[10] Brian Costilow, a 10-time finisher of the race, concentrates his advice on the family aspect of the Leadville 100, recommending to "Make it a goal to enjoy your fellow runners." With the exception of elite runners, it is hard to find runners who are singularly focused on their podium spot in the Leadville 100 crowd.

Ben can relate to Brian's advice about enjoying the experience for what it is and he too revels in the simplicity of running. Ben speaks affectionately about experiencing a full day of running, from sunup to sundown, doing the exact same motion for hours on end. Even better, Ben gets to experience the day in his absolutely favorite place, high up in the Rocky Mountains. When the conditions are right, it is hard for Ben not to zone out when running. He lets go of any anxiety or discontent bottled up over the course of his day, exchanging this for the pure existence of the moment. This feeling of escapism is shared across many types of fanatics, from those who engage in virtual reality to the roller coaster enthusiasts profiled later in the book. Yet beyond escapism and consistent with many other ultramarathoners, Ben also achieves a state of flow. Beginning after about 2 hours into a race, Ben gets giddy and feels on top of the world. He finds his pace, settles into a steady rhythm, and enjoys the passing scenery. If there exists a scratch of extrinsic motivation for Ben, it is when he contemplates how many people have actually finished an ultramarathon. Yet, this pride of being a finisher is far outweighed by the experience itself as the primary motivator for Ben's competition in ultramarathons.

The race itself can be broken up by segment, each playing on the physicality and psyche of the runner as they attempt to cope with bodily stress. Early morning excitement and nervousness transitions to disciplined effort and self-affirmation. Starting the race too quickly causes a great number of issues later in race, as bodily resources are expelled too quickly. By the time runners hit the halfway mark, they have completed nearly two marathons and are in desperate need of nutrition and emotional support. This is the point where I was to meet Ben for the Leadville 100, at Winfield aid station. Ben would have just completed a rapid ascent from Twin Lakes, gaining in elevation from 9,200 feet to 12,600 feet at the top of Hope Pass, followed by a descent into Winfield involving a rapid drop of 2,400 feet, which actually puts more strain on the legs than the climb. As the race has an out-and-back design, Ben would have the luxury of doing that exact same climb and descent in reverse order.

The challenge posed by Hope Pass sets the Leadville 100 apart from other ultramarathons, as runners often state that the 60-mile mark is where things

---

[10] Leadville Trail 100 Run. Athlete Guide. https://www.leadvilleraceseries.com/wp-content/uploads/2019/08/Leadville-Athlete-Guide-100-RUN-Read-Only.pdf (accessed August 17, 2019).

get serious and the desire to pull out from the race peaks. At this point, non-elite runners would have been running continuously for 15 hours and burned through most of the body's strategies for generating energy. Runners experience a shutdown of their digestive tract, which means that any food consumed past that point sits longer in the gut, causing nausea, cramps, and sickness. It is not uncommon for runners to experience gastrointestinal bleeding after an ultramarathon. In fact, close to 80% of ultramarathon finishers complain about digestive problems due to running, with nausea being the most common. It is no wonder that digestive problems are cited as some of the main reasons runners give up competition.

The 60-mile mark also coincides with sunset for nonelite runners at the Leadville 100. Beyond Hope Pass, runners must traverse two additional climbs at Mt. Elbert and Sugarloaf Pass. Completing these segments, in the middle of the night after a full day of running, puts the body at extreme distress, and hallucinations are not uncommon. Dereck, a fellow pacer at the Leadville 100, described the hallucinations of his runner during the prior year's race. His friend saw blood pouring down the faces of all the other runners he encountered, believing that he was living in some sort of real-life horror movie. Only through Dereck's continued reassurance did he stop yelling and accept that he was hallucinating. Partially due to this experience and the general state of runners at this point in race, Dereck nicknamed this segment the Zombie Apocalypse. As a sports medicine practitioner, he actually prefers pacing during the early morning, as he feels this is when he can be of the greatest use.

Getting the motivation to continue running during the dead of night is not easy, and runners use any source of encouragement to keep going. In Ken Chlouber's words, "When it comes to that point, when it hurts beyond hurt, when your lungs are burning, your leges are dead, and you've still got miles and miles to go, that's when you dig deep."[11] Ben thinks about the commitment he has made to his friends, family, pacers, and crew to keep going. Quitting, in his mind will be a letdown to both himself and those who are there to support him. In the words of a previous finisher of the Leadville 100, Danny Bundrock, "Once the gun goes off, we cannot change our level of physical ability. We can only affect our outcome by using our mental component, by keeping our pre-race goal in mind and not giving in to some temporary discomfort." Having accurate expectations about just how bad it will get can make a difference for runners; when a runner feels like death, calling out the feeling for what it is makes the challenge easier to move beyond it.

---

[11] Leadville Trail 100 Run. Athlete Guide. https://www.leadvilleraceseries.com/wp-content/uploads/2019/08/Leadville-Athlete-Guide-100-RUN-Read-Only.pdf (accessed August 17, 2019).

When I asked Richard about how he helps clients "dig deep," he returned to the notion that the appeal of sport is overcoming adversity and the unknown. "Sport is a story of perseverance and seeing what is physically possible." By the same token, "Preparation allows the athlete to recognize adversity and to remind them why they are there," drawing on their training to successfully navigate obstacles. "When the event is done, athletes rarely talk about all the situations that went well, but rather talk about periods of struggle and the elation they felt when they overcame them," explains Richard. When an ultramarathon runner underperforms, "their first reaction is typically 'how do I sign up for the next one?'" During the tough moments, keeping the right mindset by putting anxiety and pain in perspective, accepting these feelings as part of the journey, and employing well-rehearsed strategies all contribute to the outcome. It is no wonder that Richard's most successful clients are those who are most interested in understanding their own psyche and put in the time to developing their mindset alongside their physical prowess.

Having an answer to a range of "what if" questions allows for an immediate and practiced response to stressful situations. Yet in the middle of the Zombie Apocalypse, when hallucinations are in full swing, it is nearly impossible to employ any of this training, as Ben experienced firsthand. During his last 100-mile race, he saw houses, street signs, and cars of a city that simply did not exist. He heard and saw an old couple sitting on a bench wearing grotesque masks, followed by a group of women cackling and talking suspiciously. Whatever Ben happened to think about would all of sudden appear in his field of vision, making it especially frustrating when he thought about and then hallucinated a much-needed aid station. Without his pacer there to comfort and reassure him, the emotional distress of the hallucinations could have caused a premature end to the run.

Other runners cope with exhaustion by giving in to the urge for sleep. A crew member at Winfield recounted what happened to his son during the prior year's race. His son was over 4 hours late coming into the last aid station, causing him a great deal of concern. When he finally staggered into the aid station, his son stated that he simply could not run anymore and decided to take a nap in the woods. Bedding down on the ground a few rows away from the trail meant that no other runner or pacer could see or prevent him from sleeping in the elements. Cold, exhausted, and wet, the ingredients were in place for developing hypothermia. For this reason, many ultramarathons forbid runners from sleeping outside of aid stations. When absolutely necessary, they dictate that naps be taken in the middle of the trail so that other participants can provide assistance. And sometimes, the need goes much beyond sleep, with runners losing consciousness, as was the case for a runner this particular year at Winfield. Halfway up the slope of Hope Pass, a Search and Rescue team were deployed to collect a fallen runner and airlift him by helicopter to the closest hospital. Like any other extreme activity, ultramarathons test the limits of the human body, and even the most seasoned athlete can fall prey to a fast deterioration of health.

From a health perspective, runners at Leadville are forewarned of the dangers of the four H's. Hypoxia occurs at elevations above 10,000 feet, where there is less oxygen to breathe compared to sea level. Acclimation can take up to 3 weeks at altitude to adjust fully to the lack of oxygen. Hydration is a particular problem in Leadville, as the relative humidity can be as low as 5%, resulting in runners losing fluids more rapidly compared to other races. Hyponatremia occurs when runners drink too much fluid, flushing minerals and electrolytes out of their bodies. These minerals are necessary for cellular functioning, as well as for maintaining the heart and neurological system; as such, hyponatremia can be life-threatening. Lastly, hypothermia can easily occur in the mountains, where snowstorms during the night in August are not unheard of. If runners have to stop for weather, the heat they have generated through physical exertion will not sustain them.

Emphasized again and again across my interactions with ultramarathon runners and their crews is the goal of simply finishing the race safely. In the words of another Leadville 100 finisher, Wyatt Hornsby, spoken to first-time runners, "Patience, patience and more patience. Keep it simple—it is a very, very long run in which the greatest goal is to just finish."[12] There is no wonder why races like the Leadville 100 have very clear cutoff times for different segments of the race. If runners are not on pace to complete the race in a reasonable amount of time, they are pulled from the race at the closest aid station. For this particular race, the runners needed to complete 50 miles under 14 hours. If they completed the full 100 miles under 25 hours, they would receive a "Big Buckle," whereas a "Small Buckle" was awarded to runners who completed the race within the 30-hour cut-off.

Ben's initial foray into the running world occurred when he was living abroad in Cyprus, where he completed his first 5k and got heatstroke along the way. Ben would be the first to admit that he had historically never been great at sport and found comfort that most runners gauge themselves not by where they placed in the race, but rather by whether they finished. Ben moved on to a 10k race and, with some encouragement from a friend, then began contemplating a marathon. Short runs are like a gateway drug into marathons, which

[12] Leadville Trail 100 Run. Athlete Guide. https://www.leadvilleraceseries.com/wp-content/uploads/2019/08/Leadville-Athlete-Guide-100-RUN-Read-Only.pdf (accessed August 17, 2019).

for a select group, become a gateway to ridiculously long runs. Within a few years, Ben had five road marathons under his belt and was feeling confident he could do more. Ben was drawn to the simplicity of running and what success in this particular sport meant. You either completed the race or didn't; you either got a buckle or left empty-handed.

It didn't take long for Ben to get bored of marathons. The pain he felt recovering from a marathon no longer had the same sting, making him wonder, "What if I went further?" He convinced himself that 50 miles would be more than enough, but when that milestone came and went, a nagging re-emerged in the back of Ben's brain, "What if I could do more? What would 100 miles feel like?" Ben soon found out. With greater mileage comes increased risk of injury. On his first attempt at 100 miles, at the High Lonesome 100 in Colorado, Ben found himself running in the pouring rain, after dark, and with probably the worst running partner in the world. Unlike the communal dialogue he had grown accustomed to with ultramarathoners, Ben found himself in lock step with a self-acknowledged expert who piled on unwanted advice for miles on end. This triggered some distant memories set deep in Ben's psyche, and he quickly fell prey to a bad case of imposture syndrome, letting his self-doubt consume him mid-run.

Ben desperately wanted to escape from the know-it-all and when an opportunity came to fill up his water bottle from a stream, he gladly took it. Ben edged down toward the stream, filled up his bottle, took a sip or two, and turned back toward the trail. The only problem was that the trail wasn't where it was supposed to be. Ben had lost his bearings. Cool-headed and in control, Ben decided to climb a ridge to get a better vantage point about where he was. This extra jaunt in the woods added three miles to his run, took 1.5 hours, and cost him physically. By the time Ben limped into the next aid station, he was in bad shape. His body was soaked and his arms were frozen. He was dehydrated, low on calories, and suffering from hypothermia. Rolling up in a sleeping bag, his pacer attempted to do his job and get him back in the run, but it wasn't meant to be and Ben pulled out with more than three-quarters of the race behind him.

Unlike the rest of us, Ben wasn't scared about being alone, lost, and suffering from hyperthermia, but rather mad at himself that he was not disciplined enough to keep his confidence or correctly attend to his hydration and energy needs. As Ben put it, "Pride got in the way and that lady got in my head." Ben sought redemption and registered again for the High Lonesome the following year. This time around, Ben went all in on his preparation. He set and stuck to his mileage goals, with four trail runs per week, including a long run that peaked at 32 miles a week before the race. During the race itself, Ben put into practice techniques for "brain-hacking," which involved decoding what his body needed without overthinking or judging the signals.

During his second attempt at the High Lonesome, Ben didn't tempt fate. He stuck to his running routine, started with a slower than normal pace, and was wary of breaking superstitions, like wearing the official run shirt before completing the race. He paid attention to his body and was cognizant of his surroundings. When things got tough, Ben implemented his coping strategies, from setting realistic expectations of time goals to relying on the encouragement of his pacers. Ben's discipline paid off and when he crossed the finish line, his immediate feelings were both of elation and thankfulness to his family for giving him the opportunity to run. These emotions are in stark contrast to his first attempt, which left Ben reeling that he let both himself and his family down. With such an accomplishment under his belt, it wasn't long before Ben wondered whether he could do it again and, potentially, build up to traveling internationally for runs, such as the ultramarathon around Mont Blanc. Ben was setting his sights high.

Ultramarathons put an amazing amount of stress on the human body and a runner's brain is not immune from their effects. Alarmingly, a study conducted on runners in the 2009 TransEurope-FootRace, a formable challenge of 4,487 km, found some major brain loss following the run.[13] Participants were scanned using an MRI before, during, and eight months after the race. On average, the runner's volume of gray matter in the brain decreased by 6% across the 2-month run, which was found unrelated to issues like dehydration. In comparison, brain volume reduces by .2% per year due to normal aging, while Alzheimer's patients experience a drop of 2% per year. Using basic math, extreme running reduced the participants' brain volume to the equivalent of 3 years living with Alzheimer's or 30 years of normal aging.

The decrease in volume doesn't occur universally, but is localized in specific brain regions, those most associated with visuospatial and language ability.[14] For the most part, walking and running are only challenging during the period of learning it and much of the process is highly automated thereafter. As a result, there is not much gray matter dedicated to running and the body looks for other areas to shave off the top. The cognitively demanding tasks of language and visuospatial perception on the other hand are prime picks for energy conservation; they are complex in nature and take up a lot of real estate.

---

[13] Freud, W., et al. (2012). Substantial and reversible brain gray matter reduction but no acute brain lesions in ultramarathon runners: Experience from the TransEurope-FootRace project. BMC Medicine, 10, 170.

[14] Freud, W., et al. (2014). Regionally accentuated reversible brain grey matter reduction in ultramarathon runners detected by vowel-based morphometry. BMC Sports Science, Medicine and Rehabilitation, 6, 4.

This finding should provide some caution to any runner thinking about completing an ultramarathon before taking a college entry exam.

The good news is that runners don't appear to suffer brain lesions due to extreme running. Even better news, their brains were found to gain back all the missing gray matter before the 8-month check-up. In a separate study of endurance athletes, extreme running appears to build up connectivity in working memory and executive functions (like planning, attentional switching, and decision-making), as well as in motor control, sensory, and visual ability.[15] The stress placed on the brain to navigate rough terrain at speed seems to pay off with improved structure, function, and connectivity that has the potential to impact overall brain health.[16] It is no wonder that athletes who flex these cognitive muscles during running, rather than letting their minds wander, tend to experience improved performance. In sum, once the immediate effects of the run wear off and brain matter is restored, the net result on the brain for ultramarathoners appears positive.

Beyond brain structure, ultramarathons affect the chemistry of the runners' brains, with the release of naturally produced compounds increasing with the speed at which the runners compete. Of particular importance is the pain-reducing chemical endorphin, which is produced within the brain by the pituitary and adrenal glands. Chemically similar to opiates, endorphins are many more times powerful than opium (one type in particular, beta-endorphin, is 20–50 times more powerful) and cause the release of other chemicals, like cortisone, which aids in converting sugar into energy. Although powerful for pain suppression, any connection between endorphins and reports of runner's high has proven quite illusive. A different family of chemicals, the endocannabinoids, appear the likely suspects for runners' feelings of relaxation, analgesia, and calm that kick in during a long run.[17] As the name implies, this is the same system involved with the active ingredient of cannabis, THC.

To research the phenomenon of runner's high, scientists have focused their efforts on capturing the sensation using runners' own words. They described it as a "lift in the legs," "heightened mental awareness," "euphoria," "laughing and crying at the same time," and "being at peace in the world." Miranda, an ultramarathon runner profiled by the BBC, described her experience, "After about an hour, I can feel my mind start to settle and that's when I start to zone

[15] Raichlen, D., et al. (2016). Differences in resting state functional connectivity between young adult endurance athletes and healthy controls. Frontiers in Human Neuroscience, 10, 610.
[16] Minds Run Free by Christian Jarrett and Ella Rhodes, Psychologist, May 2017.
[17] Raichlen, D., et al. (2012). Wired to run: Exercise-induced endocannabinoid signaling in humans and cursorial mammals with implications for the "runner's high." Journal of Experimental Biology, 215, 1331–1336; Fuss, J., et al. (2015). A runner's high depends on cannabinoid receptors in mice. PNAS, 112, 13105–13108.

out and slip into a meditative state. Afterwards, I'm so relaxed—you just don't have the energy to get angry about anything!"[18] The runner's high is by no means guaranteed for runners, but rather often occurs unexpectedly and only with a select proportion of the running population. When it does occur, studies using EEG readings of the brain shows that the runner's high clicks in after about 25 or 35 minutes of continuous running.[19] It appears that humans are not alone in experiencing it and similar brain mechanisms are activated in a variety of other mammals, although they are unable to express it to us in words. Evolution appears to have given some species the means to cope with extreme aerobic exercise, giving incentive to expend more energy and risk potential injury.

As their brains cope with the immense stress created by the run, ultramarathoners experience a range of psychological states. Some report that their minds are freed of constraint during a run, allowing them unhindered time to be more creative and organized to tackle tough problems. Runners often report the sensation of flow, characterized by intense awareness, centering of attention, loss of self-consciousness, feelings of control, and a sense of timelessness.[20] Flow occurs most often when ability and challenge are in balance; if the challenge outpaces ability, runners can quickly become anxious about their ability to finish the run successfully. The sensation of flow increases significantly after 1 hour of running, then decreases steadily from that high point for the remainder of the run. Although flow is related to higher performance in nearly all other sports studied, this is not the case for distance running. It appears that runners have to act a bit like a dictator, continually forcing their bodies to run further or in the words of Ken Chlouber, to "dig deep."

Any associated tensions or bad moods held by runners prior to exercise are reported to fade away through the exertion of a long run. After the run, they even tend to revise their memories of just how painful it was. Comparisons between ratings provided by runners just after the completion of a marathon and those taken about 3 months later differed significantly in the level of intensity and unpleasantness reported by finishers.[21] A key factor was the emotional state of the runner. Runners who reported more distress and fear

[18] "I Was Addicted to Drugs, Now I'm Addicted to Running" by Hannah Price and Sophie Haydock, BBC Three, June 17, 2019.

[19] Raichlen, D., et al. (2012). Wired to run: Exercise-induced endocannabinoid signaling in humans and cursorial mammals with implications for the "runner's high." Journal of Experimental Biology, 215, 1331–1336.

[20] Stoll, O. (2019). Peak performance, the runner's high, and flow in M. H. Anshel (ed.), APA Handbook of Sport and Exercise Psychology, vol 2: Exercise Psychology.

[21] Babel, P. (2016). Memory of pain induced by physical exercise. Memory, 24, 548–559.

tended to be more accurate in their memory. Such revisions can cause a self-reinforcing pattern, where runners misrepresent just how horrible they were feeling at the end of the race and decide to push their bodies even further; why do one marathon when you can you register for two?

The temptation to push the body to its breaking point is commonly reported by ultramarathon runners, driven by a combination of intrinsic motivation, goal-driven behavior, and grit. According to Ben, running "brings out the best of yourself. Every day I am not running is a day away from me being my best. If I didn't get out and do a run, I feel like I would be on a slippery slope to being a sloth." Running provides a feeling of fulfillment for Ben and proof that he is doing good things with his time. Ashprihanal Aalto, eight-time winner of the Transcendence, goes further, "When you run a marathon, you feel good. When you run a 100km race, you feel even better. And when you run 3,100 miles, you feel even better still."[22]

Aalto might have an extreme perspective on this one, but there is no denying that on balance, it appears that extreme running appears more beneficial than harmful. From a physiological perspective, runners benefit from heightened pain tolerance, the ability to bounce back after physical exhaustion, and the potential to feel absolutely exuberant, due to the runner's high.[23] The act of running provides a release valve for anxiety and depression, using the body's own resources to restore positive emotions. It also provides an opportunity for runners to focus exclusively on the present, as defined by the concept of flow.[24] The cherry on top of the sundae is the increased brain connectivity for some really critical areas, like judgement and working memory, that occurs after consistent and long-term investment into the sport.

Yet, the story may be too good to be true. Health experts have increasingly been concerned that there is a very real dark side to ultramarathons and other endurance sports, with participants becoming increasingly addicted to the physical and psychological highs felt from completing such feats. To explore these potential pitfalls, I spoke with Dr. Zachary Hansen from the Hazelden Betty Ford Graduate School. Zach has spent his professional career driving to understand why individuals fall prey to addiction, motivated by his passion for seeing his clients regain their lives through recovery programs and embarking on a second chance at life. Although initially working directly with adults and adolescents in both inpatient and outpatient settings, Zach shifted

---

[22] Sri Chinmoy Self-Transcendence: The 3,100-Mile Race Around New York by Justin Goulding, BBC Sport, June 21, 2019.

[23] Boecker et al. (2008). The runner's high: Opioidergic mechanisms in the human brain. Cerebral Cortex, 18, 2523–2531.

[24] Minds Run Free by Christian Jarrett and Ella Rhodes, Psychologist, May 2017.

into a counselor educator role, building the next generation of practitioners in addiction counseling and treatment. When considering different types of addictions, Zach points out that the most recognizable are those that involve ingesting a foreign substance into the body, like drinking alcohol or smoking cigarettes, and will come up later in this book when we explore food fanatics. Exercise addiction is a different kind of addiction, termed a "process addiction," which spans a broad range of foci like excessive shopping, gaming, or working, but can result in similar life ramifications as substance addictions.[25] Process addictions involve both dependence (with signs of tolerance and withdrawal) and compulsion (with a need to suppress upsetting thoughts or emotions) characteristics.

Zach explains that similar to substance addictions, categorizing a behavioral pattern as harmful is not a binary choice, but rather rests on a spectrum determined by an individual's personality, the reasons behind their behavior, and their level of ability to keep functioning both when on and off the stimuli. Because process addictions are less studied by psychologists, clear diagnostic criteria for recognizing the tipping point into addiction is much less certain, with the major exception of gambling addiction. Similar to the difference in impact between marijuana and opium, there are certain behavioral stimuli that are much more powerful for creating addictive patterns. According to Zach, stimuli that provide easy outlets for stress and emotional coping are candidates for addiction. Running can easily accomplish both, with runners getting hooked to the pain eradicating beta-endorphins and the feel-good enhancing endocannabinoids. One of the ultramarathon runners profiled by the BBC, Catra, provides an interesting case study on the crossover between substance and process addiction.[26] As a previous methamphetamine addict, she got into running as an alternative to drugs and has taken the sport to extremes. In her words, "I definitely get a kind of high. I'm one of about only a dozen people in the world who has run 100 miles more than 100 times. You can definitely say that I'm addicted." Her story raises an interesting philosophical question: Just how close is the line between substance and process addiction, when the body itself is producing the powerful chemicals that are akin to those ingested from the outside?

Zach has seen the relationship between substance and process addiction play out with those he has counseled. In recovery, clients confronting their substance abuse, and the wreckage it has created, will sometimes find an

[25] Pinna, F., et al. (2015). Behavioural addictions and the transition from DSM-IV-TR to DSM-5. Journal of Psychopathology, 21, 380–389.
[26] "I Was Addicted to Drugs, Now I'm Addicted to Running" by Hannah Price and Sophie Haydock, BBC Three, June 17, 2019.

outlet through exercise. Not only does exercise give the client a physiological boost but also it can provide a socially acceptable way of connecting with others. This is especially true for stimulant users, who are energy people by nature and find workouts a natural fit. Zach states, "For sure, exercise is better than substance abuse, but it too can become life-consuming over time if obsessively used as an outlet for anxiety." He advises that when exercise becomes the replacement for a substance in recovery, and potentially a form of self-medication, the therapist should attend to the individual's coping skills for dealing with anxiety and raise awareness about self-harm.

Why process addiction falls under the radar is a factor of visibility and social norms, accordingly to Zach. It is hard to ignore the signs of alcoholism, with empty beer bottles providing visual proof alongside the social stigma of unsavory smells and sloppy behavior. The signs for process addictions are more obscure, where behaviors that may be seen as normal and rewarding can take a turn into obsession and self-harm. Even when working as a clinician, Zach rarely saw process addictions like chronic exercisers; clients were less likely either to seek treatment or feel social pressure to address their behavior, even if it began to dominate important everyday activities and cause physical injury. Yet over time, the harms build up with excessive exercise and typically include social withdrawal, dependency for mood modification, and irritability when skipped. Unlike the empty beer bottles, these are the signs that something might be wrong, yet rarely does a client identity the stimuli in the process addiction as the issue "to address and change their life." Zach explains that when the two overlap, substance addictions usually take priority as the presenting condition and become the focus of therapy.

So how much of a problem is exercise addiction? Data on the epidemiology of exercise addiction suggest that its prevalence is somewhere around 3% of the general population. Among serious runners, the prevalence is much higher, hovering close to 25% of this specific population.[27] As running distance increases, so does the risk of falling into the exercise addiction bucket. Ultramarathon runners have higher addiction rates than marathoners, who themselves score higher than short distance runners.[28] A detailed study of running community members in Hungary revealed that roughly 54% of respondents showed some signs of exercise addiction, which can turn into real problems for runners when they experience periods of anxiety or

---

[27] Buck, K., et al. (2018). Psychological attributes of ultramarathoners. Wilderness and Environmental Medicine, 29, 66–71.

[28] Dumitru, D., Dumitru, T., and Maher, A. (2018). A systematic review of exercise addiction: Examining gender differences. Journal of Physical Education and Sport, 18, 1738–1747.

loneliness.[29] Under such circumstances, they may use running as a means of self-medicating, yet this can get out of hand with increased withdrawal and uncontrolled exercising.

Similar to substance addiction, process addiction can build over time. Signs that exercise addiction have become serious include tolerance (more and more exercise is. required to provide the same lift), withdrawal (anxiety or irritability occurs if exercise is missed), lack of control (runners cannot stop themselves from doing it), missed intentions (consistently overcommitting time to exercise), unbalanced priorities (where running becomes all-consuming), and perseverance (continuing to run despite physical or other forms of harm). Those who fall prey to exercise addiction progress through a typical sequence, as outlined by Freimuth, Moniz, and Kim.[30] Runners begin by participating in recreational exercise, primarily motivated by its effects on improving quality of life and a sense of well-being. Runners then progress to at-risk exercise, where they start using exercise as a way to compensate for negative events happening in their lives, counteracting depression or anxiety with a boost of happiness and accomplishment. Any downsides are directly related to the exercise itself, for example, experiencing a stress fracture in the foot.

The situation gets serious thereafter and is termed problematic exercise, whereby individuals prioritize their lives around running. In a research paper by Hausenblas and Downs, the authors highlight a range of problematic characteristics to consider when evaluating whether a runner's dependence has a taken a turn for the worse.[31] For example, the runner may spend an inordinate amount of time running, where the day is built around the run rather than the other way around. Alternatively, the runner may exercise longer than intended, withdraw from other life activities in order to exercise, or feel anxious if they miss exercising. They might also start pushing themselves past the point of exhaustion, cause injury, and then continue running before the injury can heal. Most telling, runners might experience a lack of control, where previous attempts to reduce exercise have failed. If these patterns are exhibited, it is likely that an individual has dipped into exercise addiction, which is characterized as outright dependence, with running being the central point in life. Runners are no longer doing the activity for pleasure, but rather to minimize withdrawal symptoms. What was once an enjoyable activity has become a

[29] Lukas, A., et al. (2019). Exercise addiction and its related factors in amateur runners. Journal of Behavioral Addictions, 8, 343–349.

[30] Freimuth, M., Moniz, S., and Kim, S. (2011). Clarifying exercise addiction: Differential diagnosis, co-occurring disorders, and phases of addiction. International Journal of Environmental Research and Public Health, 8, 4069–4081.

[31] Hausenblas, H., and Downs, D. (2002). Exercise dependence: A systematic review. Psychology of Sport Exercise, 3, 89–123.

necessity to avoid the physical and psychological consequences of no longer living the life of an ultramarathon runner.

What makes exercise addiction much more complex is its relationship with other forms of substance and process addictions. It is estimated that between 15% and 20% of sport-dependent persons suffer from other forms of addiction, the most common involving psychostimulants (e.g., caffeine, cocaine, and amphetamines) or anabolic steroid abuse, deviant sexual behaviors, compulsive working or shopping, and eating disorders.[32] This last category is of major concern, as the research has indicated that as much as 80% of patients with anorexia nervosa engage in excessive exercise. Further, approximately 40% of patients across the range of eating disorders show signs of exercise addiction, as a means of controlling body image, demonstrating control over one's life, or escaping from everyday worries. The conditions play on each other, ramping up obsessive-compulsive symptoms and heightening the chances of relapse.

A study by Dr. Robin Kanarek on lab rats targeted the relationship between food and exercise directly.[33] The rats were separated into four groups, based on their level of activity (either free to run or sedentary) and eating habits (either enjoying one meal or continuous eating). After several weeks, the rats were given the drug naloxone, which is used for heroin overdoses and produces immediate withdrawal symptoms. Active rats responded very differently to the drug than their inactive counterparts, exhibiting symptoms like trembling, writhing, teeth chattering, and drooping eyes. Moreover, these conditions worsened for the rats who ate only one time per day. In contrast, inactive rats were pretty much unfazed by the naloxone, regardless of how much they ate that day.

The link between exercise and food has the potential to ruin lives. Stories have emerged of individuals exercising six or more hours a day, in order to maintain an abnormally low body weight or to maintain a specific body shape. Natalie was profiled by *The Telegraph*, sharing her story as a means to raise awareness about people suffering with exercise and food addiction.[34] Natalie started at a healthy weight when she trained for her first triathlon, but a compulsive thought got into her brain that her body was inadequate in comparison to her gym mates. She became obsessed, waking at 5 AM to squeeze in a

[32] Manea, M., Milea, B., and Campean, A. (2018). Problematic exercise: A new behavioral addiction. Civilization and Sport, 19, 37–44.

[33] Kanarek, R., et al. (2009). Running and addiction: Precipitated withdrawal in a rat model of activity-based anorexia. Behavioral Neuroscience, 123, 905.

[34] The Rise of Anorexia Athletica: I Ran Until I Was Sick and Swam Until I Fainted by India Sturgis, Telegraph, August 15, 2016.

6-km swim, followed by two 3-hour sessions of cycling or running per day. She stopped eating foods high in carbohydrates and self-imposed a rule where she only ate half of the food on her plate. She occasionally became bulimic, a sign that she was attempting to take ultimate control of her body. In Natalie's words, "It became quite chronic quite quickly. I was drained, falling asleep in lectures. I lost my relationship with my long-term boyfriend. I changed, I became very insular. When I went home, my family were shocked by my weight loss. It was a cause for concern, but they assumed that was part of being an elite-level athlete." But it wasn't and instead, Natalie had pushed too hard and didn't know how to stop.

When speaking about substance abuse, Zach identified the point at which people should seek help. "It is not just the quantity of the substance being ingested, but the distress caused to life that is important for addressing addiction." Following this thread, it is not the fact that person consumes 20 beers a day that is the issue, but rather the withdrawal and impairments to life that determine that help is needed. We each have our own set of tolerance levels for drinking or running and it is against these limits that we may need help determining whether the situation has gone too far. For runners, this knowledge is essential and just as important as all other forms of preparation and training taken on to survive an ultramarathon. As a fallback, pacers are there to provide objective advice on how the race is going and whether the runner is acting too risky and should stop.

I was waiting for Ben at Winfield aid station, ready to pace him on his return journey back over Hope Pass and into Twin Lakes. This leg of the run is the most challenging, not only because of the brutal climb in altitude but also because of its placement at the halfway point in the run. During this particular year, getting to Winfield was challenging for pacers and support crews, as the narrow dirt road to the abandoned mining town was washed out during the Spring runoff. No personal cars were allowed on the road, leaving race organizers little choice but to organize buses between Twin Lakes and Winfield, a solution made difficult by the newfound popularity of the race. Buses were delayed and support crews were missing the rendezvous times with their runners. After waiting over an hour for a bus, followed by another hour crawling up a single-lane mountain road with questionable shoulders, I was on the verge of missing Ben. I realized that I had no backup plan about what to do if he was running early and we missed each other. I decided that if his drop bag was gone, I would run as fast as possible up the pass in an attempt to catch him.

I got to the rendezvous point with 5 minutes to spare. It was 4:15 PM, and I was excited to help my friend back up the mountain. At 5 PM, Ben had yet to arrive. I double checked that his drop bag was still at the aid station. It was. At 5:45 PM, I spotted Ben shuffling into Winfield. From afar, he appeared to be in pretty good shape, but as we spoke, it was apparent that Ben was both dehydrated and having issues with his legs. The descent into Winfield was grueling; his legs buckled under him, causing him to fall multiple times on the way down. The pain Ben was experiencing is a common occurrence in races like the Leadville 100, with dramatic changes in elevation. Distance running creates a measurable inflammatory reaction and swelling in the thighs, with the down passages causing the most damage. Beyond the swelling, the legs experience a reduction in skeleton muscle mass that can be felt for up to 18 days after the run.

Ben had a decision to make. He just made the cutoff time into Winfield and if he wished to continue, he would need to leave the aid station by 6 PM (15 minutes after he arrived). The issue was compounded by the fact that he would need to increase his speed back over Hope Pass to make the next cutoff at Twin Lakes. It had taken Ben 6 hours to complete the Hope Pass segment. To stay in the race, he would have to do the same segment in 4 hours, under considerably more challenging conditions, with nightfall upon us. As a pacer, my job was to encourage my runner to keep going, but also to keep him safe and injury free. It did not take long for Ben to make the difficult decision to pull out of the race. Despite not getting his buckle, Ben's achievement was amazing by any other standard. He completed 50 miles of running just steps away from the Continental Divide.

In Ben's words, "A good day is when all things come together." Despite the pristine weather, the conditions were not 100% right for Ben. Crowding was an issue early on. Unlike Ben's experience at the High Lonesome, which had under a hundred competitors, the Leadville 100 had closer to a thousand runners. Ben wrestled with traffic for the first 12 miles, making him run behind his ideal time. To compensate, Ben sped up on the downhills, which in turn ate up his stamina for the larger descents at Hope Pass. Another side-effect of the crowds was the amount of jostling and bumping between runners. Contrary to the expectations set by the Leadville 100 organizers about feelings of community, Ben only had one conversation during his entire journey into Winfield, making the event far less enjoyable than he had anticipated.

For whatever reason, the race organizers failed to plan for pacers and support crews needing a lift back down from Winfield. Buses stopped operating at 6 PM (the cutoff time), abandoning hundreds of people up on the hill. Worse still, nearly half of the Leadville 100 runners did not finish the race, and many of them were now standing in skimpy clothing in the dark with rapidly deteriorating temperatures. After 3 hours, the Sheriff's office was called and helped organize buses back to Twin Lakes. The growing pains of organizing a big event were obvious, leaving Ben and me to question whether ultramarathons in their present format are sustainable. Moving thousands of people, providing facilities, and cleaning up the damage done to the trails and fields is a million miles away from the origins of ultramarathons. At what point do the issues of crowding overshadow the experience of running in nature among a friendly community of like-minded people?

For Ben, he didn't get the same lift of exuberance from the Leadville 100 as he did from the High Lonesome. The hook that keeps him attached to ultramarathon running was not around that day. Ben already had a 100-mile race under his belt and had nothing to prove, while the experience of the race itself was more frustrating than enjoyable, especially during the last 3 miles when his legs gave up on him. On the bus ride back to Twin Lakes, I attacked the issue head on, asking Ben whether he would do another ultramarathon, to which Ben simply responded, "I don't think so. I think I'm done." For my part, I was disappointed not to follow through on my job as a pacer. Although I was able to witness the excitement and spectacle of the sport, I did not get a chance to test my own endurance of running long distance at high altitude and at night. With this bittersweet taste in my mouth, I decided to run my first, and probably last, marathon a year later. Although I do not regret the training time invested to finish the marathon and can chalk it up as a life achievement, I was not bitten by the marathon bug and don't feel compelled to run another. Rather, the experience heightened my appreciation for Ben's commitment to train his body to such an extent that he eclipsed the furthest distance I could run by a factor of four. By the end of the marathon, I had given the race all I could give and no doubt, Ben felt the same way at Winfield.

Ben's resolve to never run another was short-lived. Within 2 months of our bus ride together, he had registered for not just for one ultramarathon, but two. Ben was guaranteed a place in the following year's Bighorn 100 held in Wyoming. He was also entered into the lottery for his dream run, the Ultra Trail du Mont Blanc, which is held in late August in Chamonix, France. The pain he experienced coming down from Hope Pass was a distant memory, providing some anecdotal evidence about how runners tend to revise their memories about pain. Instead, Ben prefers to remember the immense beauty coming over Hope Pass, as well as thinking about any lessons learned about preparing better for the downhill sections of his runs. Ben's not quite done with ultramarathons and I personally wonder when that day will come. For now, the appeal of conquering a different mountain trail on a beautiful summer day overpowers any negativity hanging over him from Leadville.

For many in the ultramarathon community, the combination of improved pain tolerance, clear-headedness, and mood enhancement is just too attractive to give up. What's more, an ultramarathoner's internal drive for accomplishment is self-fulfilling; the greater the number of miles accomplished, the more intense the drive to see just how far the body can be pushed. Ultramarathon runners not only risk bodily injury but also sacrifice time and energy that would normally be invested in friends and family. With a lifestyle that tends to be all-consuming, the ultramarathoner's fanaticism is one of physical resilience and introspection. They feel their best running in the deep forest, where they can cherish their connection with nature and the simplicity of their sport. The rewards of running are hoarded, occurring entirely within the mind of the runner. It is there where runners experience their sense of presence and flow, tucked away from the pacers and crew who have come to witness their achievements. Maybe only other ultramarathoners can truly appreciate what it means to push the body to such extremes, creating that bridge for social connection that is contained within the running community. For the rest of us, we can only look on in wonder at how a runner's fanaticism can transcend pain and allow them to dig deep.

4

Virtual Escapism

"It was a small spherical room. A gleaming haptic chair was suspended on a jointed hydraulic arm attached to the ceiling. There was no omni-directional treadmill, because the room itself served that function. While you were logged in, you could walk or run in any direction and the sphere would rotate around and beneath you, preventing you from ever touching the wall. It was like being inside a giant hamster ball."

As the character Wade Watts from Ernest Cline's *Ready Player One* slips on his headset, he is about to enter a virtual world that is ahead of our present reality, but a reality much closer than it seems.[1] A giant hamster ball rig is very different from the Oculus Quest 2, as is the virtual world Wade experiences, itself light years ahead in complexity from the best massively multiplayer online game. Yet, what binds this future vision to our reality is a similarity in personal motivation for Wade that mirrors that of countless gamers today. Specifically, gamers seek to escape their current reality for an alternative world, to gain space from life's troubles, break social norms, or even try out a new identity.

Picking apart the motivations for why someone would want to escape, with the various ways in which they accomplish that end, provides a mechanism for understanding why gaming, and especially virtual reality (VR) gaming, can be so addicting. On the motivational side, people often seek escapism to take a break from the mundane or relieve some pent-up stress. Your traditional *Street Fighter* or *Mortal Combat* does well to replace the stress busting accomplished through a trip to the gym for a kick-boxing class. On a more positive note, people may seek escapism simply for the pleasure that it provides or to create space for their imagination to run wild. Whether to embellish our lives or restore balance, escapism takes four basic forms.[2] Activities can be evasive in nature, where participants avoid something they prefer not to do (like staring out the window instead of writing a term paper). Alternatively, activities can be characterized as either passive, requiring little to no participation

---

[1] Cline, E. (2011). Ready Player One. New York: Random House.

[2] Warmelink, H., Harteveld, C., and Mayer, I. (2009). Press enter or escape to play: Deconstructing escapism in multiplayer gaming. Conference: Breaking New Ground: Innovation in Games, Play, Practice and Theory. Proceedings of DiGRA 2009.

Fanatic. Joe Ungemah, Oxford University Press. © Oxford University Press 2024. DOI: 10.1093/9780197783894.003.0005

(like watching TV), or active, requiring input from the participant (gaming fits this category). Some activities achieve the fourth distinction as being characterized as extreme, where society has deemed that the negative consequences of the activity probably outweigh any positive outcomes (like binge-eating or dare devil stunts). Watching Joey Chestnut consume 75 hot dogs in 10 minutes at Nathan's International Hot Dog Eating Contest might be highly entertaining, but that activity is probably best reserved for the very few of us who have two or three stomachs to spare.

Like the other topics of fanaticism explored in this book, there is a dark side to escapism. As with the ultramarathoner who overly prioritizes their runs, escapism like gaming can lead to a severe disruption in the fulfillment of normal life responsibilities. Minor bouts of procrastination can be expected from just about anyone, but losing a string of jobs shows that something more harmful is going on. Excessive escapism can lead to addiction to the activities underlying it, denial that the pattern is causing harm, and potentially psychosis, where the line between virtual and real is blurred beyond recognition.[3] For nongamers and researchers who are looking from the outside-in, attention seems to be squarely focused on these negative consequences of escapism, with pundits concerned that frequent gamers spend too much time attempting to forget about the real world or avoid investing the time and energy to resolve the problems that made them look to escape in the first place.

Looking back over the history of video gaming, its potential to encourage escapism was evident from the beginning. In Netflix's documentary series *High Score*, developers and players alike spoke about their experiences in building what has become the largest entertainment industry in the world today.[4] From an interview with Tomohiro Nishikado, the creator of the first major breakthrough game *Space Invaders*, to a conversation with Roberta Williams, cocreator of the first graphical adventure game, *Mystery House*, the evolution of gaming is chronicled with distinct jumps in how developers programmed and incorporated storytelling that has led to the depth and variety of the current gaming catalog. Early games like *Space Invaders* and *Pac-Man* transformed the medium of video (e.g., TV) from passive to active. It was all about gameplay and keeping players enticed enough to complete levels and achieve high scores. From there, pioneering gaming companies like Nintendo loaded characters, stories, and worlds on top of good gameplay to make them more enticing. The evolution continued with games like *Star Fox*, which

---

[3] Siricharoen, W. (2019). The effect of virtual reality as a form of escapism. Conference: International Conference on Information Resources Management. Proceedings of the Association for Information Systems 2019.

[4] Costrel, F. (2020). High Score, Netflix documentary mini-series. Great Big Story.

fashioned first person perspective and 3D graphics, and *Doom*, which introduced the multiplayer format.

What is intriguing about the evolution of gaming is just how much early games got right in providing gamers with an opportunity to escape. In an interview with Rebecca Heineman, the winner of the first Space Invaders US national championship, she describes how the game provided her an outlet to be herself and establish a sense of flow, where all that mattered was the spaceship and its ability to shoot down the invading aliens. Early developers realized that key to maintaining the players' attention was to continually challenge their skills, otherwise players would get too good at the game; one player highlighted in *High Score* played *Asteroids* continuously for 31 hours, demonstrating that there was an upper limit to how challenging early games could be. A trick of the trade was to introduce competition between players through leader boards, where players sought to enter their initials for achieving a high score. Such tactics could only go so far in creating perpetual escapism and games evolved with the introduction of characters, narratives, fictional worlds, first-person perspective, realistic graphics, multiple players, freedom to create avatars, and the ability to personalize the experience, which cumulatively made a feeling of escapism inevitable for most players.

I have known Felix for nearly a decade, and one thing that I learned early is that he is a serious gamer. Growing up in a single-parent household, Felix was scratching around for ways to entertain himself, developing interests in such diverse areas as drawing and painting to Manga. When Felix bought a Gameboy in 1998, he was transfixed by the game *Pokémon*, finding himself immersed in a world of trading monsters. Two decades later, he still catches and trains Pokémon, but this time on his phone with *Pokémon Go*. He is fanatic about gaming of all varieties, from titles that are filled with fantasy and beautifully rendered, to those that allow for mindless exploration and disconnection from the real world.

What Felix discovered in gaming was much more than a way to pass the time, but a safe and engaging place where he could be himself and connect with others. The community he found is akin to the one that Kris discovered with the Minnesota Force, where people support each other on a deeper level than casual friends. His introduction to gaming occurred at a crucial time in Felix's life, when he was feeling the pressure of being openly gay in a rural community; online gaming opened a pathway to a much broader social world. So deep are Felix's social connections that he is still actively playing the same game of *Final Fantasy 14* (FF14) with a group of friends that he started over 5 years ago. In FF14, Felix has created an avatar, built a mansion, held parties with guild members, and gone on heroic missions. The relationships he has formed in the game are both real and deep, not that different from friendships made entirely in the real world. Through gaming, he was able to escape the confines of his rural community, to explore the possibilities of his own identity and the types of communities he wanted to know more about. Felix's transition into adulthood might have happened exactly as it did without his virtual friendships, but no doubt gaming provided a much more supportive and enjoyable experience.

Felix's escape motive for gaming is only one narrative about the hooks that keep players gaming. Escape can take the form of therapy, entertainment to be experienced either alone or with others, a break from the social norms that govern real life, or an enabler for trying out a new version of oneself. We will meet a thrill-seeking fanatic in Chapter 7, who shares a need for escapism, but does so by riding the twists and turns of roller coasters. In a virtual world, the limits of the experience are pushed out further as the player becomes a star-fleet captain, a great warrior, or billionaire property developer. These narratives also extend to how others view the gamer, with nongamers often misconstruing the intentions or benefits of an immersive gaming world. The good of gaming is in providing the space for players to explore both themselves and the world they live in, taking their mind to a place where the body cannot go.[5] This is in stark contrast to the bad of gaming for escape, where a player trades the broader world for a narrower or safer one, to avoid difficult situations and choices. Sometimes, perceiving the difference between these realities can be difficult, especially to the nongamer.

A peek at this difference between negative perceptions of gaming and reality is provided by Vicky Schaubert, writing for the BBC in February 2019.[6] In her story, we are introduced to Robert and Trude Steen, who were mourning the loss of their son Mats. At the age of 4, Mats was diagnosed with Duchenne muscular dystrophy (DMD), a rare disorder that leads to a degeneration of muscle and a shortened life expectancy of around 20 years. Mats wasn't able to participate in the physical activities of his peers at school and instead was confined to a wheelchair and provided an assistant that helped him get through the day. With things looking rather bleak, Mats's world changed at the age of 11, when his father provided him with the password to the family PC. Mats discovered freedom through a new identity that captured somewhere between 15,000 to 20,000 hours of his life. Mats became Lord Iberian Redmoore, roaming the planet Azeroth in *World of Warcraft*.

---

[5] Stavropoulos, V. (2019). My avatar, my self: Exploring the world of online gaming and avatar-related wellbeing. InPsych, 41, 43–48.
[6] My Disabled Son's Amazing Gaming Life in the World of Warcraft by Vicky Schaubert, BBC News, February 7, 2019.

Mats was free of his physical restrictions, joining his online peers in running, swimming, and exploring. Mats wrote in a blog post titled "My Escape," "There my handicap doesn't matter, my chains are broken and I can be whoever I want to be. In there I feel normal."

Yet, this transformation was not without its costs. His parents were troubled by how much time Mats spent online, taking precious, limited time from family and friends, as well as playing through the night. Robert states, "We thought it was all about the game. And just that. We thought it was a competition that you were supposed to win." That perception changed when Mats passed away at the age of 25. The day after his death, Robert decided to contact Mats's digital friends via a post on Mats's blog. One by one, responses came into Robert's email account, sharing stories and condolences. Robert soon realized that Mats was part of an "entire society, a tiny nation of people," who had shared in Mats's life at an intimate level. Robert stated, "We cried and cried from an intense emotional joy that came from seeing what kind of life Mats had in fact lived. With real friends, sweethearts, people who cared so much that they would fly from another country to the funeral service of someone they had never met. That was powerful." Kai Simon, a member of the Starlight guild that Mats was a member of, addressed the congregation at Mats's funeral: "While we are gathered here today, a candle is being lit for Mats in a classroom in the Netherlands, a candle burns in a call centre in Ireland, in a library in Sweden there is a candle lit, he is remembered in a little beauty parlour in Finland, a municipal office in Denmark, many places in England." Online gaming did for Mats what the physical world could not; it provided him the freedom to explore and build relationships without limitation. In Mats's words, "It's not a screen, it's a gateway to wherever your heart desires."

Such stories highlight the benefits of gaming that are often overlooked in the popular media. Sweeping comments about the ills of gaming were common from the advent of the technology, even though the scientific link between gaming and well-being was not solidly established. To resolve the issue, an ambitious longitudinal study was conducted by a research team led by Matti Vuorre, with a group of nearly 40,000 gamers studied over 6 weeks to identify whether longer play times affected personal well-being.[7] The gamers were active on a range of titles, including *Animal Crossing: New Horizons*, *Apex Legends*, *Eve Online*, *Forza*, *Gran Turismo*, *Outriders*, and *The Crew 2*. At three points during the study, the gamers were asked to report on how they were feeling, how much time they spent gaming, and whether they were feeling

[7] Vuorre, M., et al. (2022). Time spent playing video games is unlikely to impact well-being. Royal Society Open Science, 9 (7).

fulfilled in the amount of autonomy, competence, and mastery achieved in their gameplay. The game publishers also provided real data on game time to evaluate whether the player estimates were accurate. When all the data was tabulated, the researchers found gaming to have little to no relationship on well-being in either direction.

Rather, well-being was predicted by the type of motivation held by the player. When players wanted to engage with a game and were given the opportunity, they received a boost in positive feelings, as long as they did not feel that they were feeling compelled to play. This finding resembles the signs of process addiction highlighted in the last chapter on ultramarathoners, where enjoyment of the running was overshadowed by the need to do it. When I interviewed Dr. Zachary Hansen from the Hazelden Betty Ford Graduate School, I asked him about the similarities and differences between gaming and exercise forms of addiction. He confirmed that gaming addiction is similar to other types of process addictions, whereby the activity itself is not usually the problem, but rather the cycle of behavior that emerges from it. For gamers, symptoms can include building days around gaming, missing significant life events, paying more on games than they can afford, and feeling anxious if they miss their gaming time.[8] In such cases, normal impulse control is circumvented, mirroring substance dependency. Zach's advice for treatment is first to understand the underlying motivations for gaming and then develop healthier coping skills to deal directly with those motivations. In addition, he recommends building a player's recognition about the real-life consequences gaming has on normal functioning at work or at home.

Despite the similarities, there are two critical differences that set gaming addiction apart from other forms of process addictions. First, Zach makes the distinction between natural and "supernatural stimuli." Games, even the more traditional types involving a joystick and TV, do not exist in nature, and as such, humans have not evolved coping strategies to moderate themselves against too much stimulus. The latest VR technology amps up this risk considerably, by providing an alternative 360-degree world that effectively isolates the individual from the real world. Zach summarizes that with games, "there is a potential to be completely immersed in the simulation, heightening the chances for addiction." People looking for an escape can find it through gaming, providing gamers a reason to reprioritize real-world responsibilities and ignore social relationships.

---

[8] Siricharoen, W. (2019). The effect of virtual reality as a form of escapism. Conference: International Conference on Information Resources Management. Proceedings of the Association for Information Systems 2019.

To test out the relationship, field research by Daniel Kardefelt-Winther on *World of Warcraft* gamers uncovered a pattern for how escapism can lead to maladaptive behaviors and addiction.[9] In his study, the magnitude of life problems determined how strong a player's need was for a coping strategy, which in turn influenced the amount of time dedicated to the game. Acting as a moderating role across this chain of events was the player's level of anxiety and self-esteem. This insight provides further support that gaming itself does not universally influence personal well-being or that the need for escapism on the surface is harmful. Underlying life problems, especially if experienced by vulnerable people, are at the core of gaming addiction. When thinking about such vulnerable groups who are in need of an outlet, Zach commented, "players might start thinking 'I'm good at this game and this is who I am.' If the player's world shrinks to just other gamers, this can become problematic."

The second defining characteristic, according to Zach, between gaming and other forms of process addiction is the high potency of the player's experience. For those hungry for escapism, current labels provide environments where characters are constantly facing extreme and evolving situations, which are more complex and exciting than everyday life. "The gaming experience is effective at creating a flow state, but one that is artificial and goes beyond the physical limits of the natural environment," states Zach. This is great from an entertainment vantage point, but can solidify unreal expectations of what life is all about. Players find themselves in hyped-up reward patterns that can be particularly concerning if they already have tendencies toward hyperactivity. Zach points out, "games can change a person's sense of homeostasis, where everything else in a person's life seems boring." When an addicted player responds to requests by loved ones to spend more time in the real world, they might find their reality cannot fulfill them in the same way, leaving them with feelings of withdrawal and craving to become immersed again.

As mentioned before, diagnostic criteria for process addictions are lacking and, as a result, effectively identifying and providing help for gaming addiction is spotty. Rather, therapists are attuned to the underlying factors driving clients to escape, whether to provide an outlet for anxiety, create an emotional boost, or provide a distraction from dealing with underlying trauma. For now, the speed of technological change is outpacing our ability to provide targeted diagnostics and interventions for gaming addictions, with a near open door for those seeking escapism. The scale of the potential societal harms is gigantic, considering that processing speed and the wide availability

---

[9] Kardefelt-Winther, D. (2014). The moderating role of psychological well-being on the relationship between escapism and excessive online gaming. Computers in Human Behavior, 38, 68–74.

of devices has allowed for massive multiplayer online games, with hundreds of thousands of users experiencing the same environment at the same time. Meanwhile, choice in gaming has expanded beyond recognition from the early video arcades, abandoning the need for rigid rules or linear progressions in the story. Pac-Man was defined by the maze in which he raced, while Dirk the Daring progressed from room to room in search of Princess Daphne in *Dragon's Layer*. Such games still exist, but sit alongside open platforms with limitless potentials in storylines and interactions between gamers. Escape of all kinds is everywhere.

Felix's gaming spans nearly all of them. He enjoys the fast and furious play of *The Elder Scrolls V: Skyrim*, where players take on identities as humans, orcs, elves or other animal-like creatures and freely explore an open wilderness full of dragons, fortresses, and dungeons. He likes how these types of games react in real time and guarantee that nothing will play out exactly as it did in the past. Battle and ambushes are great, but Felix also appreciates using the open world format as a means of exploration, "There is always the possibility of doing nothing at all—you can create the world and just be in it sitting on a hill and staring at the stars." Due to the nature of the game, a relaxing walk toward a virtual mountain can be drastically interrupted by a giant spider lunging at you or a group of mercenaries deciding that you are an easy target. Yet, it is this randomness that makes the game that much more captivating for Felix. When nothing can be taken for granted, the level of presence in the virtual world is kept high and preserves the feeling of escapism.

In the wake of the COVID-19 pandemic, the wider portfolio of gaming platforms and experiences on offer were a sanctuary for players wishing to escape from the daily onslaught of negative news. With the lockdown beginning in March 2020, the gaming platform Steam reported its highest number of concurrent users, while weekly game sales surged 40%–60% across titles.[10] Yes, players were buying new titles that created an adrenaline rush and a sense of excitement while they were confined to the living room, but they were also seeking out games that provided social connection and respite. For this reason, the *New York Times* called *Animal Crossing: New Horizons* "the Game for the Coronavirus Moment" for its ability to transport players to an immersive world where they could engage with others in activities ranging from fishing to playing music. Players met up in big numbers to hold virtual birthday parties or even go on virtual dates within the game, and sales of the title outpaced all previous iterations of it.

---

[10] Why Computer Games Are More than a Lockdown Distraction by Chris Baraniuk, BBC News, April 12, 2020.

Felix relates to the heightened need for escapism during the pandemic and also turned to gaming for some much-needed distraction, "I bought every good game out there." Whenever Felix buys a new game, he dedicates any-where between two and four hours to playing. During the pandemic, the time invested in gaming was a savior for Felix, in "creating the space to be with others. It was better than using the phone, as I just wanted to switch off from what was happening" in the real world. One of the games that Felix played during the pandemic was *Friday the 13th*, an online survival horror game where up to seven players take on the role of Camp Counselors and attempt to escape an 8th player, who takes on the role of Jason Voorhees. Although each player is ultimately alone in the quest to escape Jason, there are opportuni-ties and rewards for working together. Maybe a horror game is not everyone's cup of tea for switching off during a pandemic, but it did for Felix what *Animal Crossing: New Horizons* did for the masses. Gaming helped Felix es-cape feelings of seclusion, while providing a sense of accomplishment, even if homebound due to virus restrictions.

Games that were previously dismissed as garbage for their lack of story, conflict, or goal achievement got a boost from the pandemic. Kate Spicer writing for the BBC describes her experience with the games *Everything* and *Mountain* by Tru Luv, "Conspiracy theorists are bombarding my social media feed, and everyone is an armchair expert on the pandemic. But for now I am okay, because I am a moose . . . I move around this game of infinite possi-bility, not doing much, occasionally communicating with other things . . . [the games] both have calmed me and made me forget the lunacy and drama of life online and in lockdown."[11] Gaming during the pandemic did not en-tirely replace the physical world, but allowed for immersive experiences that allowed players to either break their boredom, connect with loved ones, find new romances, or simply relax.

The promise of VR is to take the adventure of gaming one step further, by breaking down the physical barrier between players and the worlds they enter. Sales growth in VR headsets has grown from just shy of 10 million units in 2016 to an estimated 10 times that number in just 5 years.[12] To pave the way for widescale adoption, hardware design must converge with greater bandwidth, processor speed, and a library of fun and interesting games and experiences to explore. What this future looks like has been painted with bright colors by science fiction. *Neuromancer* by William Gibson popularized the concepts of

[11] How Gaming Became a Form of Meditation by Kate Spicer, BBC Culture, April 13, 2020.
[12] Hartl, E., and Berger, B. (2017). Escaping reality: Examining the role of presence and escapism in user adoption of virtual reality glasses. European Conference of Information Systems Proceedings.

the "matrix" and "cyberspace" in 1984, blurring the lines between man and machine when the main character, Henry Case, relies on neurobiology to jack into the digital network.[13] In *Snow Crash* by Neal Stephenson, a pizza delivery man named Hiro lives an alternative existence in the Metaverse, one where he lives in a prized neighborhood just off of the Street; the equivalent of the Champs-Elysees, which wraps around the equator of the virtual globe.[14] In the real world, Hiro shares a 20-by-30 U-Stor-It unit as a home, but in the Metaverse he lives among Frank Lloyd Wright reproductions in spitting distance to a downtown unlike any other, described as a "Las Vegas freed from the constraints of physics and finance."

This is not to say that inequality does not exist in the Metaverse, it is just decoupled from reality. The best avatars, those with highly realistic features, are reserved for hackers or people who have the financial resources to buy the work of designers. Late adopters to the Metaverse are forced to opt for off-the-shelf avatars with limited facial expressions and to materialize in a public Port rather than waking up in a personal home. A parallel disconnect between the real and virtual exists in Ernest Cline's *Ready Player One*,[15] where the protagonist, Wade Watts, lives in the Stacks, a sprawling array of RVs, shipping containers, and other tin boxes tied together with an array of pipes, girders, support beams, and footbridges. When Wade powers up his console, puts on his haptic gloves, and slides on his visor, he is transported to the OASIS, an endless universe of thousands of worlds for people to explore "rendered in meticulous graphical detail, right down to bugs and blades of grass, wind and weather patterns." Unlike the Metaverse, OASIS is presented as open source, where users have the freedom to design both who they are and the environments they want to explore. With environmental collapse coupled with an energy crisis as described in the book, adoption of OASIS surged and, with it, "the lines of distinction between a person's real identity and that of their avatar began to blur. It was the dawn of a new era, one where most of the human race now spent all of their free time inside a video game."

Hiro's desire to escape his pizza delivery job in favor of becoming the world's greatest sword fighter, just like Wade Watts's need to escape his dystopian existence in the Stacks, illustrate what today's psychologists fear about a future dominated by technology. They worry that the line between real and virtual can go too far, with the virtual overwhelming what otherwise could be a healthy and balanced life. If gamers fuse their identity with their online

---

[13] Gibson, W. (1984). Neuromancer. New York: The Berkeley Publishing Group.
[14] Stephenson, N. (1992). Snow Crash. New York: Bantam Books.
[15] Cline, E. (2011). Ready Player One. New York: Random House.

representation, allow their online needs to overwhelm real-world priorities, and compensate for perceived real-life deficiencies in appearance or personal attributes, potential risks emerge for gamers to withdraw from the real world.

There is still much to do for developers to get close to the version of VR described by Stephenson or Cline. Beyond the physical logistics of having an apparatus that allows for 360-degree movement and bodysuits equipped with the ability to both sense and produce pressure, the strain on the human brain may be overwhelming. Slight inconsistencies between the senses can cause motion sickness, as can the prolonged light produced by VR headsets, termed "cybersickness." Even if a player is spared nausea and dizziness, their eyes are working overtime in VR, especially if the tasks in the game are repetitive and require close inspection. The ultimate desire of VR developers is to fully avoid these pitfalls while also creating an experience that delivers the characteristics of presence, immersion, and interactivity.[16] Presence is the subjective feeling of being within a given environment, even if your physical body is somewhere else. A really engrossing movie can sometimes create a feeling of presence, where viewers forget that they are sitting in a theater with a sticky floor covered in popcorn kernels and spilled soda.

Yet, the experience of watching a movie falls short of immersion, which is the psychological experience of being completely enveloped by the experience, forgetting both time and space. A greater range of sensors, larger field of vision, or a more agile apparatus could all play a role in heightening a player's feeling of immersion, allowing them to forget that a real world even exists. These technical capabilities also play a part in determining interactivity, which is the extent to which a player feels that they are able to interact with their virtual environment in the way that they would choose to do so. Hardware is only part of the equation, as intuitive design and ease of use help boost perceptions of interactivity. Layered on top of that are the psychological components of the game. The best examples allow in-game characters to progressively evolve and integrate into their virtual environments, while maintaining a level of believability that what occurs on screen could actually happen. Together, highly interactive VR setups boost feelings of presence, which together allow players to feel immersed in the environments they are experiencing.

My first encounter with VR was in the early 1990s. I remember entering an arcade filled with four standing pods, identical except for a strip of color indicating which player you would be when you joined the game (e.g., yellow, blue,

[16] Mutterlein, J. (2018). The three pillars of virtual reality? Investigating the roles of immersion, presence, and interactivity. Conference: 51st Hawaii International Conference on System Sciences. Proceedings of the University of Hawaii at Manoa 2018.

red, or green). An attendant orchestrated the coming and going of players, while TV screens showed live gameplay to people standing in line. When it was my turn, I stepped up into a circular shaped platform, equipped with a waist-high ring to keep me from wandering too far away from the equipment. Placed on my head was a headset that looked like it was designed for the 1970s version of *Battlestar Galactica* and in my hand was a single "space joystick" that was tethered to the pod. The game being played was *Dactyl Nightmare*, created by W Industries in 1991, involving a battle royale between four players, set in a free-floating series of five checkered platforms connected by bridges and elevators. The goal was to find and shoot the other three players, while avoiding the occasional pterodactyl that would swoop down and drop you from a great height.

I was terrible at it. There was so much I had to get used to in the game before I was able to feel comfortable enough to battle effectively. First, I had to adjust to looking in the right direction when trying to move or shoot. Spatial orientation in the game was solely controlled by where your head was pointed. Navigation was pretty easy on the checkered platforms, but stairs and elevators were a challenge, with one misstep resulting in a free fall through space and your avatar screeching out in terror. Since there were no sensors on your legs, walking was done with a button on the joystick, which was not 100% intuitive for a VR experience. Then there were the pterodactyls. Hanging around too long in any given place put you at risk from dying a tragic and unnecessary death. After an incredibly short 5 minutes, the experience was over and it was time for four new players.

Thirty years later and the memory is still fresh in my head; it was that much fun. What I didn't fully appreciate at the time was just how much of a technological marvel the game was. Although by current standards the gameplay is a bit clunky, *Dactyl Nightmare* successfully combined a number of cutting-edge features by mixing multiplayer functionality with first-person, polygonal graphics on top of its VR capabilities. Breakthrough titles using the same format, such as *Wolfenstein 3D* or *Doom*, were not released until 1 or 2 years later. This headstart unfortunately did not translate to long-term success for the company behind *Dactyl Nightmare*, which fizzled out even after expanding beyond its entertainment portfolio into practical business applications involving safety, medical, and construction simulations.[17] Even a high visibility partnership with IBM could not keep W Industries from going

---

[17] Virtual Reality Society. Virtuality—A New Reality of Promise, Two Decades Too Soon. https://www.vrs.org.uk/dr-jonathan-walden-virtuality-new-reality-promise-two-decades-soon (accessed January 8, 2021).

bankrupt in 1997, due to a lack of sustained interest in its core entertainment offering.

Fast-forward to today, and gaining experience using VR has never been easier, with interactive experiences like the VOID popping up in tourist hot spots and fairly affordable home systems like the Oculus Quest 2 hitting the market in late 2020. Despite the fact that the Oculus Quest 2 was preordered five times more than the previous model, a sure sign of growing consumer interest, widescale adoption of VR in general is likely still many years away. Like other forms of technology adoption, an individual's expectations about the device's performance, the effort and cost they expect to invest in the activity, hedonic motivation (like need for escapism), habits, and social influences all play a part in making the technology sticky.[18] What sets escapism apart in this list of enablers is its secondary role of lowering the player's expectations about how good the technology needs to be in order to create feelings of presence. When viewed against these enablers, it is not surprising that adoption of VR as envisioned by W Industries waned. A 5-minute experience did not provide enough time to promote escapism, while paying $10 per game in an arcade did not establish habits for long-term VR use in the same way as a home setup.

Felix was an early adopter of VR and has his own headset, playing the latest VR titles alongside his normal repertoire of multiplayer online games. He enjoys the heightened level of immersion that the technology provides, where you can take in the full visual field of the world you are in. When mixed with the right audio, the experience transports you far away from the living room. Yet, the technology exhausts Felix much faster than a traditional setup. Games requiring a lot of physical movement, like swinging or ducking, feel physically repetitive. Felix too has fallen prey to cybersickness when flying around in *No Man's Sky*, a game he describes as the loneliest game ever created. As the center of their own universe, players in the game explore countless planets each with their own unique flora, fauna, and alien life, but with early releases lacking multiplayer capability, space felt really empty. This experience sums up VR for Felix, to be used when he wants to be alone, recently discovering *Real VR Fishing* as the "next level of chill."

When I first slipped on my rented Oculus headset, I was filled with anticipation. Although I am an inconsistent gamer at best and not a big fan of high-adrenaline experiences, I was curious to see just how far the technology has progressed since the early 1990s. I heard great things about *Beat Saber* and started there, finding it fantastically fun. The game reminded me instantly of

[18] Hartl, E., and Berger, B. (2017). Escaping reality: Examining the role of presence and escapism in user adoption of virtual reality glasses. European Conference of Information Systems Proceedings.

Guitar Hero and its offshoots, captivating players through its simple and addictive gameplay, pushed along with beat heavy songs and deep 3D graphics. After I dabbled around in a few other games, I turned my attention to the growing library of pseudo-educational VR experiences on applications like Within and streaming services like YouTube. I began by taking a spacewalk made possible by a successful launch onboard a 1965 Voskhod-2 rocket. From there, I kept with the aeronautical theme and traveled into near orbit on a high-altitude balloon, followed by a plunge into shark infested waters. In the first 2 hours of wearing a headset, I decided that the Oculus delivered everything I was hoping for with VR; the videos and games were immersive, created a sense of presence, and provided a degree of interactivity for me to feel in control of what I was doing. I was particularly impressed with how developers avoided creating sensations of cybersickness, by using smooth and natural filmmaking that prevented a disconnect between visual and physical sensation. I was also impressed by how the gameplay kept players from wandering around in their headsets by creating a virtual boundary that was overlayed on the real-world environment.

What I found in the next 20 minutes blew my mind. I heard about the VR documentary *Traveling While Black* and was interested to check it out, but was not prepared for just how good it was. This documentary by the Oscar-winning director Roger Ross Williams, in collaboration with VR makers Felix and Paul Studios, premiered at the Sundance Film Festival in January 2019 and takes the viewer on a history ride from the 1950s to the present day, sharing what it is like to be Black in America. The film uses Ben's Chili Bowl, an iconic Washington, DC, establishment featured in *The Green Book*, as a congregation point for discussing the legacy of segregation and discrimination in the United States. What makes *Traveling While Black* truly unique is how VR transports the viewer into the restaurant, as a silent participant in conversations they would likely never be part of. In an interview with *Forbes*, Williams says this is why he chose VR as his medium: "When you experience this documentary in VR it's all around you, and you can't escape it. Once the headset goes on, there are no external distractions. In the same way, we can't escape our blackness or the reality of being black in America, I didn't want people to be able to escape the experience they have when watching Traveling While Black and this immersive feeling could only be achieved through VR."[19]

The intimacy and honesty of the dialogue requires a maturity in production that wasn't taken lightly. Paul Raphael of Felix and Paul Studios is quoted

[19] Why You Need to See This VR Documentary "Traveling While Black" by Jennifer Kite-Powell, Forbes, February 25, 2019.

by *The Guardian* as saying, "We really wanted to do the material justice. It's not the kind of subject you want to approach and not be respectful of."[20] The choice of Ben's Chili Bowl was very deliberate, as it provided an environment that combined both ease and discomfort, as described by Williams: "We wanted to basically take people back to the time when they needed the Green Book and they needed spaces like that. We wanted to connect that to the present because we still need spaces like that to show how much hasn't changed." With Ben's Chili Bowl as a background, the scene was set for viewers to experience a conversation that might be out of reach or too difficult to confront. Williams states, "If you're not African American, you get to go into a space and be part of a conversation that you probably normally would not be privy to. If you are black, you get to delve deep into that inner trauma that we all carry with us in America as black people. I think that's really powerful in the way that 2D storytelling can't provide."

Raphael was just as cautious in how the material was constructed and presented to the viewer. He states, "You could actually overwhelm a viewer very easily and have them shut down," which would be the polar opposite of what the team was attempting to do with *Traveling While Black*. He continues, "You need to be careful with it, but when you do it right, you can affect people in a way that I think is out of reach for cinema." From my perspective, the team got it 100% right. The experience was intimate, moving, and felt real. It handled difficult content in a way that respected the stories and experiences of the people being interviewed and provided access to viewers who might never have these types of conversations in the real world, but probably should. The choice of VR created a level of depth that could not be replicated with other media and for that, I am a convert in believing that VR has the potential to do great things.

To explore just how bright the future of VR is, I interviewed three entrepreneurs who are collectively building the case for VR. Amir, Chuck, and Thong are each fanatics of VR and see its potential to change the world, albeit in different ways. Amir Berenjian is founder of REM5 VR Lab and is working to do his part to push adoption of VR. When I met up with him, he described it as "the next big thing for the last decade." He sees the current situation not so much as a problem of technology, but rather one of perception about what VR can do. Born in 1983, Amir is old enough to remember what a low-tech household looked like and considers himself lucky to have had exposure to the internet early on. Although he went on a decade-long hiatus

[20] Traveling While Black: Behind the Eye-Opening VR Documentary on Racism in America by Dream McClinton, Guardian, September 3, 2019.

from computer science with a career in investment banking, the launch of the Oculus Rift in 2016 proved to be reawakening for Amir. What Amir saw in the headset was not only immersive gaming but also untapped potential for both human connection and learning. He became obsessed by VR, decided to quit his job, and made the decision to go all in by establishing REM5 VR Lab. Amir believes that VR is the next big computer platform, integrating mobile and wearables into an integrated, immersive experience. This vision is evidenced in the name of Amir's company, with the "5" in the name REM5 VR Lab nodding to the influence of all the five senses for creating immersive environments.

To Amir, VR is a democratized experience, which places each person on a level playing field to learn and enjoy in a shared virtual world. Unlike a semester abroad for a lucky undergraduate who has the access and resources to live in another country, all that is required for VR is a headset, internet connectivity, and software. Amir believes it is therefore "one of the most powerful tools for learning" that can scale for broad social change. As Amir puts it, "It is just not scalable for everyone to meet my grandma," but in a virtual world, you can. All that is needed is to put the technology in the hands of users and Amir has an answer for that, beer and pizza. Amir turned to this trusted social hack by positioning VR as a form of entertainment with the hope that a portion of users will see the potential in the technology to do much more. And there is no better accompaniment to entertainment in a state-of-the-art arcade than party food. From families with older kids to corporate events catering to organizers searching for something new, Amir successfully established a foothold for social good.

Amir's mission follows two distinct paths. The first is geared toward children, where he dreamed to bring the beloved Magic School Bus to life. Like Ms. Frizzle from the bestselling books, Amir welcomes children to explore the world around them by bringing far-away experiences right into the REM5 VR Lab. Children can take a spin on an Apollo mission or tour the Eiffel Tower, and unlike the real world, every adventurer is guaranteed the same chance of being invited on the trip. The VR experience is more intuitive than that on a traditional desktop or handheld device, as children use their bodies to explore and learn. With the children firmly in the driver's seat of their personal experiences, they are also building confidence and skill in navigating the world around them.

Amir's second educational offering offers the same level of control for the participant, but is geared at building social competence and addressing tough issues like prejudice and discrimination. Amir has built a safe space for adults to step into the shoes of another person and experience the world as they see it. Without judgment, and placed into the role of passive observers, participants get to experience unconscious bias firsthand and to see how privilege manifests itself in every day social interactions, whether walking down a virtual street as a visible minority or being interned at a refugee camp. After the experience, participants are invited to discuss and unpack their experience, building cultural competence and emotional intelligence along the way. Amir sees the potential of VR to scale experiences that sit outside the mainstream, while simultaneously eliciting real reactions that are appropriate for the story unfolding in front of them. It is through self-reflection and conversation after the VR experience that Amir is betting will create social change. Amir has welcomed more than 3,000 participants through his cultural competence experience and has no intention of stopping any time soon.

Like Amir, Chuck Olsen is also on a mission to use VR for good. With a career built in journalism and filmmaking, he saw potential in VR from the moment that he sculpted mountains and dug canyons using his body in a 2014 VR design lab. Despite the slow burn of VR's breakthrough moment to the mainstream, Chuck has not lost his faith in the medium because of its ability to lift storytelling, provide a higher level of immersive entertainment, and, above all else, create interventions for both the mind and body. Similar to how hypnosis can be used as an alternative to pain reduction for patients allergic to anesthesia, VR can trick the mind into interpreting physical sensation differently than what is truly occurring. Hunter Hoffman and David Patterson at the University of Washington were technology pioneers in creating SnowWorld in the late 1990s, as the first immersive environment created to reduce pain among severe burn victims. By tricking the brain to reinterpret a wound dressing as an altercation with a snowman, patients reported feeling up to 50% less pain during their medical procedures.

Using SnowWorld as inspiration, Chuck founded an applied VR company called Visual. When he brought his corporate vision to a group of Angel Investors, Chuck resorted to an example from pop culture by describing the technology as a real-life Holodeck; the imaginary world of holograms depicted on *Star Trek: The Next Generation*. With funding in hand, Chuck began exploring both content and applications for the technology, beginning with a 360-degree panoramic of Lake Superior's North Shore, to be used as a distraction for patient's undergoing dental procedures. Although the premise was sound—there are few encounters hated more universally than getting a root canal—the partnership was shelved after Chuck realized that it was "not the best use of 360 views, especially when the dentist instructs you to sit still."

Chuck moved on and found a sweet spot in applying VR to promote wellness among seniors. He partnered with Ebenezer Senior Living to explore how to transport residents, especially those with severe mobility restrictions, to environments where their physical body cannot go. One group of seniors was studied over a period of 4 weeks, with two sessions held per week, involving wide range of content including nature, travel, arts, and performances, to gauge the impact of the technology on a broad range of psychological variables. At the conclusion of the study, all of the participants reported that they enjoyed VR, to the point that they even created "The VR Club" to talk about their experiences. Across the board, approximately 95% of participants reported feeling happier, more relaxed, more positive, and less worried while taking part in the study.[21] Beyond these immediate results, the effects of VR spilled over into the real world, with seniors increasing the frequency of their social interactions (from 35% to 50% reporting daily socializing with friends). An anecdotal exception to the findings was for one senior who was transported into a virtual aquarium, who frantically declared, "I'm out" when a small shark was spotted in the simulation.

The match between personal preferences and choice of experience is clear in Chuck's third application of VR for wellness, this time focused on memory care. A recording of the opera *La Traviata* by Giuseppe Verdi returned a former opera singer to the point where she was singing along with every word. Another resident who had difficulty sitting still was transfixed by her experience and decided to kick off her shoes and sit still for its entirety. Seniors in assisted living generally crave novelty and play, characteristics that are often devoid from regimented mealtimes and limited recreational options and off-campus travel opportunities. VR provides escapism to places well beyond the routine, to wherever your mind can dream it, as conveyed by one participant, "When you live on the 20th floor of this building you don't get a lot of opportunities to think about going boat riding—so that's cool." The most heartwarming story that Chuck shared was about a senior who was transported back in time to her grandmother's front porch, a place of love and harmony that has not existed in decades. Complete with randomized birds that flew around the sky, the experience sparked memories of loved ones who had long been forgotten.

To recreate grandma's porch goes beyond 360-degree filmmaking, using animation as a means to replace what is really hard or in this case, impossible to film. But it also has its limitations, for not everyone will have a developer devoted to recreating their specific grandma's porch. Beyond that, not everyone will have the most up-to-date technology to experience it as intended. Chuck fears the inequality that comes with any new technology, where some

---

[21] Visual, WellnessVR Evaluation Study, 2018.

participants are fully rendered and able to enjoy their virtual environments, where others are literally given avatars without hands due to limitations in gear. These inequities are in the same vein as those predicted by the science fiction writers, where lack of resources or know-how can limit the VR experience and its potential to be a social leveler.

Yet, the example of grandma's front porch demonstrates what VR as a medium can do. When mixed with elements of the real world, the experience is overpowering. For example, Chuck describes a game built for the Minnesota Wild, where hockey fans defended a virtual goal using a modified hockey-stick that replicated what an on-ice experience must have felt like. VR provides the brain every opportunity to revisit memories or create new ones, especially for people who are limited in physical or cognitive capabilities. Chuck is on a mission to "make real life better with VR, by heightening health and mental well-being." And people might just enjoy the experience along the way.

Thong Nguyen, founder of Roomera, recognizes that achieving good from VR will take rounds of experimentation to the get the economic model right. To state the problem directly, Thong has been pondering "how to make money and change the world," landing on the notion that both the technology and the user experience must be top-notch, an opinion held in common with Amir and Chuck. Amir recognized the importance of the user experience when creating his fun and relaxing pods, which are perfect for first-time VR users. The good times of eating pizza and drinking beer transfer into a feeling of positivity for the technology. For Chuck, the user experience is addressed by his efforts to match the right content to the user, from a deep-water dive to grandma's front porch, understanding that when the match between user and environment is right, the experience can be transformative.

Thong twists the user experience in a different direction for his specific application of VR, using it as a platform to experiment and measure architectural and product design. Thong's pathway into VR shares similarity to the others'; a chance encounter with the technology sparked curiosity into the art of the possible. Thong's company, Roomera, started as an extension of a very practical question about how best to design his own family's kitchen. Would a kitchen island get in the way of cooking or would it provide a gathering spot for friends? Thong turned to VR as a way to envision how his family and friends would navigate the space, and in so doing, optimized his design choices. Through his personal experience, Thong recognized the potential of VR to visualize design concepts without the significant expense typical of traditional prototyping. "The problem with visions is that they are flawed; either too idealistic or lacking in complexity," states Thong, "VR allows the intricacies to be worked out." Thong aims to provide freedom in designing the future unhindered. Instead of looking backward to see how a product worked out, Thong seeks real-time user feedback about an imagined future offering, allowing the designers to walk away, learn, and try again until they land on perfection. "Crazy ideas often get dismissed," states Thong when talking about a typical design process. Leaders make decisions to get rid of the noise and by doing so, shut down ideas that have real potential to disrupt how physical environments are used. VR provides a safe space, with relatively lower cost, to give crazy ideas a try.

When I talked with Thong, he provided the example of working with a popular fast-food chain to help bring what he does to life. The virtual environment he created encompassed both the kitchen and front of house, allowing the chain's leaders to make decisions about everything from merchandising to cooking and serving food. Watching out for customer sight lines and potential bottlenecks where staff would compete for the same physical space, Thong helped the company interate on designs for the layout. To maximize learning, Thong recommended obtaining feedback from potential consumers, staff, and managers, to ensure all the wrinkles got worked out. For example, What happened when the restaurant experienced a rush? Would the design falter with additional, unanticipated bottlenecks? Scenario modeling is nearly as important as the simulated environment when doing VR design. The advantage of VR is that a large number of scenarios can be run with a variety of designs done in parallel, all while avoiding the large capital expenditure of constructing in the real world.

Beyond the practical implications and visual aesthetics of the layout, the user experience extends to the remaining four senses. Second only to the vision, sound plays a critical role in the user experience. For example, Thong spoke about how he simulated what a busy hotel lobby would sound like for one of his hospitality clients. Under the right scenario, the excess noise that would be created by customers in the hotel would be deafening, requiring a rethink of the lobby's architecture. Harder to address are sensations involving touch, smell, and taste. Going back to hotel example, many chains have a trademark scent that they hope will welcome repeat customers, no matter which location they have chosen for their stay, with varieties like Skyfall, Allure, or Marquee Moon.[22] Touch is also possible, with VR overlaying the physical sensation with consistent visual cues, such as Chuck's hockey stick in the simulated Minnesota Wild shootout. According to Thong, what VR can do is "put you in a different context, taking you

---

[22] Hotel Scents. Website. https://www.hotelscents.com (accessed May 21, 2023).

somewhere else, physically or in time," to gain perspective about how you would use a product or service.

Across my interactions with Amir, Chuck, and Thong, it became evident that there is a great deal of good that VR can do for society. It can provide an escape from the physical that can free up the mind to innovate, rediscover a sense of self, or walk a mile in someone else's shoes. Yet these benefits are tempered by the potential for misuse, and instead of becoming a complement to the real world, the virtual world can become a replacement. Depending on who is driving and making decisions about what is being projected, obscured, or altered in the virtual world, the technology can be the virus or the cure. This is especially true for some of the emerging business models for companies promoting VR that are not based on the sale of hardware. Headsets like the Oculus Quest 2 are not cheap to make, nor are the games that are sold below cost. If companies make their money from player data and advertisements rather than equipment or software, how comfortable should we be with these companies that are creating our virtual worlds? How close are we from Nolan Sorrento and Innovative Online Industries, as featured in *Ready Player One*?[23]

VR is a bigger hammer than any competing online experience for driving compelling and immersive experiences, hitting on the senses at a much more fundamental level and opening the cellar door to deeper levels of escapism. The next logical step for the technology is the abandonment of the physical limitations of headsets or physical equipment; *Star Trek*'s holodeck might have gotten it right. With infinite possibilities about where and when a person could be transported, there will become a point where the virtual world tantalizes even the most resilient among us as a better alternative to our physical reality. For those who grew up watching *Star Trek: The Next Generation*, it is hard to forget Lieutenant Reginald Barclay, who suffered from holo-addiction, creating doppelgängers of the bridge crew, to play out his personal fantasies.[24] From a doting Counselor Troi to a bumbling Captain Picard, Barclay created a parallel world where he was the star of the show. There are major differences between Barclay's holodeck and today's VR, for example, the ability for users to freely create their own environment and the lack of physical equipment that tethers current players to their computers, yet the potential for escapism might be the same, as it relies on a state of mind.

At the end of *High Score*, the narrator provides perspective on the quick evolution of gaming into its present form, "It was a monumental era, one

---

[23] Cline, E. (2011). Ready Player One. New York: Random House.
[24] Caves, S. (1990). Hollow Pursuits, episode of Star Trek: The Next Generation. Paramount Domestic Television.

that defined video games as a place to get lost, a place to become someone different, and go to faraway lands. But, most importantly, it defined that any player could be a game creator. So now that technology can fully blur the line between fantasy and reality, the question is . . . where will we go next?"[25] Where to, indeed? The next generation of VR provides greater presence, immersion, and interactivity on a scale light years beyond the earliest games profiled in the documentary; even those were successful in creating a sense of escapism. Thankfully, we are a few natural calamities away from the dystopian futures described by science fiction writers Gibson, Stephenson, and Cline, yet this does not mean that the human drivers toward escapism are any less real or powerful in their present form.

Being a fanatic of gaming and VR involves a leap away from the physical form into a state of flow that is disassociated from life's troubles or social barriers. It is interesting to contemplate that the sensation of flow can arise from both pushing the physical body to its extremes, as shown in the previous chapter on ultramarathons and later when we explore the world of high-risk sports in Chapter 7, and from the near total opposite of escaping the physical body through VR. For Mats Steen, gaming provided an escape from the limitations of his physical body to a place where he was able to run, swim, and romp around the world with his friends. Felix played games to escape the social boundaries of his rural community, to a place where he was able to explore his own identify and find people who he preferred to spend time with. The seniors that took part in Chuck's research escaped the limitations of their age, discovering lost memories and the feeling of being unrestrained by the routine of a care home. They even rediscovered the harmony of sitting on their grandmother's front porch.

These stories demonstrate the healthy side of escapism, one that can be exploited to drive good in society, from changing social paradigms to designing better products or social spaces. This is a different narrative than what is normally talked about, with gamers viewed as falling prey to the more addictive elements of escapism, using technology as a way of amping up reward centers in the brain and avoiding life's troubles. Instead, it is a fanaticism defined by challenging social conventions and breaking down physical barriers. From the fantastical worlds of massively multiplayer online games like *Final Fantasy 14*, to the very intimate experiences of 360-degree video like *Traveling While Black*, users have a broad range of experiences to choose from, which are increasingly disconnected from the stereotype of gaming and VR as reserved for adrenaline junkies. With the technology accelerating in its ability

[25] Costrel, F. (2020). High Score, Netflix documentary mini-series. Great Big Story.

to create greater presence, immersion, and interactivity, its position as a superior medium to tell new stories, unlock lost worlds, and dream the possible becomes clearer. The challenge is how to keep players from descending too far down the rabbit hole, by remembering that the virtual world exists to complement the real world and not replace it.

PART 3
THE COGNITIVE

5

One Person's Trash

Different from either an ultramarathon runner confronting the pain of the present moment or a VR fanatic dreaming about the future, other fanatics are busy at work uncovering the past. As the old saying goes, one person's trash is another person's treasure. I've never experienced a more direct application of this phrase than the experience I had on a gorgeous late summer day in a town called Chaska. The city itself dates to the second half of the 19th century, gaining notoriety for brickmaking and being a primary supplier to the growing cities of Minneapolis and St. Paul. Nowadays, Chaska has been absorbed as an exurb and is more famous for its proximity to the Renaissance Festival and playing host to the Ryder Cup. On this particular morning, I drove into the middle of town and met with a group of bottle collectors at a vacant property next to City Hall that had just been cleared to become a new municipal parking lot. Once standing on this particular site was a Victorian era single-family home that had one essential feature that made it appealing to this particular group of treasure hunters: it was built prior to indoor plumbing. This was the day that I dug in someone else's outhouse to find treasure.

So, what makes someone dig around in another person's trash and worse? The answer for the most part resides with the humble bottle. In the United States, bottle collecting has become one of the most popular hobbies, falling just short of the notoriety shared by coin and stamp collecting. Famous bottle collectors have included Andrew Carnegie and Henry Ford, while enthusiast clubs are dotted around the country. Individual bottles have sold for astronomical sums, like a blue Homestead Bitters bottle fetching $200,000 in a private sale in 2010 and a blue firecracker GI-14 flask selling at auction for $100,000 that same year.[1] Driving this fascination is a huge number of innovative and unique specimens, estimated to be in the hundreds of thousands of different bottle types being produced between 1800s and the 1950s.[2] Collectors judge the rarity and craft of each bottle by looking for the manufacturing date, typography, style of glassmaking, color, base type, and

[1] Antique Auction Forum. The Current State of the Bottle Hobby. https://antiqueauctionforum.com/blog/guest-blogs/the-current-state-of-the-bottle-hobby (accessed July 9, 2022).
[2] Bottle Store. The Bottle Blog. https://blog.bottlestore.com (accessed July 9, 2022).

Fanatic. Joe Ungemah, Oxford University Press. © Oxford University Press 2024. DOI: 10.1093/9780197783894.003.0006

finish. Bottles typically fall within the categories of milk, soda, beer, ink, per-fume, liquor, snuff, and apothecary types, each shaped for a given purpose, whether to hold powder, pour and drink, or warn of poisonous contents. Cobalt blue, deep amethyst, red, or green bottles are rarer and therefore more desirable, as these colors were typically avoided for common food products. Mouth-blown bottles, rather than those that were machine made, score extra points, but what matters most is the condition of the bottle and whether it is free from blemishes and chips.

It is not lost on bottle collectors, and collectors in general, that they have a deeper interest in their particular hobby than the general public. Edward Leahy, a collector of books, demonstrates this awareness when writing about his interactions with noncollectors, "I am often asked what kind of books I col-lect. Over the years . . . I've diligently recounted the two or three areas . . . then five . . . then eight . . . now ten or twelve areas where I have serious collecting interests. Typically, the very recitation exhausts the inquirer's attention span. After all, he was merely being polite and was probably looking for a simple an-swer like 'history books.' "[3] This is one of the reasons why collector clubs exist, to provide a public forum for like-minded individuals to share their discov-eries, contemplate what an item represents, and build personal connections to it. When reflecting on why he owns multiple first-edition copies of Charles Dickens's *A Christmas Carol*, Edward has concluded that collectors are driven to collect their past, "No matter how we phrase it, we collectors all collect our past, whether real or imagined—books we had or books we missed. So as we move inexorably into the future, some part of us, with every old volume, wants to cling to the past—not the 'long past,' but our past."

The motivations underlying the need to build and maintain collections are varied, but generally involve a combination of being a sentimental and so-cial activity, creating enjoyment, building knowledge, and forging friendships for the collector. In a study about the motivations for collecting led by Sally McKenzie,[4] the link between collecting and sentimentality was clearly illus-trated by a participant who collected beagle-themed figurines and stamps. Her fondness for these objects stemmed from the fact that her pet beagle died while she was traveling overseas, "I was really, really upset about it because I wasn't there and I couldn't go home and funny enough, I was in China at the time, I found a resin Beagle so I bought that and it (the collection) just took off from there . . . So, I guess it was just a way of dealing with the loss." For other

[3] Beck, K., Bilder, M., and McDonald, A. (2002). Collectors on collecting. Rare book exhibition programs, Boston College of Law School.
[4] McKenzie, S., et al. (2015). Collecting in an urban context: Relationships between collections and space in the home. Australian Journal of Popular Culture, 4, 15–27.

participants, collecting was a means to build and strengthen relationships with each other, much the same as other types of fanatics attending science fiction conventions, playing massively multiplayer online games, or attending an outing as a roller coaster enthusiast. The last group of collectors studied by McKenzie were motivated in an attempt to relive a bygone era, notably by one participant who maintained a collection of 54 retro washing machines and dryers.

On arriving at the vacant lot in Chaska, I found my amiable host for the day surveying the property and unpacking tools from his car. Dave has been a bottle collector for decades, digging up and exposing long-lost items in privies across the country. Until meeting Dave, I never made the connection between bottle collecting and privies, while the whole notion of digging around in someone's else's toilet was unthinkable. Standing back from it now, the activity really isn't that odd. Without municipal trash or sewer service, the privy was a one stop shop for everything being discarded and the biological elements were just one component. In cities, privies were often lined with stone and could be rather large, up to 20 feet wide. There are often many privies on the same site; as one privy filled up, another would be dug out. Dave remembers one property that had 14 separate privies, which marched around the lot as the years went on and different families moved in. Although many towns and cities had ordinances that privies should be cleaned of the biological elements before being covered up, either by the property owner or by hired help known as honey dippers, the rules were rarely followed. The good news is that a hundred years stands between the modern treasure hunter and the really gross stuff, allowing for nature to work its course and turn it all to soil.

The range of items that are found in privies is truly mind boggling. Items that were meant for consumption and disposal are to be expected, yet even bottles are not equal in their value. For example, soda bottles are a rare find due to the refund that was offered to consumers when they returned their empty bottles. More common are the pharmacy or grocery bottles that were intended for single use. Then there are the broken household items, like dinner plates, cups, and cutlery, which were thrown away and replaced. A third type are the items that fell in the privy by accident, like eyeglasses, pipes, coins, or jewelry. Going to the outhouse in the middle of the night, potentially in bad weather, carried its own risks, no different than today's stray iPhone ending up in the toilet. Lastly, there are the truly unusual items that need some detective work to find out why they ended up in the privy. Dave personally has found guns, false teeth, opium pipes, and on one dig, over a thousand leather shoes. A couple of years ago, he found some heirloom tomato seeds, representing varieties not seen in over a hundred years, surviving the human gut and resting at the bottom of a privy for the last century. Dave successfully cultivated the plants, and his kids now sell each season's harvest. Probably the most extreme story is about Dave's friend, who uncovered the skeletal remains of a body dating to the 1870s—that required a call to the county coroner. Privy digging is not for the faint-hearted, although for different reasons than I initially feared.

Collecting was all around Dave when growing up. His grandmother collected baskets that were displayed on basket trees throughout the home. A generation later, his mother amassed over 5,000 ceramic bears that took over Dave's old bedroom, displayed in semitransparent cases that march around the periphery of his room. His father was more modest in his collecting, focusing on coins. Dave's great aunt traveled throughout Europe in the 1920s, 1930s, and 1940s, acquiring spare change that became valuable through political instability and currency recalls. These coins made it into a jar alongside silver dollars and buffalo nickels, which fascinated Dave. Beyond interest in the physical differences between the coins, Dave wanted to know the story behind the items and learn about that European "trip that I knew nothing about. All those items were tied to certain events." Dave began to attend the local collectors' club and frequented a coin store run by a World War II vet. When the owner went on break, Dave was left to run the store and loved it.

Growing up in the outskirts of the Twin Cities, Dave was fascinated by the abandoned buildings and farm equipment that dotted the fields, and pondered what life was like for the people who used to live there. One day, he came across a drainage ditch that got washed away and exposed a heap of Civil War–era bottle and crock shards. Most of the items were broken and not of huge value, but the find nevertheless gained him some local notoriety and was written up in the newspaper. From that moment, Dave was hooked and began his hobby in earnest. Finding whole specimens, that demonstrate craftsmanship with either unusual or decorative embossing, is part of the appeal. Yet for Dave, the cognitive component of unpacking the everyday history of the person living at the site is even more captivating. How rich or poor they were becomes evident in what they threw away, as well as what they enjoyed consuming. If enough privies are dug up in a town, a broader picture is built up. For example, Dave wrote a paper for the Stillwater historical society based on the soda and pharmaceutical bottles found in the area.

Dave is not driven by the blind acquisition of items. He doesn't go out and buy bottles from other collectors. Nor does he have a fascination in broad collectibles—he has a noticeable disdain for anything that is remotely commercialized. Dave is fanatical about bottle collecting for its unique combination of the physical, with a spike in adrenaline whenever digging, and the cerebral, when piecing together the history of the item and its user. Bottles typically had "a limited location and time of use. They are a time capsule of another age." Dave is highly aware of what drives him in his hobby. He loves discovering "something new and unique" as much as cataloging and understanding what the object is. Dave enjoys seeing the specimens he unearthed on display and has no problem discarding bottles that have little personal or historical value. As a parent of teenagers, Dave has found a new richness in his hobby by bringing them along for a dig. Each dig provides a personal experience for Dave and connects him to a bygone era, demonstrating that he is true collector at heart. There are some notable parallels between Dave's collecting and Marj's fanship from the first chapter, as well as a roller coaster enthusiast we will meet soon. All individuals are captivated by their passion and use it as a means to collect memories, experience life, and connect with others. It also has become a core feature of who they are, going beyond just a fun activity pursued on the weekend.

A couple of days before the dig, I got a text message from Dave that he got special permission to dig anywhere on the property, but to do so quickly as some parking lot construction was to begin soon. What got Dave excited about this particular site, beyond the fact that it was uninhabited, was a detailed plot map from the city that showed the location of the first privy. Using this as a guide, our small group of six treasure hunters got busy prodding the land to find the exact location of the hole, using long thin metal probes. When pushed into the earth, the probe will typically travel with a bit of friction and requires steady force, especially through layers of clay. Yet, when pushed into a former privy, the probe travels effortlessly and when pulled up, a noticeable change of color is seen in the dirt, from the black of topsoil to an ashen gray. Clues in the landscape can help treasure hunters avoid just randomly probing the ground. For example, they can spot slightly sunken spots in the grass, typically near property lines or trees. One member of our group has a much less typical, but apparently pretty successful way of finding the privy. Using two metal wire dowsing rods, he works to locate the brick or stone walls that can sometimes line the privy. Once a shortlist of potential sites is established, several additional pokes of the probe confirm the location of the privy and then the real work begins.

We began digging about an hour after our arrival, being careful to cut and remove the sod in a way that would allow us to restore the ground to the way that we found it. Our probes discovered two likely spots that were adjacent to each other. As noted earlier, it was common for households to work through multiple privies before municipal sewer and trash services arrived. After a family filled one hole, they would dig another nearby and move the outhouse that sat over it. We began digging a rectangular hole that was roughly 4 feet wide and 7 feet long. If it weren't in the middle of the day at a site across the street from City Hall, a passerby could easily have mistaken our group for a bunch of grave diggers. We did look suspicious enough for a couple of concerned citizens to come by and check on what we were doing, but as we had a printout from City Hall in hand, the locals of Chaska stood down and responded more with curiosity than concern. In fact, one neighbor suggested that we come back later in the year, to dig up the privy in his own backyard.

The group took turns digging, two people working at time, removing boulders, metal pipes, tree roots, and over a dozen of Chaska bricks before signs of the use layer became evident. A change in the composition and color of the dirt is the first sign of the use layer, with grayish ash becoming visible. As with everything else from the household, ash from the fireplace or kitchen was chucked down the hole, with the beneficial effects of both breaking down biological matter and dissipating bad smells. The first couple finds were promising and unique, specifically a microscope slide and elaborate broken clock. From there, we uncovered two chamber pots, broken Scandinavian China, a few spoons, and plenty of beef and pork bones. At this point in the dig, the bigger spades and shovels were replaced by trowels and gloved hands, to ensure that glassware and other fragile items were not broken in the process of excavation.

Our first few bottles were not particularly noteworthy, just the run of the mill nonembossed ketchup types. Although the professionals were nonplussed, I particularly liked an extracts bottle and kept it as a memento from the morning. Lunch was upon us and the group opted to go for a burrito from a joint smashed between the coin laundry and corner grocery. Thinking that the best find of the day was going to be the burrito, I left the group for another commitment and unfortunately missed out on the true treasures. Postburrito, the group uncovered five Chaska embossed pharmacy bottles, 15 bottles for medicinal vapors, a Glencoe MN soda bottle, Costco-sized maple syrup jugs, a store sign advertising "Pictorial Patterns Review" for dressmaking, a porcelain chicken, a statue of St. Christopher, the rest of the microscope, and loads more plates. More noteworthy, the team uncovered five porcelain dolls that when found in the dirt looked incredibly creepy, but provided evidence that kids once lived at this house. Probably the most encouraging find was a George Benz appetine bitters black glass embossed bottle that if whole, would have fetched $800 at a collectors' convention. This specific specimen was missing a single two-inch piece, but still represents a top 10 bottle find for Minnesota.

When I caught up with Dave post dig, I was glad to hear that the site was by far the best one of the 70 privies dug up in the area. They were able to dig to very bottom of the use layer and hit the clay bottom, dating the materials to around the turn of the century. This left the possibility that the other privy dates before it, as the house was known to predate the clay layer by at least a couple of decades. When the team returned a few weeks later, the dig went from good to epic, scoring Dave's top experience for treasure hunting in Minnesota. They continue to speculate on who exactly who lived at the house. From the clues unearthed, they knew that children were likely and that the family was relatively wealthy, as evidenced by imports from China, Japan, and Germany. A snake skeleton might indicate that they had at least one pet. What is less clear is how the microscope and store sign played in. Were the family the owners of a general store or potentially connected with a pharmacy in some way?

Such speculations are part of the fun and allure of the dig. Since the actual physical hole would only allow for two people at any given time, the remainder of the group were left to sit in camping chairs and watch. With every scrape of the soil, the anticipation built up about what would be found. Any discovery would prompt conversation about what exactly it was and how the item fit into the emerging story about the people who lived at the house. In Dave's words, "These items have not been touched by anyone in over a hundred years," and for the treasure hunters, that is a key part of the thrill. The dig requires perseverance and problem-solving, sprinkled in with knowledge about common-use items and an eye for spotting the unusual. The type of fanaticism that tied the group together was much more cognitive than physical, rooted in the past and the importance of local history. That morning, the group members stopped being business owners, students, and parents and were instead treasure hunters on the pursuit on uncovering long-lost items and putting together the puzzle of a family that once lived on Pine Street.

Even if they don't offer the firsthand experience treasure hunters enjoy, collections and museums have the potential to transport observers to a different time and place. If you look hard enough, there is a museum for everyone, from medical devices to boardwalk arcades, where individual interests are catered to. Atlas Obscura is a fantastic source for finding the more idiosyncratic collections out there, acting as a collection of collections. Touting itself as "the definitive guide to the world's hidden wonders," the guide never fails to disappoint, and I use it whenever I find myself in a new city. My personal highlights include seeing the skull of Phineas Gage in a display case in Boston, having my fortune told by an automated typewriter in San Francisco, and visiting the birthplace of SPAM, all found through the guide. One particular museum in London brings to life the definition of a collection like no other, interweaving the collector's intent and the collection's purpose in society. It also is unique in its future-forward purpose, going beyond celebrating the past to inspiring a future generation of creative talent.

Sir John Soane established the museum that carries his name through a special act of Parliament agreed during his own lifetime, turning a vast and eclectic mix of "antiquities, sculpture, casts, timepieces, furniture, stained glass, paintings, and oriental objects" into a "treasure trove of a museum," as described by Atlas Obscura.[5] According to the entry, "The highlights of Soane's crammed-in collection of art, sculpture, and antiques include the sarcophagus of Egyptian pharaoh SETI 1—held in the Sepulchral Chamber, an acquisition that so thrilled Soane he threw a party that went on for days—and a bevy of paintings by William Hogarth. . . . In the courtyard on the lowest level is buried Soane's Dog Fanny, the grave for which reads: 'Alas! Poor Fanny!'" If you have not visited the museum, you might be fooled into thinking that the museum is large and sprawling. The reality is that the museum is contained in a single house, conceived as a total work of art, where John Soane himself lived, in the heart of London.

Soane's path to fame was far from guaranteed. Born in 1753, Soane began his life from modest beginnings. As the son of a bricklayer, he worked during his adolescence and stopped his formal education at age 15, when he joined his older brother to work the family business in and around Reading. His fortune changed dramatically when his drawing skills were noticed by a surveyor and he was introduced to the architect George Dance the Younger. Soane moved to London to join the architect's practice, enrolled at the Royal Academy, and won a number of awards for his drawings, including a scholarship to travel abroad and see architectural masterpieces firsthand. Soane's ultimate destination was Rome, where he spent the next 2 years, in his own words, "seeing and examining the numerous and inestimable remains of Antiquity." This appreciation for the classical world and antiquities would remain with him for the remainder of his life. Soane returned from Italy in 1780 and soon received his first commissions to build country houses, before landing the chief architect and surveyor role for the Bank of England in 1788, a position he held for 45 years. Beyond the bank and the design of the Dulwich Picture Gallery, his most notable work was his own home at Lincoln's Inn Fields, which gained recognition for how much could be accomplished aesthetically within a limited interior space.[6]

[5] Atlas Obscura. Sir John Soane's Museum. https://www.atlasobscura.com/places/sir-john-soanes-mus eum (accessed September 21, 2021).
[6] Curl, J., and Wilson, S. (2015). The Oxford Dictionary of Architecture. Oxford: Oxford University Press.

How that came to be was less of a grand design and more of a lifelong work in progress. With his business practice established, Soane bought a house at 12 Lincoln's Inn Fields in 1792, demolished it, and built a new one to his own specifications. From the beginning, the home was intended to showcase Soane's abilities and tastes, as well as build confidence in potential clients that Soane was distinguished among his peers. In 1807, Soane acquired and moved into the house next door at 13 Lincoln's Inn Fields (the current location of the museum) and used that as an opportunity not only to expand his office but also to create a purpose-built domed area to showcase his rapidly growing collection of antiquities and beautiful objects. The acquisition also coincided with his appointment as a Professor of Architecture for the Royal Academy. Over the following decades, he transformed the house from a personal home to a museum for students of architecture. Initially, by invitation only, students and special guests could inspect his collection and bask in the aesthetic beauty of how the items were arranged and interacted with the building. He hoped that the future generation of architects would lose themselves in his collection and be inspired to create something new.

In 1822, when Soane was in his 70s, he held the first public exhibition of watercolors of his museum. A year later, he acquired the house at 14 Lincoln's Inn Fields, with the intent of adding an extension to his house and displaying his collection of paintings from Hogarth, Canaletto, Turner, and others. Yet, all the success, attention, and accolades Soane received were bittersweet. He initially had hoped that both his sons would take an interest in becoming architects, yet they shunned the profession. His older son John suffered from chronic health issues, while his younger son George had an uncontrollable temper, eventually falling out with his father and becoming estranged from the family. Outliving both his wife and eldest son, Soane effectively barred George from inheriting his vast and quite valuable collection by negotiating a private Act of Parliament in 1833, four years before his death. The museum's website summarizes the Act's intention "to preserve his house and collection, exactly as it was arranged at the time of his death, in perpetuity—and to keep it open and free for inspiration and education."[7]

Standing back from John Soane's collection, it could easily be mistaken as a mass of valuable clutter. Personally, I have been to the museum on a number of occasions and always walk away feeling a bit bewildered, questioning whether I took it all in or appreciated the right elements. As summarized by the museum's website, "The organisation of the Museum can at first glance seem crowded and even chaotic. However, it is, in fact, purposeful, with each

[7] Soane. Our History. https://www.Soane.org (accessed September 21, 2021).

interior being a work of art in its own right. Soane was constantly arranging and rearranging the collection, not just to incorporate new acquisitions, but to enhance the objects' poetic qualities through creative and inspiring juxtapositions." Luckily for us, we know what Soane was trying to accomplish and can trace back the motivations for his fanaticism to both the personal enjoyment he felt for his collection and the larger purpose of inspiring the next generation of architects. Without such guidance, the line between a collection and hoard could get rapidly blurred. If John Soane's collection was made up of less valuable items or not kept up to pristine conditions, would we still be recognizing his legacy in the same way? Alternatively, if we did not know he was one of the greatest architects of his day, would we lose the relevance behind the collection and just consider it eccentric?

The distinction between a collection and hoard gets progressively blurred with each term that gets added to the normal English vernacular, with phrases like "passionate collectors," "pack rats," "impulsive buyers," or "accumulators" pointing to something potentially deviant, but not quite making it clear what that is. Society's awareness and concern over hoarding is much greater today than in Soane's time. Societal events like the 1930s financial crash and the 1970s oil crisis raised popular concern about what exactly is normal consumer behavior, instead of something that warrants corrective action. Additionally, today's consumer culture hinges on single use and discardable items, which is categorically different from the items Dave digs up in old privies or what Soane would have bought and used. Granted, the level of luxury experienced by Soane is seldom found in the normal turn-of-the-19th-century privy.

Psychologists distinguish between collecting and hoarding across three variables. First, collections are relatively common in society, with 30% of the general population reporting that they maintain a collection of some variety.[8] Second, collectors use their items or invest time putting them on display. Third, collectors are likely to demarcate a specific space within their home for their collection. Collectors are typically eager to talk about their items, show them to others, and engage in trades with others who share the same interests. This behavior is very different from hoarding disorder. Hoarders rarely use their items, allow them to spread across their livable space, and do not invest the time in organizing and decluttering what they have accumulated. Dave and Soane are cut from the same cloth in how they showcased, curated, and engaged others in their collections, despite having very different motivations and interests in what they collected.

[8] Nordslettenfrr, A., and Mataix-Cols, D. (2012). Hoarding versus collecting: Where does pathology diverge from play? Clinical Psychology Review, 32, 165–176.

In a series of interviews with professional organizers (POs) working in the Toronto area, researcher Katie Kilroy-Marac learned that a key distinction between collecting and hoarding is observed in the ability or inability to sort and categorize objects.[9] One organizer commented, "I see it all the time . . . they make too many categories of things. Like, every folder on their desktop has one single file in it . . . It's not, you know, one file folder for all the automotive bills. It's 'Automotive January' and one bill . . . And then there are the other clients who are just the opposite: they create these categories that are so big that everything just gets lost inside of them." The ability or inability to categorize gets at the root difference between collections and hoards; without being able to group like with like, it is very difficult to plan, organize, and share a collection with others. In the words of another profiled PO, "A collection is a group of specific things that are treasured, displayed, and have a natural ebb and flow, so that a collection is refined on an ongoing basis." It must show signs of active consideration, be accessible, and separated from mundane, everyday objects.

What is held in common between a collection and a hoard is the focus and attachment to material items and strangely, both collectors and people who hoard can fall victim to compulsive buying. Driven as a response to negative events and feelings, both collectors and people who hoard may experience cravings or withdrawal if kept away from the acquisition of material items. Approximately 5% of the American public are thought to be compulsive buyers with unsustainable spending habits, which are often hard even for the acquirer to comprehend. One acquirer of dragon-themed books profiled in a 2017 study lead by Samantha Cross acknowledges the tension she feels when encountering a find, "My list of books that I've read that I own is like three pages long, and still, when I go the bookstore, and I see a new book . . . then I go and get it . . . and I'm thinking 'Anne, you already have too many books and you haven't read them yet.'"[10]

The distinction between collecting and hoarding is best characterized by what an individual does with the acquired items and whether or not they will ever be discarded. Although it seems harsh, much of a what constitutes a hoard can be considered as junk. Dr. James Collett, writing for the Australian Psychological Society, describes a hoard as tending "to be of low financial value, in poor condition or outright disrepair, relatively easy to reacquire if needed, and unlikely to be perceived as meaningful by others. Clothing,

---

[9] Kilroy-Marac, K. (2018). An order of distinction (or, how to tell a collection from a hoard). Journal of Material Culture, 23, 20–38.

[10] Cross, S., Leizerovici, G., and Pirouz, D. (2018). Hoarding: Understanding divergent acquisition, consumption, and disposal. Journal of the Association for Consumer Research, 3, 81–96.

kitchenware, haberdashery, ornaments, toys, hardware, and automotive parts are all common items to find in a hoard."[11] Yet, the value of the items themselves is not 100% telling of what a hoard is. Simon Evan's 2008 mixed media artwork titled *Everything I Have* makes this point directly by visually presenting his most mundane possessions as a finely curated collection that demands attention. Instead, hoarding is about the behavior exhibited across the acquisition, consumption, and disposal of material goods. People who hoard break the convention that they have control over what they consume, when in fact their behavior diverges from the typical and spirals out of control until it can be of harm to not only themselves but those around them.

Back to Soane, it was his behavior in how he acquired, curated, and discarded items that defined him as a collector, rather than the impressive beauty and value of the items he collected. His fanaticism of collecting consumed him right up until the end, with at least three acquisitions arriving at his home posthumously. The last object placed by Soane himself was a small statuette of Victory, placed in the breakfast room in front of a watercolor of his wife. For Helen Dorey, the current deputy director and inspectress of Sir John Soane's Museum, there really is no other item that would have been more fitting as Soane's last installation to display. For her, the statuette was "symbolic of victory over the grave" and a life lived "in pursuits of architecture in all its aspects."

Helen is the latest curator from a long line of professionals dating back to the museum's foundation, all of whom were entrusted in caring for and preserving the collection "as a total work of art." When I met with Helen, it was easy to see the passion and commitment she holds for the museum. Her connection to Soane goes well beyond her technical role as curator, to an appreciation of Soane as a person and a desire to make true his vision for the museum to inspire future generations. Much of Helen's work has been focused on undoing the "improvements" made to the house by her predecessors, which have acted to undermine the original intent of how items were presented and the aesthetic that they were intended to create. The museum's first curator, George Bailey, began this unfortunate trend by moving partitions and furniture to make the house more livable, which was completely understandable when considering that curators both worked and lived among Soane's possessions. Later changes became increasingly intrusive, from poking holes in the walls for electricity to replacing carpets and stained glass on the whim of the curators' changing tastes.

---

[11] Collett, J. (2019). Unpacking hoarding disorder. InPsych, 41, 5, 1–14.

Helen's mission to restore the museum relies on both tireless research and her keen eye for detail. Moving room by room, she gains an intimacy with each interior space by reviewing any and all references to what was once in the room, including household records about what was bought and repaired during Soane's occupancy. Yet, the most precious references are the vast number of sketches and watercolors by Soane's students who came to the house for inspiration. In Helen's words "it is the best documented house in the world," even if it also happens to be the most jammed together. The long history and vastness of the collection provided both immense promise and challenge. Beyond what is visible to museumgoers today, there are countless small items stuffed away in drawers, some of which were not listed in the original inventories drawn up in 1837. A difficult call was made by Helen on the items that Soane used day-to-day in his personal living space and whether these items could and should be considered part of the museum. The private apartment lacked documentation and saw the most dramatic changes over time, but with some excellent detective work, they are now restored and open to limited viewing.

Helen's lifelong interest in architecture began early in her life, sprouting from the numerous family trips to see the historical buildings that dot the British countryside. After pursuing degrees in history and history of art, she landed her first job with the museum, joining a skeleton staff as a combination secretary and junior curator. Thirty years later, she has not regretted her career choice and is just as committed to the museum as ever. Like Dave, she is motivated by "the thrill of the chase," which in the context of the museum is researching and tracking down every possible detail in order to get as close to Soane's vision as possible. For example, Helen recently had new nails fabricated to perfectly match those used by Soane to hang his pictures. They needed to be the right size, shape, and color. Getting to this level of detail might drive others mad, but for Helen, it allows her to achieve a closeness to Soane. "When every item is in the right place, everything makes sense and shows Soane's architectural genius. You are in his mind and thoughts," explains Helen.

One thing that I had to ask Helen about was the origin of her second title as inspectress. To her knowledge, she is the only person in the world to have this title, which was specified by Soane in the act of Parliament. The original role was intended for Sally Conduitt, Soane's housekeeper, to enable her to act after his death as a deputy director in charge of keeping the collection and building in pristine condition. What makes the role truly unique is that it is one of longest-running, continuous leadership roles held by a woman of any institution in the world. All this history is part of Helen's fanaticism with curation, but it really is the work itself that she finds "endlessly fascinating." She explains that "outside the context of the museum, the importance of an item could be missed." For example, Helen spoke about some twisted Ash sticks in the dining room. For Soane, the pieces of twisted timber represent the role nature plays in architecture, but if found in an open field, these sticks would lack significance. Like collectors, Helen is striving to understand the past and discover the rare and beautiful, engaging with others about what she has learned. Yet, it is her everyday role of inspectress that embodies the principles of collecting and puts them into practice.

Hoarding is the polar opposite of what the inspectress role is about, as people who hoard display a failure to engage with and discard their possessions. As a disorder, hoarding is a relatively new standalone diagnosis, first appearing in the *Diagnostic and Statistical Manual of Mental Disorders*, fifth edition, in 2013, based on the research of a group of psychologists led by David Mataix-Cols.[12] In their study, two distinct samples of participants living in London were recruited. The first set was made up of 50 self-identified hoarders found via a hoarding support group and advertisements on patient websites. The second set of participants included 20 self-identified collectors, recruited through personal connections with staff at King's College London or local collectors' shops. Within this group, collectors reported interest in a broad range of items, including comics, stamps, coins, books, and CDs, as well as the much more specific items of vintage radios, toy soldiers, and model submarines.

Through a combination of interviews and questionnaires, the research team was able to distinguish people who hoard from collectors, and establish diagnostic criteria for pathological behavior. Of the participants studied, 29 were identified as meeting the criteria of hoarding disorder, which itself was separated from a diagnosis of obsessive-compulsive disorder (OCD). This last finding is particularly important, as prior to the field study, hoarding was tied more directly to OCD, with typical symptoms including checking, counting, and washing, driven by an unrelenting need to reduce anxiety or unwanted thoughts. Whereas OCD is considered distressing and inconsistent with personal aspirations, hoarding disorder does not carry the same baggage.

People demonstrating hoarding disorder are diagnosed by range of criteria.[13] First, they have difficulty discarding possessions, even those with limited or no objective value. Second, they perceive a need to save items

[12] Mataix-Cols, D., et al. (2013). The London field trial for hoarding disorder. Psychological Medicine, 43, 837–847.
[13] Nordsletten, A., and Mataix-Cols, D. (2012). Hoarding versus collecting: Where does pathology diverge from play? Clinical Psychology Review, 32, 165–176.

and experience a great deal of distress when forced to give them up. The clutter they accumulate congests and clutters their living spaces, to the point where real harm is experienced by the individual or those around them. The hoarding then causes clinically significant impairment in the individual's ability to maintain normal social and occupational relationships. Lastly, their behavior cannot be attributed to a medical condition (like a brain injury) or better accounted for by the symptoms of another psychological disorder (such as depression zapping away the energy to engage in normal activities).

It is estimated that somewhere between 2% and 6% of the population could be considered pathological hoarders, however because the designation of the disorder is so new as a separate concept, the real number may be higher.[14] Early evidence indicates that hoarding is more common in males than females, but women are more likely to seek treatment. Hoarding does carry comorbidity, with diagnosed patients commonly suffering from anxiety disorder, major depressive disorder, and OCD. Hoarding behaviors appear early in life, with approximately 60% of normal children aged 6 demonstrating the trait. What subsides for the majority of people resurfaces in their 20s, creates impairment in their 30s, and reaches pathological status in their 50s. Once the ball gets rolling, people with hoarding disorder encounter a spiral of negative consequences for their behavior.[15] Clutter can elicit stigma among family and friends, resulting in increasing social isolation. Hoarders often have inadequate social safety nets to rely on, typically live alone, are low-income, and share the same disorder with close family members (approximately 50% of people who hoard report having a first-degree relative with the same condition). On a more basic level, hoards can create tripping hazards in the home, which is especially concerning because of the skew of hoarding behavior to older populations.

Dr. Suzanne Chabaud has seen these statistics firsthand in her practice at the OCD Institute of Greater New Orleans and in her stint on the A&E show *Hoarders*. When I spoke to Suzanne about her personal journey becoming an expert on hoarding, it became apparent just how much the world has changed in recognizing the disorder as something unique and in need of being addressed. When she was approached by A&E to take part in the show in 2009, hoarding was still entangled as a type of OCD, with a staggeringly small number of clients coming forward for treatment. As a result, Suzanne had to take a deep dive on what was known about hoarding and work out for

---

[14] Nordsletten, A., and Mataix-Cols, D. (2012). Hoarding versus collecting: Where does pathology diverge from play? Clinical Psychology Review, 32, 165–176.
[15] Collett, J. (2019). Unpacking hoarding disorder. InPsych, 41, 5, 1–14.

herself how best to approach and work with the people she would encounter on the show. Over the course of over 35 episodes, filmed between 2009 and 2016, Suzanne amassed field experience that is elusive to many psychologists working with clients today. Unlike Suzanne, who was able to enter personal homes and witness her clients' behaviors firsthand, psychologists typically interact with clients in the office and therefore miss out on witnessing the impact from therapy firsthand.

Spotting the difference between collecting and hoarding is not difficult, according to the Suzanne. The interference caused by an unchecked consumption of objects on living space is apparent as soon as you step over the threshold, as is the smell in the air. With an inability to "release or let go" of objects, the people she encountered developed "sensory numbing" to the environment they lived in, unable to see or smell their world. For example, Suzanne remembers one client who had kept a large quantity of birds, who were free to relieve themselves throughout the house. Suzanne spotted a small memo book on the floor when walking through the house and seeing that it was covered with excrement, decided to throw the book away. Within hours, her client noticed the book missing and asked why it was discarded. Ignoring or not noticing the fact that the book was disgusting, the client had a plan to use the picture on the front cover as part of an art project. Perceiving value (even if never brought to fruition) of objectively useless items is common to people who hoard and goes hand-in-hand with the sensory numbing that Suzanne described.

This example made it clear to Suzanne that people with hoarding disorder perceive their world very differently than those around them. Where the rest of us would be visually overwhelmed with the living environment, an individual who hoards has adapted to the clutter to the point of not recognizing just how abnormal it is and the potential harm that it presents to normal living. As observers, we miss the value that they ascribe to what they have acquired. In Suzanne's words, "their objects have an assigned value that is personal to them. For collectors, others are able to see how amazing the items are and why the items are of interest." The same doesn't apply to people with hoarding disorder, where items are constrained to a "personal value." What might have started as a collection turns into a hoard as the neat organization of the collection degrades to the point where only the individual knows what value the items might hold. The collection, which might have initially provided joy and fulfillment, becomes a source of distress as it takes over the home.

This gap between what the individual and an outside observer perceives creates a barrier to seek treatment. They don't see the danger in newspapers and mail piled on the stove or the risk of appliances that do not get repaired.

The hoard imposes on the ability of the individual to adequately function in the home, yet Suzanne reinforced that many people don't actively seek treatment, but instead are encouraged to seek help by family and friends. On their first encounter with a therapist, they often say that they are there not because they see harm in the way they are living, but because their family believes that "they have too much stuff." Suzanne believes it is important to take small steps in developing trust with a new client, making sure that they know that the therapist is genuinely there to help, even if extreme measures are necessary to save them or others from a dangerous situation. With time, an individual's delusional thinking that nothing is wrong breaks down into recognition that the way they are living is not sustainable. Suzanne believes that with the identification of hoarding disorder as a bonafide disorder, part of the stigma will break down and allow people with it to seek treatment more consistently. Destigmatization is the key to reduce fear of judgement and feelings of shame.

From a social vantage point, hoarding represents significant risk. According to Dr. James Collett,[16] as many as four out of five fires in the home result from excessive clutter. People with hoarding disorder clutter and congest the living area to a point where normal function of the space is severely compromised. In the words of one individual profiled in a study by Cross, Leizerovici, and Pirouz, "I would rather stand on the corner bare-ass naked during traffic than allow anyone inside my house."[17] An extreme case of the potential harm from hoarding was witnessed in 1947, when the Collyer brothers died of their 136 tons of clutter. One of the brothers was buried alive when a pile of refuse fell on him. The other brother was blind, unable to navigate the home, and eventually died from starvation.

The cost to remove hoards is not inconsequential, and one can imagine how many dumpsters were needed to clean up the Collyer brothers' house. As an individual's hoarding behavior gets worse, it creates its own barriers to change. Mounting home repairs, greater volumes of goods to dispose, legal issues and complaints by neighbors, and finding effective treatments for the underlying condition all stack up and work against the individual, preventing them from finding a long-term solution. Some people are able to walk the tightrope between hoarding and the full harms of their behavior. Termed "functional hoarders," these individuals accumulate objects privately and shield the impact of their behaviors from all but their closest friends and family.

[16] Collett, J. (2019). Unpacking hoarding disorder. InPsych, 41, 5, 1–14.
[17] Cross, S., Leizerovici, G., and Pirouz, D. (2018). Hoarding: Understanding divergent acquisition, consumption, and disposal. Journal of the Association for Consumer Research, 3, 81–96.

As with any other psychological ailment, it is sometimes difficult to look beyond the behavior to the person underneath. Emily Saltz talks about a pair of brothers in the "Editor's Message" that she wrote for a special edition on hoarding and elders.[18] Two brothers, Jimmy and Harry, lived in an urban apartment building and kept largely to themselves. Neighbors began to complain about the pair's living conditions, having experienced bad odors emanating from their apartment, junk piled up, and the occasional flood when the brothers forgot to turn off the bathroom faucet. Health officials got involved, and the landlord started to seek eviction. Before matters spiraled out of control, Saltz asked "the neighbors, the landlord, and the health department—to back off, slow down, and give (her) time to make some progress." She managed to "enter their apartment and their lives . . . and Jimmy and Harry soon became real people to her." Harry was trained as a classical pianist, while Jimmy played in the amateur baseball league. Both had no clue what the fuss was about and saw no issue with the way they were living. Through their connection with Emily, the brothers were able to make some tangible adjustments to how they interacted with the neighbors. Without her getting to know the brothers on a personal level, the chances that the city would have acted by clearing the piles of trash and forcing eviction were elevated, despite the emotional carnage left behind.

Based on these brothers' example, Suzanne stressed how the harms of hoarding extend to other family members and especially to future generations. When raised in a hoarding household, the normal development of children can be stifled and maladaptive patterns of behavior reinforced. This is a personal motivation for Suzanne, to break the hoarding cycle before it is passed to future generations. She spoke about one particular family and how hoarding disrupted the normal functioning of the household. Due to the clutter and ignoring the maintenance needs of the house, the children spent their entire childhood without the ability to take a hot shower or bath. Their hygiene was poor and no doubt influenced both the child's physical health and ability to make friends. Suzanne stressed that not all households fall into squalor through hoarding behavior, but once the wheels are set in motion, there is a tendency for low mobility in the house to create the conditions ripe for deteriorating hygiene.

Suzanne's example is unfortunately quite common for children raised in hoarding households. In a particularly compelling account, Barbara Allen describes what it was like to grow up in a world of clutter.[19] The rules of

[18] Saltz, E. (2010). Hoarding and elders: Current trends, dilemmas, and solutions. Journal of Geriatric Care Management, 20, 4–9.

[19] Allen, B. (2010). Nice children stolen from car. Journal of Geriatric Care Management, 20, 25–27.

keeping everything were applied to the entire household, "My sister Cindy and I try one day. We gather together a useless jumble of toys: headless dolls, trucks without wheels, broken pieces of plastic that once belonged to something, but no one remembers what, and bundle them into a cardboard box. We cart the box outside to leave for the garbage men; our farther carts it back in. 'It's all good stuff,' he says." With everything considered "good stuff," the piles of clutter ended up blocking hallways and clogging stairs, to the point where Cindy began to worry about dying.

Friends were barred from Barbara's house. On the one occasion when a particularly brave friend crossed the threshold into the home, Barbara was in shock, "No one has ever just come into our house before, and we are so surprised by her presence that, for a few seconds, we stand paralyzed and speechless." Her friend, Rose, made it to the kitchen; the place where the family's three unhousebroken dogs were free to roam. Rose stepped over a puddle of dog urine and accepted a cup of coffee complete with a "small island of grease floating on the surface of the liquid." After a short stay, Barbara and Rose talked outside. "Whew . . . That was really something," Rose said. Barbara replied, "You drank it . . . you drank the coffee," to which Rose stated, "Well, I had a little problem when I saw that floating scum. But then I reminded myself that you drink that stuff every day and you aren't dead yet." Barbara lived with a person who not only hoarded but was a "dirty" hoarder. Her childhood was overtaken by rules about what to keep and not clean, which extended to her own personal hygiene, as the family was forbidden to take showers in order to save water. In Barbara's words, "I hate a lot about the way we live, but the fleas are what I hate most."

The "doorbell dread" described by Barbara is quite common, according to Suzanne. Individuals with hoarding disorder and family members alike share in genuine fear that someone will come over and discover just how unlivable a house is. Also common in Barbara's story is the directive "not to tell anyone about this house," which layers additional anxiety onto family members who themselves might be dreaming for a different way of living. In many ways, it is not surprising that the majority of individuals with hoarding disorder live an isolated life and choose not to have children or marry. Suzanne mentioned that the abnormal relationship they have with items stifles their ability to form functional relationships with people. "The relationship with objects interrupts relationships with children and spouses. They are seldom more important than the object." An article by Margit Novack[20] brings Suzanne's point

---

[20] Novack, M. (2010). Rooms of shame: Senior move manager's perspective on hoarding. Journal of Geriatric Care Management, 20, 21–24.

home with a profile of Clark, who spoke about his final days with his wife: "I buried my wife yesterday. She was a hoarder. I loved her and I took care of her, especially the past few years when she was bedridden. After fifty years of marriage, her dying words to me were not 'I love you.' They were 'Don't touch my stuff.' I was surrounded by her stuff for years. I want to get rid of it and reclaim my life."

Four major psychological factors contribute to developing hoarding behavior.[21] First, people demonstrating hoarding behavior have an unusually high emotional attachment to possessions, amplified by tendencies toward poor emotional regulation, feeling negative emotions more acutely, and perceiving negative emotions as more threatening. The second psychological factor is cognitive, with people demonstrating hoarding behavior typically experiencing difficulty with concentration, categorization, planning, and decision-making. It is estimated that 28% of people with hoarding disorder hold a comorbidity diagnosis of inattentive ADHD. The third psychological factor has to do with beliefs relating to identity, personal responsibility, and material value that collectively get in the way with discarding possessions. People with hoarding disorder report feeling that their material possessions are an extension of who they are as people. When forced to discard items, their sense of self is threatened and they fear the loss of personal memories. Lastly, hoarding behavior is reinforced through a pattern of avoidance, where poor personal motivation for change and a lack of insight, denial, and procrastination create a self-fulfilling cycle. By avoiding how their hoarding impacts both themselves and those around them, they create a wall against the anxiety and regret that would occur if they embraced change.

People with hoarding disorder often feel that discarding an item wastes its unused value, causing them to feel regret and creating a cycle where future items are retained indefinitely. Robin, a participant in the study by Cross, Leizerocvici, and Pirouz,[22] reflected on these feelings, "If I throw things away, I'll get upset because I think that maybe I'll use that or maybe I could have used it or it just so happens that after I've thrown it away and it's gone, I needed that . . . Yeah, like with fabric pieces and stuff, I'll think, 'Oh if I had kept that piece, I could have done this with it.'" The narrative built around hoarding is often well intentioned, with thoughts and rationale about frugality and environment. Hoarders often balk at the single-use, machine-made consumer society that we all live in. Yet, this rationale does not follow through to healthy

[21] Nordsletten, A., and Mataix-Cols, D. (2012). Hoarding versus collecting: Where does pathology diverge from play? Clinical Psychology Review, 32, 165–176.

[22] Cross, S., Leizerovici, G., and Pirouz, D. (2018). Hoarding: Understanding divergent acquisition, consumption, and disposal. Journal of the Association for Consumer Research, 3, 81–96.

living; instead of being reused, the hoard builds up and the potential value is never realized.

Emotionally, discarding items can feel like abandoning memories of people and places that are of great importance to a person with hoarding disorder. In the words of Joseph, a participant in a 2010 study by Helene Cherrier and Tresa Ponner,[23] "To me it's like a photo, it's a historical link to a time and a memory because we can't remember everything, and when you see these things it just jogs your memory about something that happened in the past . . . again we throw away our memory. It doesn't make sense." Linda has an emotional connection with objects as a reminder of where she has been, "Wherever I go, I like to pick something up like a tangible reminder of where that is. And as a result . . . , I have now a very large collection of rocks." Such motivations are not so different from what drives collectors, but people who hoard do not make good on their intentions to enjoy and use objects as a way of connecting with memories; the items pile up and loose the connectivity that drove their acquisition in the first place.

Suzanne summarizes that hoarding disorder is a "disorder of intentions" and many of these will never be realized. To break through, Suzanne attempts to "uncover the treasures from within," working with her clients to unpack what an item can tell her about them. She acknowledges the emotional attachment that people with hoarding disorder have to objects, using this as a basis to explore whether there are more healthy ways to demonstrate attachment. For example, if a person with hoarding disorder has an affection for Christmas decorations, could they envision a way to clear space in the house, removing items that would be in the way of the decorations? Could they envision a situation where they would like to host friends for a festive winter night in the newly decorated room?

This type of progress is often elusive for people experiencing hoarding disorder and requires diligent training in therapy to make long-term behavioral improvement. The most promising course of treatment has focused on cognitive-behavioral therapy (CBT), whereby personal goals are defined in counsel with a therapist, followed by building up problem-solving skills and behavioral change to strengthen emotional regulation. Although different approaches are used depending on the individual, separating the three elements of item acquisition, managing clutter, and discarding goods proves effective. To tackle item acquisition, basic math goes a long way to modify behavior; if the amount of goods coming into the house outweighs what is being

---

[23] Cherrier, H., and Ponnor, T. (2010). A study of hoarding behavior and attachment to material possessions. Qualitative Market Research, 13, 8–23.

discarded, the hoard is building. Individuals are often surprised with just how many items flow into their homes on a weekly basis. When it comes to decluttering and removal of possessions, small steps are key. Breaking rooms down by corners or shelves can make the process feel more achievable and counteract the emotional anxiety that individuals experience. Therapists will also attempt to tackle indecisiveness by reinforcing the rule that each possession can only be handled once when sorting, to avoid items continually popping up in the "keep" pile. For a successful decluttering to occur, the ultimate decision to discard an item will always sit with the individual; forcing them to remove items against their will is detrimental in the long term and will stir up intense feelings of grief or regret.

With time, reducing the clutter and gaining living space creates hope. Stories about how friends and family begin to visit again or how children regain their bedrooms result in a virtuous cycle where improvement builds upon itself. The individual effectively has traded their clutter for personal relationships and free time away from endless item acquisition. Progress begins when a therapist is able to assess the mental and physical factors that might be underlying the behavior. For example, with elders, the combination of social isolation, feelings of loss, memory impairment, and trauma can all contribute to pathological behavior. The therapist will in parallel need to build a trusting and positive relationship with the client, to encourage those small steps in curtailing the acquisition and discarding of items. If full-scale change is out of reach, the focus sometimes switches to increasing personal safety rather than attempting to eliminate the hoarding behavior itself. Termed "harm reduction," the approach provides an alternative to CBT with goals to improve the safety, health, or comfort of the client. Yet since a true solution is not being sought, the approach requires a greater degree of understanding among friends and family, as well as partnerships with protective government agencies.

Suzanne stressed that society has further to go before clinicians will be able to offer marked improvement across the population. Even if the right therapeutical practices are in place, there are not enough helpers on the ground to accurately assess the harm being experienced or reinforce the strategies taught through therapy. For example, Suzanne talked about the lack of screening questions that could be built into interactions with health practitioners. Asking questions during medical screenings like "Are you having friends or family over for the holidays?" or "Are there services at your home that you cannot get access to (like the family that lived without hot water)?" could flag up that a person is suffering from the disorder. Once therapy is underway, a person with hoarding disorder requires a village to ensure that change sticks.

Suzanne spoke about the importance of peer groups, to provide a psychologi-cally safe environment where people with hoarding disorder can speak about their struggles without shame or judgment. Ensuring that they feel valued and heard is critical to empowering them to deploy CBT techniques. Suzanne strongly believes that the personal and societal harms caused by hoarding disorder call out for more action. Fires, trip hazards, missing work, strained relationships, and physical disability only scratch the surface on the real im-pact that the disorder has on society. "Treatment is not a clean-up. It is about making the home safer." Thankfully we are now having a conversation specifi-cally on hoarding, which is the first step toward systemic help.

On the surface, the fanaticism held by collectors or people who hoard appears to have much in common, especially if the focus is on their attrac-tion to and acquisition of physical items. At first glance, it would be difficult to tell the difference between a collector and person with hoarding disorder as they scanned the tables at a rummage sale looking for treasure. Equally, both collectors and people who hoard may go beyond their financial means to build up their personal stash, although in different ways. Whereas collectors typically overspend their means acquiring a rare or missing artifact, people with hoarding disorder largely represent a lower income bracket and buy volumes of low-cost items. This difference between quality and volume cracks the window on a key insight on the psychological motivations for the two groups. Whereas collectors are focused on the positive elements of buying, specifically to add to or embellish their collection, people with hoarding dis-order often acquire items to fill an emotional hole that only gets worse when the hoard reaches an untenable level. The hoard is intertwined with the iden-tity of the individual, to the point where discarding items feels like they are giving away memories and a part of who they are. There is a great sadness to hoarding, where individuals get caught up in a web of acquiring items for a future utility that never transpires. The hoard takes over and dominates per-sonal relationships, freedom of movement, and healthy living.

The story for collectors couldn't be more different. With great pride, collectors exert effort in organizing, curating, and pruning their collections, using it as a mechanism to connect with other like-minded people. They show fanship for items as others would show fanship for artists in popular films or music. Without diminishing the positive social elements of collecting, the most striking feature for collectors' fanaticism is just how cognitive it is. Dave shared with me a book, written for bottle collectors, that chronicled every fea-sible specification to look out for, such that the treasure hunter could decipher the rarity and value of the find. This is part of the thrill, not knowing what you have until doing a deep dive on it. Better yet is discovering something that has yet to be chronicled. The collector then moves into inspecting the artifact, evaluating how pristine it is, what repair is needed, and whether it makes the cut into the collection, where it should belong, and how prominent it should be.

Beyond the physical attributes of the find, collectors strive to place the artifact in a larger historical context and ascribe value to what it might represent. They ponder what it might say about the people who once owned it or the community in which the object emerged. It is hard not to think about the children who once played with the porcelain dolls living at that house in Chaska or wonder about the many hands the coins of Dave's great aunt passed through before World War II. Sometimes the collector's story is very personal, like the beagle figurines bought to remember a childhood pet. Other times, the story is someone else's and unearthed by peeling back layers of history and filling in the gaps with some healthy speculation. Edward Leahy may have gotten it right by surmising that collectors collect the past, whether real or imagined.[24] The collector's fanaticism is a complex interweaving of sentimentality for the past, a thrill for the hunt, and puzzle-solving. I would be hard pressed to say whether collecting retro washing machines is more gratifying than dragon-themed books, as both have shown the potential for fanaticism. For both, it is the act of collecting that drives the pleasure rather than the strict ownership of goods, a theme that will come up again when exploring chocolate fanatics. Dave taught me that one person's trash can indeed be another person's treasure, although I imagine that Sir John Soane had some truly exceptional trash.

[24] Beck, K., Bilder, M., and McDonald, A. (2002). Collectors on collecting. Rare book exhibition programs, Boston College of Law School.

6

Compulsive Perfection

While some fanatics are looking to the past for their inspiration, others are focused squarely on the future, even if their version seems to be completely outlandish. The character of Doc Brown from the film *Back to the Future* epitomizes what a mad scientist is all about.[1] The opening sequence tells it all, from the wall of endless clocks to a dog-feeding machine gone awry, we are set up to believe that Doc Brown will be one eccentric fella. With framed pictures of Thomas Edison and Benjamin Franklin, we know that Doc reveres the scientific minds that have gone before him, while a newspaper clip of his burned-out mansion, an automatic coffee machine pouring coffee into a missing pot, and overburned toast that is inches away from catching fire hint at a cluttered mind, not overly burdened with safety or details. He is equally unworried what others think of him, perfectly happy to live in his own world of ideas rather than build extensive social relationships beyond Marty. When we meet Doc himself at the Twin Pines Mall, sporting a full biohazard suit, a breastpocket full of tools, and wild flowing gray hair, the stereotype of the mad scientist is there for us to digest.

From Henry Frankenstein[2] to Wayne Szalinski from *Honey, I Shrunk the Kids*,[3] the persona of the mad scientist provides a shorthand for what it means to be creative and innovative. Sometimes, the depiction is aloof and friendly; Doc Brown or Wayne Szalinski may be eccentric, but they are approachable and well intentioned. Any mistakes they make are mere oversights from a mind thinking about bigger and bolder ideas. With other depictions of the mad scientist, there is something more sinister going on. Henry Frankenstein bringing the dead back to life or Dr. Finkelstein from the *Nightmare Before Christmas*,[4] stitching together and keeping his daughter prisoner, tells us that the mad scientist is dangerous and in need of containment. Common to both the positive and negative versions is a mind that thinks differently than others,

---

[1] Zemeckis, R., and Gale, B. (1985). Back to the Future. Universal Pictures.
[2] Shelley, M. (1818). Frankenstein. London: Lackington, Hughes, Harding, Major and Jones.
[3] Gordon, S., Yuzna, B., and Naha, E. (1989). Honey, I Shrunk the Kids. Walt Disney Pictures.
[4] Burton, T., and McDowell, M. (1993). The Nightmare Before Christmas. Touchstone Pictures.

Fanatic. Joe Ungemah, Oxford University Press. © Oxford University Press 2024. DOI: 10.1093/9780197783894.003.0007

stretching the boundaries of conventional wisdom, complemented by a personality that has a disregard for societal conventions.

In real life, the true innovators around us are fanatic toward an idea that others might consider outlandish or unthinkable, but they persevere nonetheless. If hoarders are characterized by a failure to act on intention, innovators can be considered their exact opposite. Elon Musk's relentless push for electric cars and James Dyson's drive for the perfect household vacuum made them household names. Innovators like Musk or Dyson maintain a focus on achieving their visions that the rest of us would find exhausting. I'm sure that most people have had a fantastic, innovative idea for a new product or service waiting to be acted on. When I was a teenager, I kept a whole notebook of inventions, none of which I seriously pursued. Whenever I got excited about an idea, the risks and obstacles seemed too high, and, as the common saying goes, the juice was not worth the squeeze. Innovators look at the situation differently. Obstacles are there to be beaten and failure is not rejection, but an important step in development. Yet, what may truly set innovators apart is a confidence in their own ability, which protects their fanaticism for creation from self-doubt and allows them to take risk. Innovators are free from a fear of failure, allowing them to pursue an idea and wait for the rest of us to catch up and see their brilliance.

On a frigid January day, I drove to the outskirts of the twin cities, past the McMansions to where the real farms begin. I turned my little city car up a country road, freshly covered with snow, wondering if I would be lucky enough to be able to make it back up the hill that I just drove down. I turned to the right and entered through a rustic metal gate, following the tracks in the snow made by the last driver, careful not to slide off into the ditch on the side. In a few hundred feet, I spotted two incredibly excited dogs bounding toward me at full speed, apparently oblivious to the fact that it was -4 degrees outside. They promptly stopped in front of the car, prideful that they were able to stop the intruder in his tracks. We played a game where we each took turns. I distracted the dogs and advanced the car a few feet. They then countered by repositioning themselves and blocking my way again. After about 20 turns, I gave up and met the victors exchanging pets for sniffs and licks. They escorted me to my destination, an amazing, converted barn that is part home and part workshop. With a combination of the rustic and the modern, it is an environment perfectly adapted to its owner, whose passions for invention and the countryside compete for first place.

Scott Olson in many ways grew up as a typical Minnesotan, embracing the cold and outdoors with vigor. Scott played ice hockey from an early age, hunted, and even started his own taxidermy business in high school. His dad was an elementary school teacher and carpenter, which might have played a role in shaping Scott's innate skills for coming up with new ideas and thinking through the engineering and physics of everyday items. Yet, for the first part of Scott's story, it was his talent on the ice that took prominence. Shortly after high school, Scott became one of a few Americans to play in the Canadian junior ice hockey league, as goalie for the Brandon Wheat Kings. Unlike the other members of the team, Scott was in his element living in Manitoba, "I was able to drive a half hour to the best hunting spots. I was the only member of the team into bird hunting."

From time to time during our interview, Scott would interrupt the conversation to point out a flock of trumpeter swans landing on the lake directly behind his house. They arrive in groups of five or six to take advantage of the open water Scott created by submerging an aerator just off the water's edge. Or maybe it has to do with the abundant corn Scott provides for them to feed on during the winter months. With the help of some binoculars, Scott observes his winter oasis, taking great joy from seeing the largest of the waterfowl species, which were once endangered and almost extinct. There is little doubt in my mind that Scott is still the same man who relished living in rural Manitoba decades ago.

Scott would frequently travel back to Minnesota to visit family and friends. On one of those trips in 1978, he noticed that his brother had bought a pair of Super Street Skates and immediately rushed down to the local sporting goods store to get some. Between him and his younger brother, it is safe to assume that they represented nearly the entire local market for inline skating. Yet for Scott, it was a dream come true when he first got on the skates; he was so fanatical about the product, he decided to wear them to a party that night. His mind began racing about the potential for inline skating. At this moment during the interview, it is not exactly clear the train of thought that led Scott from being a product advocate to an entrepreneur and reseller of the skates. However, there he was the day after the party buying the last four pairs the store owned. Feeling lucky to rid himself of the product, the owner wanted nothing to do with inline skates and instead gave Scott a single business card from the California manufacturer. Scott pressed on and phoned the company, "I didn't know what I was doing. I decided that twelve pairs seemed like a good order and then I referred to myself as 'Ole's Sporting Goods,' thinking that they would treat me more seriously if I was a store." With money lent from his father, Scott received his first shipment as a cash-on-delivery transaction.

This version of the skates only vaguely resembles what we normally consider to be an inline skate. First off, there was no boot; the skates needed to be attached to an existing ice skate boot minus the steel blade. Second, they came only in one size, such that the ideal balance point would differ depending on the user. Lastly, the bearings were nowhere as fluid as a modern inline skate or skateboard, requiring much more effort for the user to get momentum. Scott recognized that only one potential audience could look past these deficits and see the potential of this early version of the product, namely his hockey buddies. In an interview with *Newsweek*, Scott reflected, "I realized that this thing could be huge. I definitely knew all the hockey players would buy them. And as I made them smoother and faster, I realized it had mass appeal."[5] Not only did the hockey players have tons of old skates hanging around that could be easily converted to wheels but they all were on the outlook for ways to keep training during the off-season, using the same skating stride as done on ice. Scott had found his customers and soon developed a successful side gig to playing professional hockey.

When Scott was 21, the side gig became his main hustle. He was selling the skates out of his parent's basement and offered a five-day money back guarantee to any new buyer, never questioning that his product would be the next big thing. He started to make modifications to the design, experimenting first with making the skate adjustable, so as to better fit different sized boots. When he presented the design to the Super Street Skate company, they passed on the idea, which led Scott to question whether the company even owned the design rights to their product. Working with a friend-of-a-friend, who was a patent attorney for a major manufacturer, Scott discovered that his adjustable boot design fell more closely under a different patent held by one of the largest roller skating companies of the time, the Chicago Roller Skate Company. They had attempted to sell a booted version of inline skates and even had a glossy advertisement on the back of the Sears Roebuck Christmas catalog, but the product was overshadowed by the four-wheeled version that is now synonymous with Disco, polyester, and all things from the 1970s. Being persistent as always, Scott hitchhiked his way down to Chicago, skated to headquarters through a very unsafe section of town, and convinced the owner to sell the patent to Scott for a marginal fee, as Scott demonstrated that he "really believed in it." The 1966 patent had only a few more years remaining on it, so he had to move fast to establish his business. With that move, the Rollerblade was born.

It is strange to think, but inline skating has a longer and richer history than the roller skate.[6] It was a more natural extension to its ice-loving brother,

---

[5] Blading on Thin Ice, Newsweek, December 11, 1994.

[6] Roller Skating Museum. The History of Inline Skating. https://www.rollerskatingmuseum.org (accessed February 10, 2022).

with wheels arranged in a straight line to replicate the blade. Although early examples date to the 1760s, the first patent for an inline skate was filed in 1819 for a three-wheeled version by M. Petitbled, which did little to settle the debate on design. Inventors continued to tinker with designs sporting two to six wheels, each attempting to solve for the skate's notoriety for being difficult to turn, maneuver, and stop. Early versions used steel or wooden wheels, which kept the skates from holding the edge and with that flaw, prevented them from developing any mass market appeal. This all changed in 1863, when the first quad skate was patented by James Plimpton. With wheels arranged in rows of two, the skate provided the grip, balance, and maneuverability that was lacking with its processor. Manufacturers quickly shifted to the new design, putting the inline skate on the back burner and establishing the quad skate as the future favorite of disco lovers everywhere. As proven by a prominent display of 107 framed patents in Scott's barn, innovation on the inline skate didn't stop completely. His collection starts with a very basic, angular four-wheel version from 1860 and progresses all the way to the highly specific versions executed during Scott's watch during the 1980s and 1990s.

Scott doesn't give up on a concept easily. Being an avid user of his product, known for commuting over 15 miles to downtown on his blades every day, as well as wearing them through airports when such things were allowed, Scott pushed to make his own experience better. With an inherent understanding of physics, Scott knew that with a range of modifications, the inline skate could overpower the quad skate in speed and stability. His timing was perfect; as the rest of the skating industry was reaping the cash cow of quad skates, Scott pushed relentlessly for innovation on the Rollerblade, introducing dual bearings (alleviating much of the friction to attain higher speeds), higher grade urethane wheels (to gain an edge that was not possible with the original hard plastic), and more fitted boots, through partnerships with specialty manufacturers. With every successful modification, Scott was transforming a niche product loved by hockey players into a form of recreation equipment that first attracted Nordic and Alpine skiers for off-season training, before becoming accessible to everyone. Ex-runners liked the low-impact workout, while adrenaline junkies liked the speed.

Even as the product moved away from hockey, the hockey player never really left Scott. Early in our conversation, Scott mentioned what it was like to be a goalie. I was surprised to hear Scott's perspective, "I always thought of being a goalie as an individual sport," he said. "As a goalie, you spend a lot of time alone on the ice." The confidence that Scott built to stand on his own played out beautifully in his career both on and off the ice. Even when no one else seemed vaguely interested in his product, Scott persisted without losing faith or passion for inline skating. A belief that his product just had to work moved him forward, even when it appeared that all the momentum was going in the opposite direction, similar to the persistence seen with Michael in Chapter 2 when establishing CareerTrackers. Beyond being the loneliest position on the ice, being a goalie is also the highest pressured. Goalies are the last defense between the opposing team and a game win. Scott talked about the resiliency needed by goalies to "overcome the bad times" and pick themselves up after a major loss, to "learn how to live with the ups and downs of the game." As will be discussed shortly, Scott's unfaltering belief in himself and his products came under fire multiple times over the decades, but somehow Scott was able to pick himself up and play another day. His passion for skating never wavered, as Scott organized long-distance events (like courses from Duluth to Grand Forks), a roller-hockey league, and even roller-tennis tournaments.

In 1986, Rollerblade began to market skates explicitly as fitness equipment, pushing interest for inline skating to new levels. Soon after, aggressive inline skates were introduced, paving the way for dedicated sporting events, first with the USA Roller Skating inline speed skating event in 1992, followed by the X-Games aggressive inline competition in 1995 and then inline hockey at the Pan American Games in 1999. Inline skating had become a billion-dollar industry, reaching close to 30 million Americans at its height. It was estimated that nearly two-thirds of all American 11-year-olds owned a pair of inline skates in 1997. Yet all these developments occurred after Scott was forced out of the business that he created. Despite a profitable year in 1984, Scott's accountant embezzled a significant sum from the company and left the books illegible. To avoid bankruptcy, Scott sought out and found an investor who sold him on a plan to raise needed funds in exchange for half of the company. Seven months later the money failed to materialize; Scott was made a final offer of cash for 95% of the company and full voting rights. Scott signed the deal, recalling during his interview with *Newsweek*, "I walked out of there in tears. The guy stole my company and there was nothing I could do."[7] After six years of legal proceedings, Scott eventually secured a 1% royalty on sales with a term that ran out in 1997.

Being the goalie that he is, Scott picked himself up and decided to play again. At first, he focused on innovating new types of inline skates under the names of SwitchIt and Nuskate. Among his innovations was an interchangeable mounting plate on the bottom that allowed for wheels during the summer and a metal blade during the winter, as well as a solid heel for walking in between the two. After seeing the pair that Scott showed me, I have been

---

[7] Blading on Thin Ice, Newsweek, December 11, 1994.

trawling the internet attempting to find a vintage pair in my size. Scott didn't stop there and branched out into a range of other recreational products, including the RowBike and Kong Pong. In the feature by *Newsweek* from 1994,[8] a bicycle messenger is said to have cruised up to Scott, who was rowing down Manhattan's Avenue of the Americas and shouted, "That's a kind of bike I ain't never seen before," to which Scott replied, "The first time I laced on a pair of Rollerblades and skated around Minneapolis, I got the same kind of response." In Scott's workshop, I saw a wide range of equipment being invented and perfected, all taking advantage of Scott's natural inclination toward sport and mobility. His website sums up his passion, "His fitness products are designed to create a new, healthy way of life that focuses on full-body fitness . . . they provide the exhilarating sensations of speed and motion." Although his departure from the Rollerblade was premature, Scott may have avoided the inevitable, as the inline industry now represents more of a generational fad than an enduring sport. In comparison to the heights of an estimated 30 million users in the United States, the number for inline skaters dropped to just 5 million in 2017, retreating into a niche sport for only its most ardent supporters.[9] The death knell for inline skating occurred in 2005, when the X Games pulled its inline skating events.

Today, Scott is working on the Skyride, which involves a self-propelled car, either rowed or pedaled, suspended from a track well above the ground. It was easy to spot the test tracks peeking through the barren trees when I pulled into his farm. When he presented his idea on Shark Tank, the sharks didn't bite, yet that didn't faze Scott one bit; he achieved some free marketing for his product. Scott has already found a foothold, selling the Skyride as the newest attraction featured on Carnival Cruises. Described as a "flying bike" by the *Daily Beast*,[10] the Skyride was named the Best Cruise Ship Feature by CruiseHive in 2017, when it was introduced aboard the Carnival Vista. Carnival describes the experience for passengers, "Skyride is a bit like riding a bike—you'll never forget it. But Skyride is also completely unlike riding a bike, because when was the last time you biked around a ship, high above the deck and even higher above the sparkling blue sea?"[11] Scott is still aiming higher, contemplating how the Skyride can become part of "making fitness exciting," through broader applications in fitness clubs, hotels, and resorts. It is not hard to contemplate

[8] Blading on Thin Ice, Newsweek, December 11, 1994.
[9] The Rise and Fall of Rollerblading by Sport History Weekly, August 21, 2022.
[10] Scott Olson Interview: Skyride, Rollerblade, Shark Tank, More by Lauren Ashburn, Daily Beast, July 13, 2017.
[11] Carnival. Website. https://www.carnival.com/onboard/skyride (accessed May 22, 2023).

how a Skyride would make a fantastic attraction for the local zoo, state fair, or really anywhere with a spectacle to take in.

Standing back from the last four decades of innovation, the root drivers for his pursuits are truly an unique combination of interests and traits that makes Scott who he is. First off, Scott is a fanatic for fitness and recreation. From skating 14 miles to work daily to rowing down the street on a RowBike or building an all-body weightlifting machine that resembles a medieval torture device with spiked standard weight plates, Scott's body is constantly in motion. At one point during our interview, Scott stood up and attached himself onto a full-length stretching board and continued the conversation, thinking nothing of the fact that his body was no longer vertical. Looking out from stretching board, Scott had a fine view of the trumpeter swans coming in for landing, as a reminder that he is also fanatic about the outdoors, with many of his inventions geared at getting people outside and to look at nature. This combination of movement and the outdoors comes together perfectly in Scott's vision for the Skyride and is shared with Ben, the ultramarathoner we met in Chapter 3.

To these areas of interest, Scott has some personal traits that drive a compulsion toward innovation. He has a natural propensity for physics and a need to tinker with an invention until it moves the way that it should. Like Ben running across the Rockies, Scott is in it for the long haul, digging deep in his own cognitive marathon to make a more perfect product. From Rollerblade wheels that replicated moving on ice to the RowBike that puts the whole body in motion, Scott is prepared to spend decades working through tough mental problems and getting the design right. In his own words, Scott confessed that he is "never done with the product and there is always a way to make it better. As a user of my own products, I know what can be done better." To this, Scott continues to have a mindset of a competitive athlete, stressing that he needs to "make it better before someone else makes it better." He wanted to be the first to make the SwitchBlade, knowing that it would be a natural extension to what the Rollerblade had become.

Beyond being competitive, goalies have a level of resilience not demonstrated by other positions on the rink. Although not necessarily to blame for a defeat, there is a degree of acknowledgment that if they played better, the match could have gone the other way. Scott has plenty of training not to dwell on defeat and failure. True to both life and hockey, Scott knows that "you win some and lose some." When Scott lost control of Rollerblade, he took a step back to reground himself. Yes, he might have lost his business, but he also had so much more than just the company. His real passion was inventing something that the world has not seen before, and to get there, Scott knew that failure was part of the process. He regularly "expects an idea not to work. I want to get to it (the failure) sooner and learn." In practice, he frequently builds his prototypes out of wood, before moving to metal. The prototypes in his workshop look like a mishmash of spare parts, but Scott knows that these are just stand-ins until the right shape and mechanism falls into place. "Failure is part of the equation . . . part of the big picture," that only becomes clear through experimentation.

Not everyone shares the same attitude that Scott or other entrepreneurs, like one chocolatier we will meet in Chapter 8, have toward risk and failure. How an individual looks at failure, whether something to be either accepted or feared, has far-reaching consequences, from influencing whether to ask out a romantic partner to building up the courage to start a new career. How an individual looks at fear sits alongside the trait of success orientation as a key psychological motivator. Those high in fear of failure show increased vulnerability to anxiety, underachievement, and in some cases learned helplessness, a condition where an individual self-destructs by giving in to failure completely. At a more nuanced level, fear of failure can act as both a friend and foe to performance.[12] On one hand, fear of failure can spur activity, as an individual attempts to avoid failure by working extra hard. When combined with a high need for achievement, a doubling down of intensity is witnessed and the individual can be characterized as an "overstriver." On the flip side, fear of failure can also be dealt with through an avoidance of the activity. When combined with a low need for achievement, such a person is known as a "self-protector," typically leading to underwhelming performance.

Although performance might turn out well for the overstriver, their journey is not without struggle. In comparison to someone who is low on fear of failure, the overstriver will likely experience higher anxiety, less regulated self-esteem, and perceptions that they are not fully in control of their destiny. If they fail despite their best efforts, the failure may provide proof of incompetence and cause the person to switch their behavior to resemble a self-protector. They might put in place obstacles to performing well, make excuses for why the world is unfair, and set unrealistically low expectations to be measured against.[13] With time, such behaviors can build up until the individual loses interest and withdraws completely from the activity. At the core of this fear of failure is shame, established early in life through an

---

[12] Martin, A., and Marsh, H. (2003). Fear of failure: Friend or foe? Australian Psychologist, 38, 31–38.
[13] Conroy, D., Kaye, M., and Fifer, A. (2007). Cognitive links between fear of failure and perfectionism. Journal of Rational-Emotive and Cognitive-Behavior Therapy, 25, 237–253.

individual's relationship to their parents.[14] If failure was overtly punished by a parent and successes went unrecognized, that child can be oversensitized toward failure, feel that success is beyond their ability, and believe that they will not be accepted if things go wrong. With failure, a strong sense of shame emerges. A child feels publicly exposed as incapable and unworthy of love or recognition.

Those children turn into adults who might have a warped perception of risk. Unlike Scott, who accepts failure as part of the learning process, these adults likely turn away from becoming an entrepreneur, preferring to put an idea on the shelf rather than take on a risky business venture. When studied, fear of failure has been shown to interfere with the whole entrepreneurial process, from fine-tuning an idea to financing and even choosing entrepreneurship as a respectable career. Compounding the potential shame of an idea gone wrong is the very real financial implications of a failed business. When Gabriella Cacciotti and her team of researchers interviewed a group of entrepreneurs, fear of failure was quickly evident.[15] One interviewee stated, "Now, it's totally my problem, it's all my problem. If I don't succeed it's completely my fault." Another went further, referencing the shame they could feel, "Well nobody likes to publicly fail . . . family and friends knowing that we took a shot at it and it didn't work out, that's kind of embarrassing . . . having them say, well how's it going, and you say, uh actually we closed that business, that kind of sucked." Several of the entrepreneurs were in the overstriver mode, using their fear of failure to drive activity, "Because it made me work harder. That is what drives me—that fear of failure. Anything I do, I have that thing of I will not fail . . . Fear drives you on."

The compounding effect of financial hardship with the personal shame felt with a failed business, weighs heavy on entrepreneurs, especially those who are early in their journey. In the words of one entrepreneur, "I think that worry and fear play a part in business. . . . If the business hadn't gone up from day one, it would have failed. I can tell you that I was scared to death, because I didn't know where I would go or what I would do if the business failed . . . The fear of failure is a part of what motivates me, and any other small businessperson who's honest about it." For those entrepreneurs who made the plunge, their anxiety can make them push harder. Fear of failure might be a friend of performance, but not a particularly good friend, as it comes with a significant emotional cost. Yet, there are entrepreneurs like Scott who appear impervious

---

[14] McGregor, H., and Elliot, A. (2005). The shame of failure: Examining the link between fear of failure and shame. Personality and Social Psychology Bulletin, 31, 218–231.

[15] Cacciotti, G., et al. (2016). A reconceptualization of fear of failure in entrepreneurship. Journal of Business Venturing, 31, 302–325.

to the fear of failure; he appears to be high on a need for achievement, but lacks the baggage associated with a fear of failure. Scott embraces learning and feedback, while relishing in the freedom to try out new, and sometimes quite outlandish, ideas. I saw very little evidence that Scott is bothered by what others think, or fazed by the strange looks that he might have received roller-blading through the airport or rowing down the streets of Manhattan.

It is this last characteristic that might be the secret sauce for what makes Scott a fanatic of innovation and creativity. Without concern for the shame associated with failure, Scott is able to push the boundaries of what people will do with their bodies, from peddling around midair on the Skyride to rowing down the pavement on the RowBike. Scott is interested more in showing others what his inventions can do than concerned with the potential scorn he could receive. Moreover, he is not overly concerned with the expectations that others might have of him. Although supportive of his entrepreneurial ideas and skating ability, Scott's parents did not have unachievable expectations for him to live up to. With a great deal of freedom to pursue his passions, Scott's success (or not) was his alone, without the anxiety of losing face or the love of others.

Scott's normal behavior of taking an idea and refining it into something revolutionary, can be categorized as the good version of perfectionism that psychologists have been researching for decades. The good type, also known as normal perfection, is characterized by individuals taking pleasure in refining their ideas and products, often reaching a state of flow, where people can lose themselves in their craft for hours on end, oblivious to the world around them.[16] In contrast, the bad type, also known as neurotic perfectionism, is not enjoyable, but laden with expectations to perform better, which has been found related to a range other psychological pathologies from depression to eating disorders. The difference between the two types was further defined in the 1990s, when a set of independent research teams identified the facets and types of perfectionists. Personal standards, level of organization, concern over making mistakes, doubts about taking action, parental expectations for success, and the extent of parental criticism were identified as key contributors for whether a person would become a perfectionist.[17] Across these attributes, a perfectionist is defined by a relentless pursuit for performance driven by either their own inherent needs or in response to satisfying social expectations.

---

[16] Stoeber, J., and Otto, K. (2006). Positive conceptions of perfectionism: Approaches, evidence, challenges. Personality and Social Psychology Review, 10, 295–319.
[17] Martinelli, M., et al. (2014). Perfectionism dimensions as predictors of symptom dimensions of obsessive-compulsive disorder. Bulletin of the Menninger Clinic, 78, 140–159.

A third type of perfectionism goes outside the mind of the individual, defined by whether the perfectionist holds similar expectations of others.

This difference between the source of the expectations, either with the individual or others, makes all the difference in whether perfection can be characterized as a good or bad thing for the individual. If driven by the individual, where high personal standards and self-organization are driving behavior, the psychological research shows a relationship to universally positive outcomes like endurance, satisfaction with life, active coping styles, and achievement. When left unchecked, the bad type of perfectionism, characterized by expectations being set by others and concern over making mistakes, has been related to low self-esteem, anxiety, depression, procrastination, defensiveness, and interpersonal problems.[18] Perfectionism has been linked to the development and maintenance of a range of serious psychological disorders (notably OCD), as well as self-harm, insomnia, and the imposter syndrome, where self-doubt overcomes a person's confidence and makes them feel like a fraud. The context matters too. Some activities like figure skating and music require a higher level of perfectionism for the performer to achieve mastery, and the feedback from coaches or judges can be unrelenting. To cope, athletes, musicians, and other performers often create a wall between the activity and other facets of their life to contain the pressure and maintain their psychological well-being.

What might be somewhat surprising is just how early in life a path toward the bad type of perfectionism gets paved, with two of the six characteristics associated with the individual's relationships with their parents. All parents strive to raise self-sufficient, well-adjusted children who strive to be the best versions of themselves. Yet there is subtlety on the yardstick used to measure what success looks like. Developmental psychologists stress that striving for excellence is different from striving for perfection and emphasizing the former sets children up for a happier, healthier life. According to clinical professor Sylvia Rimm, "When perfectionism becomes pervasive and compulsive, it goes beyond excellence. It leaves no room for error. It provides little satisfaction and much self-criticism because the results never feel good enough to the doer."[19] In one case study, Rimm describes a gifted preschooler named Charles who was reading at the 4th-grade level and doing mathematics at the 2nd grade level. Often praised for his brilliance, and the first child in the extended family, Charles focused extensively on everything but

[18] Lloyd, S., et al. (2015). Can psychological interventions reduce perfectionism? A systematic review and meta-analysis. Behavioural and Cognitive Psychotherapy, 43, 705–731.

[19] Rimm, S. (2007). What's wrong with perfect? Clinical perspectives on perfectionism and underachievement. Gifted Education International, 23, 246–253.

fine-motor skills, which he avoided completely. When asked to draw a picture, write, or cut paper, Charles would break down in tears and tantrums. He could not perform at the level of expectation set by his family and the anxiety that this was creating pushed him into demonstrating maladaptive behavior. Yes, he was good at reading and mathematics, but he was also falling behind in other key areas of childhood development. To put Charles back on a healthy track, his parents changed how they praised their son, drawing emphasis to his behaviors (e.g., I like how you solved that problem) rather than how universally smart he was. They also invested time in building his fine motor skills, by encouraging Charles to work through challenges independently and rewarding his patience and persistence. These slight modifications improved the situation rapidly and potentially avoided long-term developmental issues for Charles.

With the bad type of perfectionism, children and adults do not take as many risks or will procrastinate when forced to do so, fearful that their actions will keep them from being the best. Physically, the fear can manifest in stomachaches and headaches. Emotionally, perfectionists might enter into a state of depression or become defiant to hide their feelings. More extreme episodes can lead to interference with living a normal life and performance issues at work. This is all bad news for creativity, where taking risk is par for the course. People who shoot for greatness instead of perfection have been found experimentally to produce more creative solutions and to act with increased openness to experience. For skeptics of whether creativity could ever be scientifically measured, the research team led by Jean-Christophe Goulet-Pelletier attempted to take subjectivity out of the equation by looking specifically at each participant's level of divergent thinking.[20] For example, participants were given the task of thinking about how many uses you can have for a newspaper. Underlying the relationship between aspiring for greatness and higher creativity appears to be the flexibility allowed within a person's thinking; striving for excellence creates more room for creativity than pursuing perfection. A unique secondary finding was that perfectionists appear unaware that their creativity may not be as high as those striving for excellence, even though their expectations were acting as an impediment.

From my conversations with Scott, I am confident that he exemplifies the positive type of perfectionism. It was evident that his pursuit of a better product comes from within and that he was not overly concerned with the

---

[20] Goulet-Pelletier, J., Gaudreau, P., and Cousineau, D. (2021). Is perfectionism a killer of creative thinking? A test of the model of excellencism and perfectionism. British Journal of Psychology, 113, 176–207.

expectations held by others. Moreover, his acceptance of failure as part of the creative process, with the need to fail early to learn, demonstrates that his concern for making mistakes and doubts about taking action are both in check. Reacting to why it took over 2,000 attempts to get the lightbulb right, Thomas Edison was famously reported to have said, "I never failed once. It just happened to be a 2000-step process." No doubt that Scott would agree with this assessment; failure is part of the creative process and compels him to do better. It is not to be feared.

What is hidden from view is a change in how Scott organizes his creative pursuits. Over the course of his various business ventures, Scott has come to appreciate that he doesn't need to go it alone. He has learned how to partner with designers and craftsmen to both articulate the ideas running through his mind and build workable prototypes. Scott no longer needs to be the focal point for all his products, most recently admitting that he "doesn't need to be the Skyride guy," but rather by finding the right types of partners, his ideas can gain traction that he might not be able to accomplish on his own. He encourages kids and teenagers to send him some "unbelievable drawings," to see where their innovation can take them. One such unbelievable drawing from 25 years ago was the inspiration for the Skyride. Through such conversation, Scott shares his fanaticism, and it is addicting. His love for fitness, recreation, and the outdoors permeates who he is, but he is also defined by resilience. Being the eternal goalie, Scott does not fear failure and defeat, but uses it as a tool to go further.

Getting beyond fear can be viewed as unachievable by a person consumed by the bad type of perfectionism and can lead to a truly debilitating state of being. Instead of enjoying the pursuit of excellence, like Scott tinkering around with the blade to make it fit each skater's unique foot, a person suffering from OCD is consumed by the fear of doing things wrong. As explained by Dr. Renae Reinardy, the point at which the drive to get something perfect becomes unbearable differs for each individual, "OCD is driven by fear and is characterized by feelings of impending doom." Once established, these feelings become crippling and suck away the joy of everyday living.

I was excited to speak with Renae to challenge my own assumptions about the disorder. Like others, I find myself falling back upon popular depictions of OCD like Jack Nicholson playing Melvin Udall in As Good as it Gets.[21] Most memorable for me is the endless shower Melvin took to get himself perfectly clean before going to dinner. As his date waited outside the door, a huge cloud bellowed out of the bathroom door from what must have been an epic

---

[21] Andrus, M. (1997). As Good as It Gets. TriStar Pictures.

shower. Harder to depict for even a great actor like Jack Nicholson is the raw emotion and internal dialogue that drove Melvin to become compulsively clean. For Renae, she encounters these issues every day. She is a Licensed Psychologist who specializes in OCD, Phobias, Hoarding Disorder, Body-Focused Repetitive Behaviors, Tic Disorders, and related conditions. She is also the Program Developer of Courage Critters, an innovative approach to easing children's anxiety with a combination of online tools and a stuffed animal companion. Renae's techniques have been featured on Dateline NBC and she was a regular expert for A&E's show Hoarders. During my interview with Renae, it was clear how skilled and experienced she is working with anxiety disorders, but even more impressive is the passion and interest that she showed toward helping her patients move beyond their biggest fears. Renae is genuinely warm, approachable, and non-judgmental, qualities that are in top demand for clinicians working to tackle fears that patients find both embarrassing and near impossible to confront.

Renae helped me get beyond the popular conceptions of OCD. She explained that the intensity of emotions for people experiencing OCD is like a volume knob turned way too high for those experiencing psychopathological levels of anxiety. For example, a person experiencing symptoms of OCD would not feel excitement for the Christmas holiday, but feel a deep need for perfection, "thinking to themselves that if they don't get an ornament on the tree just right, their spouse might die or they themselves will not survive the feeling of dread." Renae stresses just how terrifying and real these feelings are, even if they are not at all rational. Emotion is in "the driving seat for obsessions" that take over normal thoughts and the enjoyment of everyday life. Obsessive thoughts lead to feelings about a lack of control, which in turn can result in compulsions or avoidance of normal everyday activity.

Key to the relationship between OCD and perfectionism are doubts about actions either taken or ignored. People who hold the bad type of perfectionist tendencies may begin exhibiting the hallmarks of OCD that include obsessing about decisions or events and performing compulsions like washing, checking, or ordering to relieve the built-up anxiety.[22] These compulsions do not need to be physical, but can occur in the head of the sufferer, such as repeating words, making mental lists, or counting. OCD is thus often referred to as a disorder of doubt, where individuals suffering from the condition are unable to tolerate uncertainty. They can often experience "not just right experiences," an uncomfortable sensation that the situation is left undone and

---

[22] Martinelli, M., et al. (2014). Perfectionism dimensions as predictors of symptom dimensions of obsessive-compulsive disorder. Bulletin of the Menninger Clinic, 78, 140–159.

not completely under control.[23] For example, sufferers report more often than the general population that they feel like they did not set their alarm quite right or that they might not have fully turned off the faucet in the bathroom. The relief provided by clicking the alarm button multiple times or checking the tightness of faucet is only temporary, as the repetitive thoughts and behavioral rituals become overwhelming and can overshadow the original fear that got the whole juggernaut going. According to the National Institutes of Health, about 2% of the general population is said to suffer from OCD, which occurs more often than mental illnesses like schizophrenia, bipolar disorder, and panic disorders.[24] The disorder usually manifests itself in adolescence or early adulthood and is chronic, sprouting up over years or decades with periods of quiet mixed in.

The tragic part about OCD is just how all-consuming it is, often sucking the joy out of what the individual desires or enjoys the most. For example, Renae spoke about an accomplished writer who had developed OCD. With associations that had nothing to do with the writing itself, such as arranging the desk a certain way, the writer began dreading the ritual so much that they gave up writing altogether. Renae refers to OCD as a "bully" that picks a fight with whatever you value most in life. From doctors who begin fearing inadvertently harming their patients to artists fearing that they will not find inspiration, every type of profession is a potential target. So too are social roles, like becoming a new parent. Renae spoke about a new mother who feared mortally harming her newborn. These were not the typical fears of parenthood, such as laying a baby on its back to avoid SIDS or installing a car seat the right way, but rather sounding more like a plot line from the next series of *Dexter*. The mother had no history of causing physical harm, nor had any motivation to do so, but the specific and persistent fear of harming her child was there nonetheless. Fully aware of just how irrational and graphic her fear was, the mother's joy of having a new child was sucked out of her. Within the mind of the patient, graphic dark images "cycle out of control in an instant" and the more the individual attempts to push them away, the worse they can become. Alone, the mother was powerless to effectively confront her bully.

This combination of irrational and disturbing thoughts with feelings of helplessness causes many individuals suffering with OCD to conceal their condition rather than seek help. The stigma of others knowing about their dark

[23] Coles, M., et al. (2002). "Not just right experiences": Perfectionism, obsessive-compulsive features and general psychopathology. Behaviour Research and Therapy, 41, 681–700.

[24] Heyman, I., Mataix-Cols, D., and Fineberg, N. (2006). Obsessive-compulsive disorder. BMJ, 333, 424–429.

thoughts can be nearly as bad as the fear that is at the root of OCD. Patients can be "terrified by people knowing about it," confirms Renae, with many individuals living with persistent obsessions for decades before seeking treatment. OCD can start in childhood, with the perceived expectations of parents or peers being in the driver's seat. Fears of not being perfect is common for the children Renae works with, where she helps them embrace what happens when they allow themselves to be sloppy. For example, she might ask a child to write a letter and put it in an unsealed envelope. With the letter left open, she exposes the child to the lack of consequences for leaving a task incomplete. Renae spoke about the increased pressures being placed on kids and teens by modern technology. The lives of others "can seem so easy with modern followership," yet being concealed behind the small TikTok snapshot is someone else's normal reality, filled with its own share of disappointment. The expectations set-up by social networking can easily set the foundations for fear of acceptance and imposture syndrome, where toxic thoughts of never being good enough take over.

In Renae's 20-plus years of experience working in the field, she has witnessed a range of intrusive thoughts, running the gambit of violent, sexual, or existential themes. Renae jokes that if anyone came into her office without knowing the context behind her work, they would have a hard time understanding what they were looking at. From baby dolls to swords and spiders, Renae has amassed a variety of props that she uses as part of exposure therapy. She did not initially plan on being an expert in OCD or even a psychologist. Renae started her studies in civil engineering, but found solving human problems more interesting than physical structures. After landing an opportune internship in graduate school, Renae carved out a specialty in OCD, phobias, hoarding, and body-focused repetitive disorders that she finds both immensely rewarding and well suited to the logical problem-solving that is shared in common with engineering.

The tricky thing about treating OCD is that if done too quickly or with the wrong tools, the cognitive pathways for obsessions can be reinforced and compulsions can turn into habit. Although treatment of OCD can include medication that can inhibit obsessions and compulsions, behavioral therapy holds the most promise for long-lasting effects. Such treatment generally focuses on unraveling a person's irrational thoughts, followed by gradually exposing sufferers to the nub of their fears. When seeing new patients, Renae starts her treatments by talking about OCD and educating them on what the condition is all about. From there, she explores the emotional elements that underly the patient's own situation, for example, what has driven the writer to abandon his craft or the new mother to avoid her child? Renae then builds a

list of symptoms and compulsions, such that she can build a behavioral hier-
archy and find ways to prevent the cascade of thoughts, feelings, and actions
that are exhibited with the patient. Renae stresses that with OCD, "it is all
about emotion and logic doesn't matter."

From there, Renae starts to employ exposure and response prevention
therapy, which is geared to short-circuit the pathway between the trigger and
the patient's reaction. Renae builds up the patient's exposure to triggers, asking
along the way how difficult they are on a rating scale, to the point where the patient can build up "emotional tolerance" to both the sensations and thoughts
elicited by the triggers. Hence, all the props that are littering Renae's office;
depending on the trigger, she might need everything from a sword to a sex
doll. During the course of treatment, OCD might initially prove elusive, going
in a different direction with new thoughts or compulsions that are driven by
the same underlying fear. In Renae's words, "it is one tree, but with multiple
branches." Knowing this, the treatment goal is not just to survive OCD, but to
extinguish it completely and ensure that it does not resurface. This aspiration
is warranted, as OCD has proven to be one of the most treatable psychological conditions. In Renae's words, "the only option for patients is to break the
rules that they have set for themselves," and put their own personal bully in
its place.

All of us have a bully or two that should be put in its place. For myself, I have
always been anxious about my voice. Despite the fact that I do a considerable
amount of public speaking, building confidence in this ability was years in
the making. As a child, I had a significant speech impediment, with adults
struggling to understand what I was saying and children poking fun at my
expense. Apparently, I developed a rather creative response, by telling adults
who struggled to understand me that I was speaking a foreign language. It
was a great way to deflect blame and maintain self-confidence, but did little
to address my slurred and fast speech. Over time and with practice, I was able
to speak more clearly and take the time to ensure understanding, but the em-
barrassment is deeply embedded to this day. When thinking about my biggest
fears to overcome, singing scores high on the list. It is the perfect storm of re-
earthing memories from childhood combined with a deficit of practice and a
lack of developed skill. In first grade, I got chastised for not singing during a
school performance and things have not gotten better since. Yet, I am fanatic
about music. I enjoy a wide breadth of musical genres and dabble in playing a
range of instruments, from mandolin to tenor saxophone. It seems to me that
I should enjoy singing, but the anxiety I feel toward my voice gets in the way. It
was time to put my bully in its place and get a flavor for what exposure therapy
is all about.

Building up some courage and putting an end to my procrastination, I called the local guitar shop and enrolled in some singing lessons, with the goal of confronting my bully and building some skills along the way, just in case that I find myself at a karaoke bar in some far-flung city. On the day of my lesson and to my own surprise, I found myself at relative ease as I entered the music studio. I'd had a relatively busy morning and didn't have the time to contemplate what the lesson would be like. I also had some positive history built up at that particular studio, as I took 3 years of lessons on mandolin with the same teacher, in the same room. The psychological safety I had for this particular encounter was solid, as there was no risk of feeling ridiculed in any way. There is little doubt that individuals going for real exposure therapy would not have the same advantages and would be entering into their experience cold, especially if they were meeting with their therapist for the first time.

We began the lesson gently, by learning about breathing and the role that the lower body plays in producing a solid and controlled breadth. Concentrating on that element was alone challenging, as I found myself fighting the urge to straighten up when inhaling, rather than drawing the air in by pushing my belly out. From there, we worked on vocalizing some sounds on the exhale. I threw out some "s" and "z" sounds, before we moved on to learning about some basic face shapes that are involved in singing, specifically the neutral, round, and smiley versions. Each of these play a role on the sound quality and especially how vowels are voiced. This is different from consonants, which apparently have either voiced or unvoiced versions in singing. Voiced consonants like B, D, or G require air and voice before encountering the accompanying vowel, whereas unvoiced consonants like T, F, or P are linked to stopping the flow of air and are inherently tied to their vowel. What I came to realize quickly is that there are a lot of component parts to singing, just like any other musical instrument and in many ways, this helped dispel any remaining reservations I had about being a full participant in a singing lesson. I was learning tools and methods, activating the cognitive side of my brain and with it, lessening the fears that I held about standing in front of another person doing the one thing I have avoided for three decades.

Then things got completely silly. We started doing vocal exercises to play around with sound and explore my singing range. We did lots of yawns, made sounds like an ambulance siren, and pretended we were cats. I have never truly experimented with my voice in the same way and therefore could not tell whether I was a baritone, tenor, or alto. Not knowing my natural range meant that I struggled to enter a song or occasionally stumbled to find the right register, causing me to pull back even more. Apparently, I am most comfortable in a baritone range, beginning at G2 and stretching up into tenor at around G4. Another thing I learned is that everyone has a chest voice and a head voice, the latter is used to hit a higher register and somehow related to those cat exercises we did. By the end of the lesson, I moved on to singing a few songs, applying the techniques that I learned for breathing and vocalizing. There was a lot to remember, especially when connecting the dots to sing the actual lyrics to the song, instead of making them up as I do when listening to music in the car. We ended the lesson by singing "Somewhere Over the Rainbow," a song specifically chosen so that I could sing with my daughter, who plays the song on Ukulele.

My minor foray into exposure therapy was enlightening on multiple counts. First, I realized that my bully is not as intimating as I initially thought and has roots in my own social confidence. The problem was never the singing itself, but rather the potential shame of standing in front of others and performing badly. I was still that kid back in elementary school being scolded by the teacher for not singing. By approaching it through tools and methods, I was able to change the script away from anxiety and fear to cognitive problem-solving. I was in control of what I was doing, and if I wanted to get better at singing, there were ways to improve. As the lesson progressed, so too did my confidence. I found comfort in finding my range and realized that the more that I breathed and committed to the vocalization, the better I was at it. If I closed down, pulled back from full breathing, and tightened my vocal cords, that is when things sounded terrible. Singing requires unhesitating commitment. Lastly, I realized that singing can be quite silly and is inherently theatrical. Getting in that mindset, especially with a teacher and peers who are game to look foolish and make ambulance sirens, is essential to batting down this particular bully.

Fear, shame, and risk taking all played a part in my decades-long relationship with singing. These same factors can help determine whether any individual will pursue a creative and innovative idea or put it on the shelf. The constraints I put in place around singing, dreading to expose my abilities and the potential shame for performing poorly in public, kept me away from even the smallest performance, whether singing Christmas carols or going out for karaoke, despite my love for music and ability to play a range of instruments. I might never love singing, but I am no longer afraid of it, and can only contemplate the relief that comes to Renae's patients after extinguishing a life-crippling anxiety. For those suffering from OCD, the bad type of perfectionism can create a perpetual state of torment; the normal joy of creation has been sucked away, replaced by talented people going through all the motions, but without the positive energy that makes art and invention possible. Their anxiety is in the driver's seat and actively works against spotting new stimuli and divergent thinking, which are core components of creativity.

By fearing failure and playing it safe, freedom and learning are compromised and over time, a vicious cycle takes over; the creativity that normally comes from flow and enjoyment has transitioned to a combination of fear and dread. Through her therapy, Renae gives us hope that even the most extreme cases of OCD can be treated by having self-compassion for mistakes, learning how to handle frustration, and building emotional tolerance for confronting fear. Moreover, nourishing creative thinking can be the antithesis of the bad type of perfectionism and can build the muscle to resist social pressure and embrace uncertainty. Writing down random ideas, indulging in creative and chaotic hobbies, or physically moving to new environments can all inspire novel ideas and divergent thinking. Through such techniques, the individual is not pushed to abandon their ambitions or to spend less time in the cognitive realm, but rather to transform into a healthier form of fanaticism.

For people like Scott, these things come naturally to him. As the eternal goalie, he knows how to face failure, pick himself up, and play again without long-term damage to his confidence or drive. He constantly changes his surroundings and doodles endlessly. Underlying these behaviors is an intrinsic drive toward achievement, low concern for the expectations set by others, and an understanding that striving for excellence is better than striving for perfection. There is a lot to respect in Scott's philosophy toward life. It has led him down a path with many twists and turns, with a destination that is never entirely known. Scott can live in that ambiguity, yet still pushes himself toward achievement. I never asked, but I am sure that Scott would show little hesitation in singing a song or two, even if he is not a natural born singer.

Maybe the depiction of the mad scientist is not that far off. A disheveled Doc Brown who is unconcerned about his appearance or local reputation is much closer to what the psychologists would describe as aligned to divergent thinking and creativity. They spend more time thinking about the next innovation or how best to push a concept forward, than how they might be perceived by others. They have chosen the cognitive above the social, driven by a fanaticism for the art of the possible. Whether or not we should fear the mad scientist is another issue altogether. As long as we are talking about personal fitness and recreational equipment, I think we are probably safe, although Scott's full-body workout machine does give me pause. In all honesty, it did look just a little bit evil.

PART 4
THE EMOTIVE

7

Cheap Thrills

Unlike the cognitive-heavy fanaticisms of collecting and innovating, there are times that thinking about nothing beyond the present moment is the perfect elixir for life's worries. If you were a teen living in New York City during the late 1980s and had a desire to live in the moment, the place to be was Action Park. A short drive from the city, located across the state line in Vernon Township, New Jersey, the park was a bastion for risk and, when pushed too far, bodily injury. Unlike other amusement parks of the day, Action Park relished its reputation for the extreme, banking on a philosophy that riders wanted to control their own destiny. Andy Mulvihill, the son of founder Gene Mulvihill, chronicles the rise and fall of Action Park in his book by the same name.[1] He describes his father's philosophy toward risk and thrill: "Unlike most theme parks, Action Park did not strap in patrons and let them passively experience the rides. A roller coaster, thrilling as it may be, asks nothing of its occupants, and each ride is the same as the last . . . He vowed that visitors to Action Park would be the authors of their own adventures, prompting its best-known slogan: 'Where you're the center of the action!'"

Originally looking for a way to capitalize on his ownership of a ski resort during the summer months, Gene built one of the first Alpine Slides in North America. With individual carts made of plastic that zoomed down fiberglass toboggan tracks, riders were in control of how fast they slid down the slope, using their best judgment to avoid flying off the track on sharp curves. Physical contact with the slide during a run would cause burns, blisters, or worse. I remember distinctly the first time I was on an Alpine Slide. I must have been around 10 years old when I rode the ski lift to the top of the mountain, with my father by my side, filled with anticipation as I stared down at the track below. I picked up my cart, sat down, and asked that I go in front of my dad and brother, as I thought I was ready for the thrill and didn't want to be slowed down in any way. In reality, I was terrified and crept down the hill at a snail's pace. The ride was way over my comfort level and ability. To this day, I still feel anxious driving mountain passes or attempting to downhill ski.

---

[1] Mulvihill, A. (2020). Action Park. New York: Penguin Books.

Fanatic. Joe Ungemah, Oxford University Press. © Oxford University Press 2024. DOI: 10.1093/9780197783894.003.0008

For Gene, this was the point. Each rider had control over their own destinies, whether they decided to blaze down the hill or crawl like I did. According to Andy, "As more riders piled on, the price of freedom began to reveal itself. The control granted by the Alpine Slide was accompanied by a measure of risk, much of it self-imposed. Attendants would tell guests to go slow and mind the brake until they got used to it. The guests would nod, completely oblivious to the safety instructions, then proceed to make every mistake they were warned to avoid." The thrill and risk of the slide was a raging success, and with it, the foundations for Action Park were firmly in place. Each year thereafter, Gene would add new attractions, from three-quarter-scale Formula One racers to a wave pool that simulated the ocean, bungee cord jumping, and early versions of indoor skydiving. Action Park was always on the front foot of the latest amusements, as long as they put the rider in control. Some of these innovations were a terrible idea from the start, such as the Bailey Ball, which held a passenger in the middle of a sphere covered with wheels as it rolled down a hill. On its maiden (and only) voyage, the ball managed to roll out of the park, cross a two-lane road, and land in a small lake. Thankfully, the rider came out dazed, but relatively unscathed, despite the harness failing mid-roll.

Of all the attractions described by Andy Mulvihill, the Cannonball Loop is the most emblematic of Action Park. Unlike any other water slide, the Loop attempted to create enough force to purposely propel a rider through a 360-degree loop. Like much in Action Park, its creation was a series of trial-and-error experiments, with an idea coming to fruition without the use of blueprints. The slogan of the ride, "Can you survive . . . the Cannonball Loop?" was fitting. Although Andy came through its first run safely, his description of the experience was far from glowing, "The descent through darkness, my body contorted by centrifugal force, was unpleasant in the extreme. Space and time ceased to have meaning. The enjoyment came not from the experience but from the bragging doled out thereafter. My father had created the first amusement ride to be endured, not enjoyed." The second rider was not as lucky. Having just applied suntan lotion, the rider flew through the loop, broke his nose, and landed 15 feet from where the ride was supposed to end. Undeterred, Gene fiddled with the design of the Loop, which eventually opened to the public with guidelines for the perfect weight and size of riders. Yet, the application of suntan lotion, slick bathing suits, disruptions in the vinyl coating, and countless other variables made the ride too risky to predict, causing injuries to pile up beyond even what Action Park was willing to accept.

The Loop closed for good, but Gene refused to tear the ride down. It was symbol for Action Park, where "Anything could happen to anyone at any time," and that was the thrill. In Andy's words, "Our problem may have been that people assumed the thrills were an illusion, just as they were at other parks. People step into a park and experience a detachment from reality, doing things they never would dare in real life." The rules of Action Park did not work this way, "There was a presumption of safety that was supported only by their belief that they couldn't get hurt at a theme park. It was a social contract that only they had agreed to." Time eventually caught up to Action Park. Laws changed, but so too did the expectations of visitors. When Action Park closed for good in 2015, an era had ended for unchecked thrill. "The thing that had distinguished us—the underlying risk—was gone. And with it, so were the people who craved that risk." I wonder if this segment of the public did not truly disappear, but rather found new outlets for thrill without limits, such as the rise of high-risk sports. Instead of going to Action Park, nature can provide the backdrop to attempt new and daring feats.

Yet thrill and safety are not mutually exclusive, as long as the ride suspends disbelief about physical harm. With the wide variety of novel contours and flips offered by contemporary roller coasters, a suspension of disbelief is achieved, even if their designs ensure the ride goes completely to plan and never approaches the variability of the Bailey Ball or Cannonball Loop. Approximately 300,000,000 riders embark on a roller coaster each year, with an injury rate of only 1.4 per every million rides, according to data from the International Association of Amusement Parks and Attractions.[2] In 2021, the association reported that 383 injuries occurred specifically on roller coasters, of which 38 were serious and required hospitalization for greater than 24 hours. Although the vast majority of injuries stemmed from the motion of the ride, 14% of injuries resulted from how riders got on or off the ride.

Research by Calvin Kuo went further and sought to understand whether riding roller coasters could cause brain damage, even if no injury were recorded at the park.[3] They compared the trauma caused by head acceleration during the ride and compared it to that experienced by either running or performing soccer headers. The researchers found that roller coasters led to brain displacements that were comparable to mild soccer headers, as well as brain strain similar to running. Although the team discovered that the amount of head motion and brain deformation was highly sensitive to individual differences between riders, riding coasters in general does not appear to present an immediate risk of brain injury, which is good news for any season pass

[2] International Association of Amusement Parks and Attractions North America Fixed-Site Amusement Ride Injury Survey, National Safety Council, August 2022.
[3] Kuo, C., et al. (2017). Pilot findings on brain displacements and deformations during roller coaster rides. Journal of Neurotrauma, 34, 3198–3205.

holder. This finding confirms an earlier finding by Douglas Smith and David Meaney that roller coasters produce head accelerations far below conventional levels for head injuries and, therefore, unlikely to mechanically deform and injure the brain.[4]

Despite these assurances, it is the perception of risk that makes roller coasters appealing for their riders. The fear created by being thrown down that first hill, as your body is hurtled toward the ground at high speeds, triggers an automatic response that transcends rational thought. Cognitively we know that the chances of train derailment are incredibly rare, but in that moment, the physical experience overpowers us and the fear is real. Paul Rozin speaks about the reversal of negative sensations, like being hurtled toward the earth at high speeds, recast as positive experiences with the concept of "benign masochism."[5] The concept is defined as "enjoying initially negative experiences that the body (brain) falsely interprets as threatening. This realization that the body has been fooled, and that there is no real danger, leads to pleasure derived from 'mind over body.'" After the realization that nothing bad is going to happen, the result of conquering our fears has the potential to transform our worldview. Previous situations that seemed at first to be insurmountable, like those addressed by Dr. Renae Reinardy in Chapter 6 when applying exposure and response prevention therapy, can become manageable and potentially a source of pride and identity after being successfully vanquished.

The reversals of benign masochism are not isolated to thrill rides, but have been shown to occur across a range of stimuli, from enjoying super-hot chili peppers to watching sad and tragic films. A similar psychological concept occurs with humor, where benign violations of social norms cause us to enjoy the cringe. Rozin and his team investigated 30 different hedonic stimuli, across the domains of sadness, burning sensations, disgust, fear, pain, alcohol, exhaustion, and bitter tastes, discovering that thrill rides (as a component of fear stimuli) were a strong example of benign masochism. Interestingly, the maximum level of enjoyment across stimuli is just below the level where the stimulation would no longer be tolerated. In other words, we enjoy eating hot peppers most when we can still stomach swallowing our food.

One other finding from Rozin's work was the positive relationship between benign masochism and individual differences in sensation-seeking. Individuals who scored highest on the need for sensation-seeking enjoyed negative experiences the most, especially in the category of fear. As a personality

[4] Smith, D., and Meaney, D. (2002). Roller coasters, G forces, and brain trauma: On the wrong track? Journal of Neurotrauma, 19, 1117–1120.

[5] Rozin, P., et al. (2013). Glad to be sad, and other examples of benign masochism. Judgment and Decision Making, 8, 439–447.

trait, sensation-seeking relates to an individual's motives for varied, intense, novel, complex, and intense sensory experiences. This hedonic drive surfaces across a range of situations and is measured across four domains: the degree to which individuals desire to take part in physically risky activities, search for new experiences, are interested in socially disinhibited activities, and are susceptible to boredom. In a study of the physiology behind sensation-seeking, Norbury and Husain discovered that individuals high in sensation-seeking have both higher endogenous dopamine levels and are hyperreactive to dopaminergic cues that reward is on its way.[6] High sensation-seekers appear to have higher tolerance for thrills and other extreme sensations and, therefore, seek them out for pleasure. Although such tendencies may lead to the substance and process addictions (like compulsive gambling), the authors speculate that this same physiology might prove helpful for surviving trauma and alleviating posttraumatic stress disorder.

Dopamine is not alone in its relationship with sensation-seeking, as other researchers have investigated its relationship to hormones and specifically, testosterone. In a study led by Stuart White, sensation-seeking individuals were more responsive to the release of testosterone during skydiving, which likely played a role in heightening the pleasure of the activity.[7] Testosterone was found to have a complementary relationship with cortisol, another hormone that is particularly busy when situations are stressful or threatening. Because testosterone responsiveness increases under challenging situations, the researchers suggest that skydiving has a rare mixture of being both stressful and challenging for its participants. Beyond the naturally occurring differences in testosterone levels, no additional gender differences were discovered.

Instead, a study by Agnieszka Boldak and Monicka Guskowska on skydivers discovered gender differences within the subscales that make up sensation-seeking as a personality trait.[8] Compared to men, women skydivers were particularly influenced by the need to seek new experiences, with 70% of the women participating in the study scoring highly on this dimension of sensation-seeking, with a particular emphasis on the mental and emotional challenges that it presents. Interestingly, women also differed from men in boredom susceptibility, which was likely a reason for a drop-off in

[6] Norbury, A., and Husain, M. (2015). Sensation-seeking: Dopaminergic modulation and risk for psychopathology. Behavioral Brain Research, 288, 79–93.

[7] White, S., et al. (2019). Putting the flight in "fight-or-flight": Testosterone reactivity to skydiving is modulated by autonomic activation. Biological Psychology, 143, 93–102.

[8] Boldak, A., and Guszkowska, M. (2016). Sensation seeking as one of the motivating factors for performing skydiving. Polish Journal of Sport Tourism, 23, 94–98.

participation in the sport after their initial experience, due to the routine and repetition required through the licensing process.

Although sensation-seeking plays a role in attracting individuals to fear-inducing situations, the specific type of outlet will differ depending on personal interest and access. Outlets for sensation-seeking can take the form of riskier occupations, like becoming a fire-fighter, or through leisure pursuits, like roller coaster riding or extreme sports. Without knowing the specific outlet, it can remain hidden from others until directly tapped. This was definitely the case for Barbara, whom I had known for just over a year when I brought up in conversation that I was writing this book on fanaticism and in particular, just starting a chapter on roller coaster enthusiasts. She immediately piped in with, "I'm one of those," and with that, provided anecdotal proof to one of the core tenets of this book. Not only are we all fanatic about something but also we can learn so much more about each other if we spend the time to ask what the other person is interested in. For Barbara, her fascination with roller coasters goes back to her childhood, riding alongside her Mom at Funtown, the last amusement park within Chicago's city limits and located at 95th and Stoney Island Avenue.[9] Chicago was once the amusement park capital of the world, with more parks within its city limits than anywhere else, but fell prey to the exodus of parks to the suburbs, where land was cheap and accommodating to giant structures. Although Funtown was the last park standing during Barbara's childhood, it was modest in size at 8 acres and containing 25 rides. It made up for this deficit in size with nostalgia, felling more like a traveling carnival than a modern-day amusement park. The star attraction was the Himalayan Express roller coaster, which twisted and jerked its riders in cars arranged like a toboggan. It was not the tallest and fastest coaster of its day, but with a low-priced ticket and lack of lines, riders could go on it again and again.

Barbara remembers vividly waiting to get on the ride, watching her mother who was normally quite restrained "let her hair down" and share in her fear and excitement. Holding her mother's hand as they rode, Barbara savored the experience. Not only did Barbara conquer her fears by riding the express but also she locked in a lifelong memory of seeing her mother out of her element and having fun. From that moment onward, Barbara was hooked on coasters. As a teenager, she sought out the thrills of the latest and greatest coasters, offering g-forces and hang times that resulted from technology advancements that allowed for corkscrews, loops, and different ways of riding, from laying down to standing upright. Barbara smiled as she recounted her memories of

[9] Back when Chicago was Fun Town by Darnell Little, Chicago Tribune, June 17, 1997.

holding her hands above her head as a teenager, as a way of saying to herself that "I'm tough." After college, Barbara found like-minded people at American Coaster Enthusiasts (ACE), the world's largest such club currently boasting 6,500 members from 16 countries.[10] The organization states, "Among its members are the most educated, dedicated, and passionate amusement park guests." Their mission is to "foster and promote the conversation, appreciation, knowledge, and enjoyment of the classic wooden roller coaster and the contemporary steel roller coaster, to create fellowship among its members, and to promote the continued operation of roller coasters."

Barbara's time as an ACE member brought her to parks throughout the country, from Hersheypark in Pennsylvania to Six Flags Magic Mountain in California and Busch Gardens in Florida. "Enthusiasts don't go to Disney," states Barbara, "for us, the place to go is Cedar Point. This is where the true thrill-seeker goes." Cedar Point is known as "America's Roller Coaster," offering 15 notable coasters, five of which tower over 200 feet in height. It is said that during a clear day, you can make out the Canadian side of Lake Ontario from the top of one these coasters. Cedar Point was named Best Amusement Park in the World by Amusement Today for 16 consecutive years, from 1997 to 2013.[11] During her prime, Barbara would go to Cedar Point twice a year, along with a visit to King's Island and one bonus park, which she took great pleasure in researching and planning. She remembers fondly planning a trip to ride the X2 Coaster across the country in California; after reading about it, she just had to go and experience it.

For the roller coaster enthusiast, the experience is much more than the ride. There is the planning of how to navigate the park and what to ride first. Then there is the study and anticipation of the ride, best done in conversation with others in line. "It is a global community of riders, all there to experience the same thrill. You talk to people not just in your group, but whoever happens to be standing there with you. The anticipation is especially high for new rides, where no one around you has had the experience yet," recaps Barbara. She is quick to spot the experienced riders, who can be found helping ride attendants getting people settled or securing their own harnesses. There is etiquette to follow, like not jumping line, and strange social norms to observe. When I was a kid, I remember the bubble gum tree at the old Elitch Gardens, where teenagers would stick their chewing gum to a tree (which rapidly became more gum than tree), before ascending the ramp to the coaster platform. Once off the ride, the experience carries on, as enthusiasts dissect the

[10] American Coaster Enthusiasts. Website. https://www.aceonline.org (accessed December 4, 2022).
[11] Cedar Fair Parks Take Top Honors in Annual Poll, Cedar Fair Press Release, September 8, 2013.

ride's design and share what they liked most about the experience, potentially buying an on-ride photo to memorialize the achievement. Such behavior is not so different from what bottle collectors like Dave from Chapter 5 perform, but instead of chronicling items, the coaster enthusiasts are capturing experiences.

When riding Millennium Force or Top Thrill Dragster, Barbara relished the feelings of adrenaline as she, "smashed against the back of her seat," dropped from great heights, or banked through endless twists and turns. Riding puts a smile on her face, instantly changing her state of mind and creating a positive response. When riding, she becomes carefree just like her mother from decades before riding the Himalayan Express at Funtown. She describes the on-ride experience as "feeling like a state of freedom, of letting go and not having anything to do. In that moment, in that experience, you put your cares aside. There are few times in life where you are fully present in the moment and there to just have fun."

After talking with Barbara, I was ready for my own slice of freedom and to pretend to be a roller coaster enthusiast for the day. As I drove north from O'Hare International Airport on Interstate 94, I scanned the horizon for any signs of Six Flags Great America. Tucked away behind an expanse of warehouses and extended stay hotels, it was easy to spot the towers of steel and wood that broke up the suburban monotony. An exit off the highway and a right turn later, I drove into the park's entrance just in time for the gates to open. A chill was still in the air, as it was an unseasonably cold October day, which seemed appropriate for the Halloween themed decorations. The beautiful part of coming late in the season is the lack of crowds, and I was able to quickly enter the park and travel to my ride of choice. I was on a mission, there to experience Goliath, a relatively new and still record-holding wooden coaster that was the focus of my goal to become a novice roller coaster enthusiast. According to the Six Flags' website, Goliath held three world records at its debut in 2014.[12] It was the world's fastest wooden coaster at 72 mph, held the tallest drop for a wooden coaster at 180 feet, and featured the steepest drop for a wooden coaster at a near-vertical 85 degrees. Thanks to its Topper Track design, where the engineers were able to twist beams of wood and cap the track with steel, Goliath features two inversions, which is still a relative novelty for wooden coasters.

I was excited to ride Goliath, as I am a huge fan of traditional wooden coasters and have ridden on a few notable versions, including The Beast at

---

[12] Six Flags. Website. https://www.sixflags.com/greatamerica/attractions/Goliath (accessed October 5, 2022).

Kings Island, which is the record holder for longest wooden coaster, and Mean Streak at Cedar Point, which was the previous record holder for height and speed when it was built in 1991. Coming off of Mean Streak, I remember just how rattled I felt, with parts of my head feeling like they were shaken loose and left on the ride, which was terribly appropriate given its name. Others had a similar experience, and it is rumored to be one of the primary reasons the ride closed permanently in 2016. Goliath clocks in at 7 mph faster than Mean Streak, which made me question how the new type of track would perform relative to the previous technology. Part of the appeal of a wooden coaster is the rickety feeling, heightening the sensations of feeling out of control and experiencing something inherently risky. Earlier in the summer, I rode one of the oldest wooden coasters still in operation, the Giant Dipper at Belmont Park, built in 1925.[13] Despite going a leisurely 48 mph and attaining a maximum height of only 75 feet, the coaster twisted, turned, and provided great airtime that, when mixed with the rickety feel of its classic design, made for a thrilling and fun ride. The Giant Dipper was perfectly paired with the total boardwalk experience, where the postride debrief involved eating a churro or two, adding to the nostalgia of what a classic coaster is all about. How would Goliath stack up? Would it strike the right balance between having a smooth ride and offering a thrill?

After passing through the gates, I wound myself through the park, first through Carousel Plaza, then through Orleans Place, DC Universe, Yukon Territory, and finally to the Country Fair area of the park. Themes too play a major part in the coaster experience, adding that extra bit of interest to the ride, especially when a twist brings you close to a water or fire feature, and provide some much-needed distraction when lines are long. At the back stood Goliath, which embodied the very notion of what a roller coaster should be, even though my walk brought me past Superman: Ultimate Flight, where riders lie on their stomachs as they soar through twists and curves, and the Joker, which rocks riders head over heels as they descend from the top of the structure downward. Steel coasters have pushed the physical limits of what riders can endure and provide additional layers of thrill beyond the classic design, but there is something about the classic wooden version that resonates with me personally. The smell of a wooden tunnel or the feeling of a vinyl cushion hark back to my first experiences on coasters as a preteen, a sensation that is hard to replace even with a more contemporary design. I think Barbara would understand this sentiment.

---

[13] Belmont Park. Website. https://www.belmontpark.com (accessed November 22, 2022).

As I arrived at Goliath and walked up to the station, I attempted to get in the mindset of a true roller coaster enthusiast. I thought about my interview with Barbara and attempted to take in as much as I could before, during, and after the ride. For my first ride, I decided to sit in the back seat. When the train pulled in, the previous rider gave me two thumbs up and declared it the best seat and ride ever. I took my seat. With restraints that lock you in by your lap and shins, it felt like a serious ride and yet also different from steel coasters that use over the shoulder restraints. Every coaster has its announcement when leaving the station and Goliath was no different. When the ride operator declared, "All clear. Are you ready to battle Goliath?," we were off. We took a quick left turn before heading up a steep 165-foot-tall chain lift. With such an incline, I was less worried about the ride itself than being stuck on the lift hill and the potential of needing to walk down the catwalk. This fear was not helped by the stutter in Goliath's ascent, where it felt like the chain missed its catch for a second.

From the top, the train dropped by 180 feet, traveling 15 feet below ground level when achieving its record-holding 72 mph. The speed was exhilarating and smooth, unlike my experience on Mean Streak and countless other wooden coasters. We then ascended quickly into an overbanked turnaround, followed by a small hill before hitting the dive loop, where I was inverted briefly before descending a half loop. I had little time to contemplate the flip before entering the second inversion and a zero-gravity stall, where I experienced the sensation of floating upside-down. From there, it was a quick journey through a second overbanked turnaround back to the station. A hat from the rider in front of me flew by, which I failed to catch in midair, which reminded me that a friend had lost her mobile phone earlier this summer when visiting Chicago and riding Goliath. Total ride time on Goliath was 105 seconds, and all I could think was, "that was amazing."

With no lines to speak of, I was able to get right back to the station and go for a second ride, this time in the front seat. It was a totally different experience. With nothing to obscure the view of the track or hang on to, the fear level was amplified. Staring down that near vertical drop, waiting for the last car to release from the chain, felt like eternity. Coming off the ride, I checked my on-ride picture and decided that it was definitely not the most flattering photo. Seeing the photo reminded me of Marj's communicator badge from Chapter 1, where artifacts like a photo memorialize the experience and provide an opportunity to share a fanaticism with someone new. With two rides under my belt, I decided to top it off with a ride in the middle seat. In comparison to the fear factor of the front seat or the heightened roughness of the back seat, the middle was a relatively tame affair and one that I would describe as more fun than thrilling.

The science behind roller coasters backs up what I felt that day. In a study by Alessandro Foschi and Fabio Ortolani, the experience of riding in the front, middle, and back seat of the same roller coaster was tested using an on-ride barometer and accelerometer, mapping out the profile of each seat in the train.[14] Unlike a single particle, a roller coaster train experiences tension between cars, which adds an additional physical force for the riders. On the downward hill, front seat riders initially are being held back by the back cars and will feel a tug against their bodies. During the descent, it is riders at the back that will feel the greatest feelings of weightlessness, as their seats are tugged away by the front cars. A different pattern is experienced at the bottom of the hill, where the middle car reigns supreme with the fastest velocity and the tension of the other cars pushing riders down into their seats as the approach the next hill. On the ascent, riders in the front seat experience the greatest tension, providing a feeling of being thrown upward and forward. In short, the best seat in a roller coaster depends on where in the ride the experience is measured; all are thrilling, but in different ways.

After three rides on Goliath in short succession, I felt the novelty of the ride was wearing off on me. The experience of that first ride would always be characterized by the unknown. What would the ride feel like? Would I enjoy the ride or be terrified? Would the ride hurt or cause me to feel woozy afterward? By the end of the third ride, I knew the answers to all these questions and my screams were replaced by smiles. It was still fun, but not as thrilling as it was the first time around. I felt I had conquered Goliath.

Beyond the repetition of the ride, my experience that day was atypical and may have played on my feelings of anticipation and fear. Waiting in line amplifies the anticipation of the rider, giving them time to look around, take in the theme and structure, and wonder whether they are indeed ready to ride. For new riders, they may become anxious and talk to strangers to gauge their level of fear and anticipation. With excited chatter in the wind, a tentative rider may bow out and decide to ride another day. I saw this on my second ride, when a pair of teens decided to jump out of line for Goliath, despite the encouragement of their friends who lined up at the turnstiles. Being a lone rider, I didn't have anyone to talk to about the ride or to reflect on it afterward. The picture taken coming down the hill takes on less importance when alone, memorializing the ride, but not a shared social experience. I can imagine that Barbara's

[14] Foschi, A., and Ortolani, F. (2007). Is it more thrilling to ride at the front or back of a roller coaster? Physics Teacher, 45, 536–541.

experience was very different when traveling with her coaster enthusiast club. The bubbling enthusiasm before the ride and postride wrapup probably made up more of the experience than the coaster itself. Upon leaving Six Flags, I felt a desire to share my experience and was determined to coax my family into riding Goliath the next time we happened to be in Chicago, to capture a bit of that magic that Barbara had when riding with her mother.

Riding Goliath is a relatively low effort way to gain a thrill, with nothing much expected of me beyond traveling to the park and meandering my way to the ride entrance. As an alternative means of gaining an adrenaline rush, a large swath of the public has taken up high-risk sports. Ralph Buckley took on the task of defining exactly what classifies as a high-risk or extreme sport, rather than something that could be considered as just adventurous.[15] He concluded that extreme sports are "those activities, conditions, and levels, where participant survival relies on moment-by-moment skill, and any error is likely to prove fatal." The duration of the sport does not matter so much, as skydivers are done within minutes of jumping from the plane, whereas climbers will spend hours or days on their pursuit. Both adventurous and high-risk versions may require fitness, training, practice, and split-second decisions, however participants in adventurous sports can afford to make mistakes and survive. This definition also allows for comparison within the same sport and can help contextualize the jump in responsibility from trainee to expert, the latter now fully responsible for their own choices and actions. Buckley suggests that making such a leap can involve a range of motivations, whether for the immediate rush, longer-term self-esteem, personal transformation, or social recognition of achieving something amazing.

A model by Richard Celsi, Randall Rose, and Thomas Leigh provides a mechanism to understand how motivations for taking part in high-risk sports build on themselves.[16] Initially, skydivers might be attracted to the thrill, with sensation-seeking playing the same role it does for the patrons of Action Park or members of a roller coaster enthusiast club, with jumpers seeking out their own optimal level of excitement. In the study mentioned earlier by Stuart White, the researchers found that skydiving created a substantial physiological response across a range of neurotransmitters and neurotransmitters.[17] By itself, the leap from the plane in flight produced an acute autonomic nervous

[15] Buckley, R.C. (2018). To analyze thrill, define extreme sports. Frontiers of Psychology, 9, 1216. https://doi.org/10.3389/fpsyg.2018.01216 published under the Creative Commons Attribution License (CC BY), https://creativecommons.org/licenses/by/4.0/.

[16] Celsi, R., Rose, R., and Leigh, T. (1993). An exploration of high-risk leisure consumption through skydiving. Journal of Consumer Research, 20, 1–23.

[17] White, S., et al. (2019). Putting the flight in "fight-or-flight": Testosterone reactivity to skydiving is modulated by autonomic activation. Biological Psychology, 143, 93–102.

system response, with a combination of biological systems relating to both the challenge (testosterone) and stress (cortisol) that sensation-seekers crave.

The sudden physical change experienced by skydivers also affects a person's emotional state. Similar to scuba divers mastering buoyancy, skydivers immerse themselves in a physical context with little relationship to navigating normal life and therefore are separated from their everyday worries and anxieties. Research conducted by Hetland and Vitterso differentiated between hedonic and eudaimonic emotions of skydivers, the latter of which are related to fulfilling one's potential and finding meaning in life.[18] The researchers argued that what makes high-risk sports special were not the hedonic emotions (e.g., satisfaction, pleasure, and happiness) that can be accomplished through other thrills (like roller coaster riding), but rather the eudaimonic elements. During the jump, skydivers were shown to experience a shift in their emotional states, with lower feelings of anger and sadness than the personal baseline they had outside of the sport. This was complemented by high levels of eudaimonic emotion that interestingly occurred both during the jump and reappeared when the participants watched a home movie that chronicled their dives.

The emotional separation with normal life plays a critical role for newcomers to risky sports, according to Celsi, Rose, and Leigh, and is key element of their fanaticism.[19] As one skydiver is quoted as saying, "The minute I throw my gear in the car, that's all I think about. I don't think about work, paperwork, or sales. Period. I release everything." This quote resonates with me, as I once worked with a particularly anxious manager who could rarely think of anything beyond his work. His only release was through scuba diving and the strange new environment he found on the sea floor. With no reference point for what he was experiencing, as well as a need to keep focused on his technique and equipment, all of his anxieties faded away. The manager was hooked on the sport and from that point onward, every vacation was to a prime scuba destination.

The most frequently stated reason for trying a high-risk sport, as discussed by Celsi, Rose, and Leigh, was interpersonal influence, specifically, knowing a classmate, friend, or relative who was hooked on the sport. In research by Aviv Shoham, participants in high-risk sports were shown to gain camaraderie, which is a sense of community that transcends typical social norms, overshadowing whatever their place is in the everyday world.[20] Moreover,

[18] Hetland, A., and Vitterso, J. (2012). The feelings of extreme risk: Exploring quality and variability in skydiving and BASE jumping. Journal of Sport Behavior, 35, 154–180.

[19] Celsi, R., Rose, R., and Leigh, T. (1993). An exploration of high-risk leisure consumption through skydiving. Journal of Consumer Research, 20, 1–23.

[20] Shoham, A., Rose, G., and Kahle, L. (1999). Practitioners of risky sports: A quantitative study. Journal of Business Research, 47, 237–251.

camaraderie was the only variable discovered in the study to explain how frequently athletes participated in their chosen sport. Athletes experiencing feelings of camaraderie appear to feel compelled to turn up more often to either compete or train with their peers and when mixed with motives for sensation-seeking and emotional release, their pastime becomes increasingly sticky and more ingrained with who they are.

Kate's journey into skydiving follows many of these elements, where a little social influence propelled her to try out the sport just once. This was not an easy commitment, as Kate's aversion to heights and fears of falling ran deep into her childhood. Kate's boyfriend, an avid skydiver with over 250 jumps, must have been convincing, and Kate was soon facing her fears, similar to the exposure therapy discussed in the last chapter. She checked the weather a few days before and with it being forecast as clear, Kate was left with few excuses to back out. Instead, she decided "not to think about it too much" in an attempt to ease her nerves. The airfield was an hour and a half outside of Chicago and she felt understandably nervous, "Cognitively I knew it was safe, but my feelings didn't agree. I kept imagining that it would feel like falling." She arrived at the drop zone, signed a waiver for the dive, watched a comical safety video that featured a wild-bearded man who emphasized that although skydiving could kill you that it wouldn't be their fault, and waited around for what felt like ages. She then met her tandem instructor, a gregarious and enthusiastic soul, intent on ensuring that Kate had a fantastic experience. As a first-time student, Kate found there was not much to do, beyond contemplating whether she would be regretting this choice for the remainder of her life.

She boarded the plane, and after 15 minutes, it was game time. The side door opened and Kate waddled with her instructor toward the gap. "Watching other people go out the door was the hardest part. My adrenaline was running wild and I ran out of rational thoughts," reflected Kate. Hanging out the door strapped to another human being provided a novel vantage point that "was not congruent with normal processing." It was Kate's turn, and her instructor prompted her by saying "don't get eaten by the door monster," and with that, they jumped. Kate was overwhelmed by sound and wind. The instructor encouraged her to scream, which helps first timers from holding their breath and blacking out. She experienced about a minute of free fall before the instructor pulled the canopy. What once was incredibly noisy became instantly silent, as the parachute caught with a "whompf." "The transition was amazing, serene, and peaceful. At that moment, I realized that I wasn't going to die and my adrenaline ramped down." Her instructor encouraged her to take it all in, but all Kate was feeling was relief. Then the ground came up on them, she slid on her butt, and with that, her first dive was over. As mentioned at the start,

Kate was terrified of heights and the sensation of falling. To her surprise, "I had neither with sky diving. I didn't get those feelings at all," recalled Kate about her first dive.

It wasn't until she watched the video captured during her dive that she appreciated just how amazing her experience was. She saw "how much fun I was having" and knew she was hooked. Kate was interested in doing it herself, "it is scary not being in control or knowing how everything works. I wanted to understand my gear and retake control. My tandem dive was amazing, but lacking in challenge. I want the challenge of mastering it." The pathway to being a certified Accelerated Freefall (AFF) skydiver starts with ground school, where Kate underwent 8 hours of classroom training focused on body positioning and safety. She also took part in two tandem dives, where she practiced the motions of pulling the release handle at the right time by monitoring her altitude. With the basics in hand, Kate embarked on her first solo dive, where she took control of deploying her canopy, under the watchful eye of an instructor. If she ran into trouble, the instructor would rapidly escalate the level of assistance and ultimately pull Kate's cord if necessary. When we spoke, Kate had just passed her AFF level 3, which tested her ability to jump, pull, and land on her own. Although she passed the exam, the landing went slightly wrong and she banged up her knee, reminding her that with each escalation of responsibility, it "becomes more of a sport than a pastime activity." After seven jumps, Kate will pass the first section of AFF and move on to "coach dives," to practice more technical skills under the supervision of a licensed skydiver. With 25 jumps, she will have the opportunity to become fully licensed. Along the way, she will have to complete two "hop-n-pops," which is a deployment immediately after exiting the plane, to train for the potential of a plane malfunction.

With every jump, Kate is becoming more comfortable and confident in her sport. She has learned how to correct her body position and anticipate when something has the potential to go wrong. Kate knew that gaining mastery would be a hook to the sport, but more surprising to her was the social appeal of sky diving. Like Barbara debriefing with her fellow coaster enthusiasts, Kate debriefs with her instructor and fellow jumpers after each dive, recounting what went well and what could have gone better. According to Kate, there are a range of personalities represented in her skydiving club, from the "happy adventurer" who relishes the experience and is out for fun, to the "drop zone bums" who are in it for life, acting as instructors and packers. They are joined by military veterans, who work to keep their skills fresh, and the "sky tourists," the once and done tandem divers. This menagerie of people has shown Kate that skydiving can be for anyone who wants to join in "the camaraderie of doing something inherently dangerous." Although the chances of death are extremely rare, especially with Automatic Activation Devices that will deploy the canopy for the diver if needed, broken ankles are not uncommon to see around a drop zone.

Kate's transition from a sky tourist to full-fledged skydiver aligns with that predicted by Celsi, Rose, and Leigh.[21] In their model, initial motivations for seeking thrills and emotional release are replaced by feelings of achievement and pleasure. Habitual skydivers continue in the sport to develop skills both for their own satisfaction and to gain social status within the skydiving community. The certification process that Kate describes formalizes these motivations, by providing tangible proof of skill progression. With special relevance here, the research by Boldak and Guszkowska unearthed a gender difference, where women were more likely to stick with their training if they were higher on experience-seeking and less susceptible to boredom.[22] From what I know about Kate, both of these motives are true; Kate thrives on experience, such as living and working overseas, but also shows great patience and diligence in her professional career.

Along the way to skill mastery, the social influence at play when first experiencing the sport is replaced by group identity, with participants increasingly seeing themselves as athletes. The high-risk subculture of skydiving provides an opportunity to construct a new personal identity by providing a clear-cut context for this identity and rites of passage that facilitate what it means for the athlete. Aviv Shoham provides support for this transition, drawing attention to how high-risk sports provide an extra elevation to identity, as the activity is often viewed as both special and distinct from everyday pursuits.[23] Other researchers like Susan Mackenzie point out that the identities of high-risk athletes often overlap with connections with nature or other lifestyle elements, making the attraction to the sport even more sticky.[24] This is true for other forms of fanaticism outside the context of thrills. Kris from Chapter 1 had immense social connections with her adopted family from the Minnesota Force, while Ben's identity as an ultramarathon runner from Chapter 3 was intertwined with his connection to the natural world and running in beautiful places.

[21] Celsi, R., Rose, R., and Leigh, T. (1993). An exploration of high-risk leisure consumption through skydiving. Journal of Consumer Research, 20, 1–23.

[22] Boldak, A., and Guszkowska, M. (2016). Sensation seeking as one of the motivating factors for performing skydiving. Polish Journal of Sport Tourism, 23, 94–98.

[23] Shoham, A., Rose, G., and Kahle, L. (1999). Practitioners of risky sports: A quantitative study. Journal of Business Research, 47, 237–251.

[24] Mackenzie, S. (2013). Beyond thrill-seeking: Exploring multiple motives for adventure participation. Journal of Outdoor Recreation, Education, and Leadership, 5, 136–139.

Beyond the thrill and social elements of the sport, Kate's fascination with skydiving was partly driven by a need for distraction. The experience is intense and requires a participant's full attention, pushing out other life worries. She likes the process of checking the weather, readying her gear, and steadying her nerves for the jump. At the end of a day full of skydiving, Kate feels absolutely exhausted mentally and physically, but equally holds a great sense of achievement. Over the longer term, her fanaticism has shifted to appreciating the craft of skydiving and the pursuit of doing it well. Kate is focused on attaining her license and knows that the path toward it is both challenging and complicated. Yet unlike other sports, skydiving requires extreme levels of trust in your own competence, to troubleshoot when things go wrong. This mixture of high cognitive challenge and adrenaline-pumping excitement has proven to be the perfect elixir for Kate, and she plans to stick with the sport for the foreseeable future.

If she does, Kate is likely to make a further jump in Celsi, Rose, and Leigh's model,[25] which is said to tap more transcendent motivations, where participants gain a sense of timelessness, special understanding about others, and profound personal identity change.[26] Becoming a skydiver is anticipated to become a core feature of Kate's personal identity, while the connections she experiences with her skydiving club would evolve to a deeper level. Celsi, Rose, and Leigh refer to communitas as a special form of camaraderie where participants in high-risk sports, representing a wide range of backgrounds, share a common bond for their past-time, which might even be considered as sacred.[27] Kate points out that skydiving is special in its speed and intensity for building trust, "Not only do skydivers take their lives into their own hands, they also put their lives inherently in the hands of those they jump with. Everyone who jumps has the potential to kill you, easily and quickly. It is also unique to be in a sport where everyone is terrified and showing so much personal vulnerability. When learning to skydive, you are absolutely going to make mistakes. You will look like an idiot at some point and it is very visible that you're scared. It makes for a really intense bonding process."

Central to the concept of communitas is that participants see everyday social roles and status as not relevant to their community and sport. In addition, they are likely to create and use language based on shared experience that

---

[25] Celsi, R., Rose, R., and Leigh, T. (1993). An exploration of high-risk leisure consumption through skydiving. Journal of Consumer Research, 20, 1–23.
[26] Celsi, R. (1992). Transcendent benefits of high-risk sports in J. Sherry and B. Sternthal (eds.), Advances in Consumer Research (volume 19, 636–641). Provo, UT: Association for Consumer Research.
[27] Celsi, R., Rose, R., and Leigh, T. (1993). An exploration of high-risk leisure consumption through skydiving. Journal of Consumer Research, 20, 1–23.

transcends its literal meaning, as a way of promoting group membership and creating a sense of pride. Understood only by insiders, this type of language is termed "phatic communication" and works to provide cohesion to the sub-culture. Kate experienced this firsthand: "There is an entire lexicon used in the skydiving community that is unknown to the world at large and kept that way on purpose." She notes that it is common for skydiving groups to keep social media channels private and require aspiring members to prove that they really do know the lingo and are not just lurkers.

Yet, the most transcending element of the journey described by Celsi, Rose, and Leigh, as well as the element that differentiates high-risk sports from other ways of getting a thrill (like roller coaster riding), is the sensation of flow. Participants in high-risk sports often describe their involvement as absolutely demanding both physically and mentally. Accompanying these demands, according to Celsi, are feelings of release, timelessness, and freedom that correspond with a peak experience.[28] As quoted in his paper, one skydiver described their experience: "Freefall is a . . . free feeling. It's one time in my life when I think of nothing else. I mean, there's nothing on my mind. There's nothing I'm thinking about other than what I'm experiencing. Everything else is totally out of my mind and I am free. There is nothing to hold me down, to hold me back. There's just nothing there." Flow, as originally conceived by Csikszentmihalyi, describes a state where actions are taken with seemingly little conscious intervention, where moments follow easily from one to the next, and where people are in control of their own actions.[29] The separation between ourselves and the environment breaks down, as does the conception of time. Csikszentmihalyi later positioned flow as the state where an individual's true self emerges, which is free of self-limitation and self-awareness.[30] Individuals in flow are freed from conscious constraints, like self-doubt and social norms, and therefore often report feeling free.

For flow to occur, an individual's coping abilities must be closely matched to the amount of challenge presented. Too much challenge and participants will become overwhelmed by the activity and will feel stressed and anxious, no different from my first experience on the Alpine Slide. With too little challenge, participants will lose interest in the activity and will feel their minds wander. Between boredom and terrifying is the pocket where flow is experienced. In addition, participants are likely not to experience flow if they

[28] Celsi, R. (1992). Transcendent benefits of high-risk sports in J. Sherry and B. Sternthal (eds.), Advances in Consumer Research (volume 19, 636–641). Provo, UT: Association for Consumer Research.

[29] Csikszentmihalyi, M. (1975). Beyond Boredom and Anxiety. San Francisco: Jossey-Bass Publishers.

[30] Csikszentmihalyi, M., and Csikszentmihalyi, I. (1988). Optimal Experience. Cambridge: Cambridge University Press.

are forced or coerced into the activity; self-direction and discovery are key components of what is meant by a transcendent experience. High-risk sports, like skydiving, provide an ever-changing context—where each experience is similar to, but not exactly like, the last one—and thus provide fertile ground for flow experiences. The predictability of my ride on Goliath does not have an equivalent to skydiving, where weather conditions, jump altitudes, and a variety of other factors all play into creating a unique experience each and every time. Where roller coaster designers attempt to provide precision in recreating the exact same thrill for all their riders, the opposite is true for high-risk sports, where the capabilities of the participant are continuously tested. Like the thrills at Action Park, the lack of constraints provides an extra layer of excitement.

Experience plays a key role for participants in high-risk sports to understand and then seek out experiences that will provide that perfect balance between capability and challenge. Training regiments like what Kate is progressing through help, by providing trainees a predicted level of challenge that should be appropriate for where they are in their learning. For advanced athletes, they are left to their own devices to know what contexts might be too much. Recall Ben, the ultramarathon runner we met in Chapter 3, who decided to stop at the halfway point at the Leadville 100. Pulling on his previous experience running other ultramarathons, he knew that continuing the race was too risky for his physical health. In the event that an athlete's experience is not challenging enough, they might be able to dial up the level of challenge by working on a new skill or attempting a new trick as a way of managing the tension between boredom and terrifying. Other ways of ramping up the challenge have more serious consequences, for example, surfers going out during a major storm or scuba divers exploring uncharted caves. Such choices provide a rush of adrenaline, but have the potential to overwhelm an individual's capability, sometimes with fatal consequences. With the development of skills and the experience of flow, athletes become comfortable with risk and become overconfident in their abilities. As quoted in the work by Celsi, Rose, and Leigh, tragic events can snap participants back to the reality that the activity is inherently dangerous, "Don't kid yourselves. Skydiving is dangerous. I've had a lot of friends die skydiving. In reality, even though we maneuver through the sky, we are falling like a rock."[31]

To understand how athletes harness their ability to drive performance, while keeping a healthy perspective about risk, I interviewed Dr. Mark Aoyagi,

[31] Celsi, R., Rose, R., and Leigh, T. (1993). An exploration of high-risk leisure consumption through skydiving. Journal of Consumer Research, 20, 1–23.

the codirector of sport and performance psychology at the University of Denver. Mark's professional background is unique in that he holds degrees in counseling psychology, kinesiology, and exercise and sport science, allowing him to truly attend to both mind and body when working with his clients. Beyond his academic credentials of attaining a fellowship with the American Psychological Association and coediting two books on applied sport psychology, Mark has deep experience working with Olympic teams, NCAA athletic departments, and professional sports teams, including the Denver Nuggets, Denver Broncos, and LA Dodgers. Mark's expertise spans individual performance, team effectiveness, and achieving meaning, satisfaction, and fulfillment through sport, work, and life.

I asked Mark about the most typical issues confronted by his clients. After some quick reflection, Mark identified the topics of identity, confidence, and purpose as the three most common issues he encounters beyond acute needs like injury recovery. As an athlete advances to professional sport, they will typically struggle with the stress of their new identity and how to square it with personal relationships. Mark mentioned how the "sport can become too big" and all-encompassing if there is nothing else to create balance. "The stakes can become super high, where everything rests on making a basket or scoring a goal." If an athlete failed to devote time to developing personal relationships or building unrelated skills, there is little to rely on if their career sours. Knowing that they are on the knife-edge, such athletes will work tirelessly to keep relevant, even if it means destroying the team dynamic and losing the game, which Mark has seen firsthand. To stretch the thinking of his clients, Mark asks them the simple question, "Who are you?," and if nothing beyond the sport comes to mind, he warns them that "it will be a problem if this sport is your sole thing. What got you here will not get you there." Mark recognizes that a high investment in sport is absolutely required to achieve the levels of performance seen today, but this drive can extend beyond its usefulness and lead an athlete down a lonely road. A coach or mentor can help them identify that it is time to refocus and reinvest in other areas of their life to maintain their mental health and avoid burnout. Relationships, interests, and a diverse skillset provide insurance to leading a fulfilling life beyond sport.

At times across their professional careers, athletes can hit a stumbling block in confidence, an issue that Mark placed second on his list of top client issues. Mark mentions that mental states were often ignored in the past, with attention placed squarely on honing the physical body. Coaches were "discouraged to look away from the sport," in fear that addressing nonphysical issues could cause "a loss of focus on performance." For professional athletes, their physical gifts provide a path to greatness, but once achieved, maintaining performance relies more heavily on their mental state. There is now broad recognition that athletes need to build skills for dealing with blows to confidence, disruptive moods, crippling anxiety, or whatever might be impeding performance at a particular moment in time. When working with clients, Mark uses acceptance and commitment therapy (ACT), whereby athletes are encouraged to change their attention from "outcomes to process." Rather than dwelling on the outcome of a match or game, Mark encourages them to ask, "Did I prepare effectively or stay true to my training? Did I follow my game plan?" Such questions allow athletes to gain a balanced perspective about their performance and open up conversations for learning.

Another core facet of ACT is acknowledging the range of mental, physical, and emotional states that arise during performance and life, accepting them, and moving on. Perceiving these states as personal flaws and replaying them in one's head can create a vicious cycle, whereby an inordinate amount of focus can reinforce a negative cognitive script that an athlete is unworthy, further jeopardizing their confidence. For example, when Kate landed badly after her jump, she had the option to dwell on her failure and question whether she is advancing in her sport. Instead, she reviewed with her coach what worked well during the jump and what she could have done differently to ensure a better landing. Equally, Ben could have given up ultramarathon running after exiting at the halfway point during the Leadville 100, but instead he recognized that his run didn't go to plan. Early traffic in the race caused him to speed up on the downhills and burn out his legs prior to the major descent at Hope Pass. Strong self-awareness, balanced appraisal, and acceptance are all part of the mental game as Mark says, "Confidence comes from inside and not outside."

The third challenge Mark highlights is highly related, but opposite to the journey Kate is on as she becomes a licensed skydiver. Kate is finding additional purpose through her sport, embellishing her life with a new area of interest and community to engage with. Yet for some professional athletes who were drawn to the sport based on their physical skills, their sense of purpose can be lost, especially if they view the sport purely as an occupation. It might sound strange at first, but sport fans can be more invested in the outcome of a game or match than the players within it; for fans it is entertainment, but for professional athletes, it is their job. To help athletes maintain or rekindle their passion for the game, Mark encourages his clients to focus on values rather than goals. It is the difference between "being a caring partner in a relationship and the act of getting married." Values are different from goals in that they exist in the present moment, have transferability across contexts, and do not get ticked off a list when completed. For much of their professional careers, athletes are told what to do by coaches, without much contemplation. Mark asks them to consider: "How do they want to be great at their sport? What do they want to be known for in how they approach the game or fellow team members?" Answers can be wide-ranging, but are rooted in the athlete's value system. Once they identify their values, Mark can help them relate to their sport in new ways, fuse their pro-fessional and personal identities, and create the foundations for the transi-tion into retirement. In Mark's words, "There is an unhelpful mindset that people have around passion. It is better to think about developing your pas-sion, rather than finding it."

It is freeing to think that there are many outlets for each individual's unique skills and values, rather than a single passion to be discovered. In the context of thrill-seeking, a number of different sports have the potential to scratch the itch for high doses of physical and cognitive challenge. For Kate, her entry was easiest into the world of skydiving, but potentially rock climbing or scuba diving could have given her the same rush and challenge. Common across active thrill-seekers like Kate are needs to fulfill the hedonic motivations of pleasure and happiness and finding ways to practice benign masochism, where negative stimuli (like falling from a plane) are channeled into feelings of a rush and accomplishment. Thrills jolt participants into the present, where little else can be contemplated beyond the immediate physical experience, and thereby replace the worries of the day with something more pleasurable. Such a transition is true whether the participant is engaged in a high-risk sport or taking on a passive role like being a first-time roller coaster rider or a sky tourist. Universally, perceptions about what is important are disrupted by the overwhelming nature of the thrill. It is no wonder that amusement parks maintain such prominence as a preferred method for escaping the rat race of normal life. Beyond the rides, amusement parks build environments of antic-ipation and reflection that wrap around the thrills, prolonging the emotional release of park goers.

For some individuals, one thrill is not enough and they become true fanatics of their chosen outlet. For Barbara, becoming a roller coaster en-thusiast brought back memories of her childhood and reinvigorated a sense of freedom each time she flew down the tracks. She also gained a sense of community from the club, as they traveled together to ride a new coaster, and gained a form of identity that provided additional depth outside of her professional world. For Kate, her chosen thrill layered in the development of skill and personal responsibility, by managing the inherent risk of skydiving. Her fanaticism is now dominated by regulating the tension between boring and terrifying, replicating the feeling a flow as she racks up the required number of dives to become fully licensed. The benefits that Barbara and Kate gain from their chosen activities, specifically identity, community, and flow, are not reserved to their forms of fanaticism, and we have seen them turn up in profiles of fanatics from other chapters. Yet, thrill-seeking might be unique in its ability to snap people out of their worries to focus entirely on the present.

8
Happiness on Sale

There are easier, yet maybe not as effective, ways to rapidly change a person's mood beyond jumping out of a plane. At its inception, soda was known more for altering moods and improving health than for its cheerful taste. The use of carbonated water for conditions like dyspepsia, nerves, and fatigue dates back over 200 years and went through multiple iterations before becoming the product we know today. During the height of its popularity, the soda fountain enabled pharmacists to make their medicines, which usually came in liquid form, palpable for their customers. Mixed with soda water and syrup, the taste of then-common medicines heroin, morphine, cocaine, and strychnine were hidden away within a tasty treat that over time became increasingly indulgent.[1] With time, ingredients like ice cream, exotic fruits, and the kola nut overshadowed any medicinal purpose and allowed the soda fountain to stand on its own as a destination for drinking and socializing. Thousands of branded sodas flooded the market during the early days of the 20th century, including Moxie, Pepsin Punch, and Dr. Pepper. Among them all, Coca-Cola reigned supreme. According to Gia Giasullo and Peter Freeman, Coca-Cola was approaching sales of 17 million gallons per year even before prohibition, the equivalent of 6 gallons of soda for every American. A string of world events including the Great Depression and the Second World War inadvertently chipped away at the traditional soda fountain, transforming it more and more into a lunch counter, with food taking center stage. The opulence and variety of soda was sidelined, and drinks became complements to burgers and fries.

Taking the Gilded Age's fascination with the soda fountain as inspiration, a new generation of craft soda makers are reinventing the industry through a network of independent retailers, such as Blue Sun Soda Shop. The brainchild of Mark Lazarchic, Blue Sun is the current record holder for stocking the greatest number of soda flavors anywhere in the world, tallying 1,300 varieties, with over 100 types of root beer alone.[2] Beyond the normal grocery store

---

[1] Giasullo, Gia, and Freeman, Peter. (2014). The Soda Fountain. Berkeley: Ten Speed Press.
[2] Blue Sun Soda Shop. Website. https://www.bluesunsodashop.com (accessed February 4, 2023).

Fanatic. Joe Ungemah, Oxford University Press. © Oxford University Press 2024. DOI: 10.1093/9780197783894.003.0009

varieties, Blue Sun carries flavors like buffalo wing, blue cheese, mustard, ter-
iyaki, and pickle, the latter a cult favorite of the local clientele. Alongside the
normal categories of cola, grape, and orange are those that inspire Mark to
collect, such as huckleberry, cactus, and juniper, with the really strange flavors
organized under the miscellaneous banner. It is there that ambiguous brands
like Bug Barf and Alien Snot are found, captivating the average 12-year-old
who comes sauntering through the isle. Yet, their attention may wander, as
Blue Sun offers much more than the bottles; a soda fountain on-site currently
boasts of 150 different flavors of soda, shakes, and malts, as well as curious
creations involving ice cream paired with donuts or cookies, ensuring that
everyone attains their full daily caloric intake. A small collection of vintage
arcade games, a collection of toys and puzzles, rare candies, and a wall of Pez
round out the offerings. There is a reason why the *Star Tribune* awarded the
Blue Sun Soda Shop a Gold Award for Best Tour and two Silver Awards for
Best Family Attraction and Best Candy Shop in 2022. With the addition of
two branches in recent years, the ability for Blue Sun to bring happiness to a
growing base of customers has only grown stronger.

The path that led to Blue Sun was not what Mark envisioned in 2015, when he
was pondering what to do with a bunch of empty office space facing a highway
service road. An entrepreneur and salesperson at heart, Mark had grown a career out of spotting gaps in the market and opening niche businesses. It is only
in hindsight that he discovered that the majority of his businesses cater to providing happiness. Alongside Blue Sun, he currently owns the largest fireworks
store in the region and a weddings supply company specializing in sparklers.
Commenting on how this unlikely portfolio took shape, Mark said, "It is easy
to sell happiness. Customers want to come in and see the soda and candy. It
makes them feel good." A glance at customer reviews would agree. Beyond
generally being impressed with the offering and fun environment, customers
feel transported to happier times. One customer wrote, "This place makes me
feel like a kid again!!! I love sharing it with my kids." Another wrote on the
store's Facebook page, "Extremely large selection of soda and vintage candy.
Love the 1950s/60s nostalgic feel!"

Two events were the catalysts for Blue Sun, which occurred roughly at the
same time. The first catalyst was a video Mark watched about a delicatessen
in Los Angeles. The 15-minute video told the story of Galco's Old World
Grocery, a 100-year-old family business that underwent a transformation
from a traditional Italian deli and grocery to specialist shop trading in soda
and beer.[3] In response to the big bottlers who asked the owner, John Nese, to

[3] Soda Pop Stop. Website. https://www.sodapopstop.com (accessed February 5, 2023).

pay disproportionately more for their products than the national retailers, he turned instead to craft soda to stock his shelves. With an affinity for craft soda, stemming in part from the many visits he made as a child to a family friend's soda-bottling plant, John grew his selection to over 600 varieties. With some favorable national and international press, his business model struck gold and his store got rebranded as Galco's Soda Pop Stop.

Watching this video coincided with the second catalyst, specifically a dinner out with friends at a local brew pub, where Mark noticed a lack of non-alcoholic choices on the menu. Compared to the meticulous descriptions of beer, like those having an earthy flavor with hints of rosemary and cherry or beer that is soft and silky with a strong malt and chocolate profile, the nonalcoholic choices were a footnote on the menu. As a nondrinker, Mark's choices involved the typical fountain drinks, except that their version of ginger ale was made by a dubious mixture of lemon-lime with a splash of cola. He was shocked by the lack of effort the pub made at tending to the needs of patrons like him, which made him angry, "Why aren't these places offering more?" To Mark, it was a missed opportunity to serve the third of the US adult population that does not consume alcohol.[4] Mark's business intuition was proven correct, as a new wave of temperance bars began to appear across the nation a few years later.

During our interview, Mark reflected on the day that he came out of his office, looked over the wasted office space and declared, "Maybe it's time to do that soda shop thing." What might be seen in hindsight as a rather impulsive act was actually well attuned to who Mark is as a businessperson. He is open to new experiences, decisive, and has a low fear of failure. Like Scott, whom we met in Chapter 6, these entrepreneurial drives are complemented by a high dose of grit, to keep things moving even when problems abound. Mark sourced 700 varieties of soda by chasing down bottlers and distributors, often just by researching the labels found on the back of an unconventional brand. He moved out the office furniture, set up and stocked the shelves, added a modest-sized candy area, and hired some local entertainment, opening the doors to the public in November 2015.

Mark's ambitions for the soda shop were modest, and he was happy if the profits would cover the rent of the building. "I didn't really think it would work. I didn't even hire anyone to run the shop." Instead, Mark planned on serving customers himself, emerging from the back office whenever someone entered the shop. He was shocked to discover a line of customers extending approximately 100 feet long on opening day; Mark underestimated the impact his

---

[4] Heavy Drinking Among US Adults, NCHS Data Brief No. 374, CDC, August 2020.

media campaign would have on drumming up business. Friends, coworkers, and the local community all turned up in droves, resulting in the shop taking in $10,000 on the first day, which is quite impressive, considering the relatively low price point for each soda bottle. Opening-day was not a fluke, and for the next 3 months, Mark found his time completely taken over by serving customers, "People just kept on coming in and the worst part is that I couldn't hear the doorbell from the back office." Mark hired some help and made the "soda shop thing" a real business.

Part of Blue Sun's magic is the natural appeal of sweet things as an easy and effective mechanism to improve mood. It is no wonder that approximately 97% of Americans consume candy at least once per year, with about a quarter of the population consuming a piece on any given day.[5] When confronted with isles and isles of soda and candy, patrons can escape life's worries and reset their mindset by recalling happier times. Underlying the relationship between sweet things and mood is a drive toward homeostasis, as suggested by Hess, Kacen, and Kim.[6] These researchers suggest that mood is inherently stable, characterized largely by the dimensions of pressure and arousal, and brought back to homeostasis by an individual's efforts to seek out and partake in behavior that can give them a needed mood boost. They specifically looked at the influence of activities involving amusement (shopping or socializing with others), relaxation (watching TV or listening to music), and dining (eating out) on an individual's perceptions of pleasure and arousal. Although all the participants' behaviors influenced mood, pleasurable activities (those related to amusement) were more long-standing than those focused on arousal and, surprisingly, the effects were stronger when the activity was done alone rather than within groups.

Before a person seeks out a mood-modifying behavior, they first have to recognize that one is needed. Research into self-gifts by Luomala and Laaksonen identified a range of antecedents for mood-improving behavior, with the most frequent related to troubles at work or school and arguments with a loved one.[7] Beyond having a reason to buy a self-gift, they will require an opportunity and resources to do so, which is where establishments like Blue Sun come in. With a low price point and easy-to-access retail locations, Blue Sun provides a pathway for potential patrons looking for a lift in mood,

[5] Duyff, R., et al. (2015). Candy consumption patterns, effects on health, and behavioral strategies to promote moderation: Summary report on a round table discussion. Advanced Nutrition, 6, 139–146.
[6] Hess, J., Kacen, J., and Kim, J. (2006). Mood-management dynamics: The interrelationship between moods and behaviours. British Journal of Mathematical and Statistical Psychology, 59, 347–378.
[7] Luomala, H., and Laaksonen, M. (1999). A qualitative exploration of mood-regulatory self-gift behaviors. Journal of Economic Psychology, 20, 147–182.

with a product perfectively suited for that purpose. Luomala and Laaksonen found that sweet things like chocolate, candy, and ice cream were among the most common items purchased, alongside cosmetics and clothes, as a means of mood-reparation. These purchases were different from their mood-maintaining counterparts, which were intended as a form of celebration, more outwardly focused, and to be enjoyed with friends. Mood maintenance also involves a degree of risk, where postconsumption guilt or frustration over bad service can spoil the good times. The conscious awareness of buyers and urgency for their mood-reparatory behavior is brought to life in a quote by one of the study's participants: "At work, somebody or something may get on your nerves. I may go browsing in stores during my lunch break then. I buy a chocolate bar or a bag of candies and eat them right away. It is funny, but it helps. Of course, it does not erase it altogether, but it is a first step. It is some kind of first aid."

The adage "When the going gets tough, the tough go shopping" effectively sums up what it means to engage in the type of retail therapy described. Through a combination of field and lab research, Selin Atalay and Margaret Meloy confirmed the influence of mood on buying behavior, with bad moods contributing to both more purchases and higher consumption of treats.[8] The researchers were most interested in the conflict that can arise between self-regulation of either mood or impulse and whether consumers in a bad mood could show restraint. They found that when given the explicit goal of showing restraint, consumers were able to strategically reduce their consumption, but still gain enough out of their purchase to improve their mood. The study also discovered that self-gifts had long-lasting effects, were seldom regretted, and not associated with the negative emotion that spurred their purchase. In all, the researchers suggest that "there seems to be little downside" to engage in retail therapy.

As a category for retail therapy, the power of sweet things like soda, ice cream, candy, and chocolate are unique in their ability to alter mood. Like other comfort foods, they are high in fat and sugar, which, when consumed, trigger a release of insulin and endorphins that play directly on brain activity. Whereas both good and a bad moods can trigger food consumption, the type and amount of food ingested differs. When studied head-to-head, people in good moods were more willing to try new foods and eat healthier foods. A series of studies led by Meryl Gardner discovered that bad moods direct individuals to attend to short-term, immediate needs that are realized in the form

---

[8] Atalay, A., and Meloy, M. (2011). Retail therapy: A strategic effort to improve mood. Psychology and Marketing, 28, 638–660.

of indulgent foods high in fat and sugar.[9] Their good mood counterparts do not feel the same pressure to enjoy something indulgent immediately and can concentrate on longer-term aspirations toward maintaining personal health.

To the relief of all of us who have turned to a sweet treat or two as a means to improve mood, candy consumption alone does not appear to be harmful to long-term health. According to a review led by Roberta Duyff of the available research on candy consumption and health, typical candy consumption by adults is in the range of 176 kcal per day, an amount that shows no significant impact on increased weight, cardiovascular risk, or metabolic issues.[10] In fact, modest amounts of coca and chocolate consumption were associated with positive cardiovascular health, improving blood flow and potentially cognitive functioning. Key to these findings is an underlying belief about what normal consumption of sweets should be. When these parameters are broken, an opposite trajectory for health is found. Individuals experiencing periods of depression can fall prey to binge-eating indulgent food, especially when they believe strongly that eating will repair their mood.[11] According to research by Joyce Slochower, Sharon Kaplan, and Lisa Mann, stressful life events can cause the overconsumption of indulgent foods for obese individuals, due to feeling out of control over their emotional states.[12] Unlike their normal-weight peers, who either maintained or reduced their food consumption with stress, food intake increased by 250% among the obese participants, as a means to cope with heightened feelings of anxiety. When feelings of stress subsided, these same participants were left with a loss of self-esteem, which could snowball and reinforce overeating for mood repair.

Thus, it is important to differentiate between typical consumption of sweet things and overindulgence, with the latter counteracting any benefits for mood restoration with long-term risks to health. When patterns of overindulgence start to surface, Duyff and her colleagues suggest that restricting access to sweets will likely be counterproductive, especially among children, by heightening the desire to obtain sweets and greater consumption when they become available again.[13] Instead, self-monitoring of behavior and using cues about the size of a typical serving show the best results. This falls in line

[9] Gardner, M., et al. (2014). Better moods for better eating? How mood influences food choice. Journal of Consumer Psychology, 24, 320–335.

[10] Duyff, R., et al. (2015). Candy consumption patterns, effects on health, and behavioral strategies to promote moderation: Summary report on a round table discussion. Advanced Nutrition, 6, 139–146.

[11] Dingemans, A., et al. (2009). Expectations, mood, and eating behavior in binge eating disorder: Beware of the bright side. Appetite, 53, 166–173.

[12] Slochower, J., Kaplan, S., and Mann, L. (1981). The effects of life stress and weight on mood and eating. Appetite, 2, 115–125.

[13] Duyff, R., et al. (2015). Candy consumption patterns, effects on health, and behavioral strategies to promote moderation: Summary report on a round table discussion. Advanced Nutrition, 6, 139–146.

with research by Meier, Noll, and Molokwu, who suggest that eaters should be mindful of every bite if they are to get the maximum benefits of indulgent food.[14] Chocolate eaters who focused on the present moment without judging their actions had a greater lift in their mood than those who blindly consumed their sweet treats.

Outside the mind of the consumer, the environment also plays a role in how sweet things are perceived. A study led by Xu looked at the influence of four different contexts on the enjoyment of eating the same chocolate ice cream.[15] Previous research has shown that characteristics of the physical environment like lighting, background music, spatial layout, and temperature can all influence a person's emotional state, which in turn can play a part in their enjoyment of food. Immersive and social environments appear to be particularly influential, where consumers report better moods after eating or drinking if shared with others. For their own study, the researchers discovered that eating chocolate ice cream in a cafe or university environment resulting in a higher affective state (with greater descriptions of joy, happiness, and pleasure) than in either a laboratory setting or bus stop. Moreover, they found that the experience of taste was also affected, with those in the cafe and university environments using descriptions like sweet and milky to describe the ice cream, whereas those at the bus stop described the same treat as bitter.

The type of consumption behavior described so far has been thoughtful and deliberate, with consumers attuned to their affective state and making decisions that will help them regain a sense of mood homeostasis or prolong a positive mood just a bit longer. Yet there is another batch of buying behavior that is dictated more by chance encounter and impulse, even if it is still focused on sweet things. Impulse buying is characterized by rapid and unplanned reactions to internal or external stimuli, resulting in a snap decision to consume a given product or service. Such buying choices are estimated to account for anywhere between 40% and 80% of purchases, depending on product category, and appear to be a growing concern, with Millennials found to be 52% more likely to make impulsive purchases than previous generations.[16] In a meta-analysis of 186 studies with empirical results on impulse buying, a research team lead by Gopalkishnan Iyer discovered that a combination of personal traits, motives, consumer resources, and marketing stimuli

[14] Meier, B., Noll, S., and Molokwu, O. (2017). The sweet life: The effect of mindful chocolate consumption on mood. Appetite, 108, 21–27.

[15] Xu, Y., et al. (2019). Changes in flavour, emotion, and electrophysiological measurements when consuming chocolate ice cream in different eating environments. Food Quality and Preference, 77, 191–205.

[16] Amos, C., Holmes, G., and Keneson, W. (2013). A meta-analysis of consumer impulse buying. Journal of Retailing and Consumer Services, 21, 86–97.

all interacted to encourage impulse purchases.[17] Specifically, the structural model discovered by their research identified two pathways to impulse buying depending on whether someone was in a good or bad mood. Hedonic motives (those geared toward pleasure) were fulfilled most when individuals were in a good mood, whereas a negative mood state was universally related to impulse buying independently of motivation, giving support to the notion of self-regulation as a key driver of buying behavior. Bas Verplanken and Ayana Sato provide some additional support by differentiating between actions that have either a promotion (such as seeking pleasure) or prevention (such as avoiding feeling of low self-esteem) strategy.[18] Preventing negative moods can creep into psychopathology in the form of compulsive buying if done at a level that impedes leading a healthy lifestyle, which was explored in Chapter 5 in regard to hoarding.

An earlier meta-analysis on psychological traits conducted by Clinton Amos, Gary Holmes, and William Keneson confirms the power of an individual's level of spontaneity on impulse buying, but also highlights the role of sensation-seeking, decisiveness, and susceptibility to influence.[19] Other traits, like self-monitoring, emotional intelligence, and self-control worked in the opposite direction by inhibiting buying behavior. A study by Melis Yigit builds on this insight by suggesting that states of mindfulness, where an individual is astutely aware and accepting of the present, can mitigate impulse buying.[20] It is thought that by heightening a person's awareness of their current thoughts and feelings without judging them, they are able to suppress the urge to consume, returning the consumer to the type of deliberate shopping as described in the discussion on self-gifts. Yet sometimes mindfulness can be undermined by the situation being encountered, as uncovered by Kathleen Vohs and Ronald Faber.[21] When cognitive resources are depleted due to tough or relentless work, it is much more difficult for individuals to avoid impulse purchases. They are likely to feel a strong urge to buy and are willing to spend more than their peers who have not experienced the same levels of mental stress.

[17] Iyer, G., et al. (2020). Impulse buying: A meta-analytic review. Journal of the Academy of Marketing Science, 48, 384–404.

[18] Verplanken, B., and Sato, A. (2011). The psychology of impulse buying: An integrative self-regulation approach. Journal of Consumer Policy, 34, 197–210.

[19] Amos, C., Holmes, G., and Keneson, W. (2013). A meta-analysis of consumer impulse buying. Journal of Retailing and Consumer Services, 21, 86–97.

[20] Yigit, M. (2020). Consumer mindfulness and impulse buying behavior: Testing moderator effects of hedonic shopping value and mood. Innovative Marketing, 16, 24–36.

[21] Vohs, K., and Faber, R. (2007). Spent resources: Self-regulatory resource availability affects impulse buying. Journal of Consumer Research, 23, 537–547.

Mark's journey to help repair his customer's mood states became much more serious a few months after he started that "soda shop thing," when he bought a vintage 1952 Crown Cork and Seal Dixie Bottler. The machine allows Blue Sun to bottle its Whistler brand of soda, each within a custom 8-ounce bottle characterized by thick glass, spiraled body, and printed white labels. Customers pay a deposit when they buy a Whistler soda, which is given back to them when the bottle is returned to the store. Crafting his own sodas on a vintage machine has been a labor of love. The first challenge was getting the sodas approved by authorities who monitor food safety standards. Although better for the environment, reusable bottles are not conducive to listing ingredients, as the same bottle may be used for a range of rotating flavors, which is a core feature of the Whistler brand. This hurdle was tackled after 6 months of idle machinery, with the addition of a micro label on the cap declaring the flavor and ingredients. It then took another 6 months to figure out the best level of carbonation, "For the first half year, we were making a pretty bad product," admitted Mark. Even after the team got better at making a consistent product, the machinery requires constant attention and with only four Dixie machines operating in the United States, any spare parts are required to be custom made.

And yet, having a bottling machine allows for constant experimentation, which is one of the major drivers for Mark's fanaticism with soda. Mark told me about a recent trip to The Wizarding World of Harry Potter at Universal Studios Florida, where he tried his first Butter Beer. He was convinced he would hate it. Mark was never a fan of either butterscotch or marshmallow, but when he tasted their combination in Harry's elixir, his mind was blown and he became determined to create his own Whistler version. Tasting and tinkering with the recipe, he was proud when his team landed on a recipe that now sits alongside the other 139 varieties of Whistler. When it comes to craft soda, there is truly a nearly infinite number of potential flavors. Extract companies routinely offer ten or more versions of flavors like orange or lemon, with the added complexity of either natural or artificial, that provide a huge palette to work with. When experimentation is taken too far, questionable flavors like Alien Snot come to life.

Mark's business has grown over the years, both in its physical footprint and reach with shipping across the United States. He crafts not only Whistler but also 48 flavors across seven additional brands in normal glass, sparing customers the need to return the bottles. What has remained the same is his attention to the customer experience when coming to the store. Customers are encouraged to browse the selection, poke their heads into the bottling area, and grab a free bag of popcorn. Bottling tours are regularly offered to the public, with school groups and retirement communities regularly streaming through. Mark soaks in the wonder of the kids as "they marvel at the way it looks, sounds, and runs." It is rare for the public to see products being made, and Mark relishes providing the opportunity. The soda business is not the most profitable within Mark's portfolio of companies, but it is by far the most fun, and in Mark's view witnessing the happiness it creates firsthand makes up for lost financial ground.

During our interview, Mark was interrupted a number of times by a friend texting him from Disney World. They were playing a game where his friend would take a picture of somewhere in the park, text the picture, and challenge Mark to identify where he was. It was through this exchange I learned that Mark is also a Disney fanatic, captivated less by the rides and more by the visitor experience. He is fascinated by the detail Disney invests in creating a sense of escapism and wants to learn the mechanics behind the Disney experience, from the tunnels that run under Disney World to the way that rowdy customers are escorted out of the park. I wasn't surprised by this discovery, as his fascination with "The Happiest Place on Earth" is 100% consistent with his aspirations for selling happiness at Blue Sun.

To understand how self-gifts at Blue Sun or trips to Disney World fit into strategies to improve long-term happiness, I spoke with Helen Williams, a coaching psychologist at Sten 10 and associate consultant with the Centre for Coaching based in London. As a chartered psychologist in both coaching and occupational psychology, Helen works with her clients to achieve work and life goals through the use of solution-focused, cognitive behavioral techniques. She is registered with the Health and Care Professions Council and is cocreator of the SOLUTION[22] and CLARITY[23] coaching models. Apparent from the outset of our conversation was the differentiation between self-gifts, which might repair or prolong mood in the short term, and alternative techniques that can lead to the achievement of longer-term goals as a source of happiness. Specifically, self-gifts might take the place of other types of anchors to remind individuals of their self-worth and ability to reach a happier state.

When working with clients, Helen deliberately develops psychological anchors that can be used to shift mind-set and change the internal narrative. "If it is happiness that I am working with, I will ask them 'can you recall an example of a time when you were really happy?' I would then ask the client

---

[22] Williams, H., Palmer, S., and O'Connell, B. (2011). Introducing SOLUTION and FOCUS: Two solution focused coaching models. Coaching Psychology International, 4, 6–9.
[23] Williams, H., and Palmer, S. (2010). CLARITY: A cognitive behavioural coaching model. Coaching Psychology International, 3, 5–7.

to relive that moment and if they are willing, to close their eyes to truly envision everything within and around them. What are they thinking and feeling? What are they sensing from their environment? Who are they with at that moment in time?" All these questions build up a picture of maximum happiness and only when found, does Helen create an anchor that will be used as a reminder for that state of mind. The anchor can be anything from a touch of a cuff link to sitting up straight, but all anchors work the same as a subtle reminder of what is possible and to provide enough feedback for the individual to change the current moment.

Key to an anchor's power to act as a disruptor is self-awareness about how the current environment is impacting an individual's mood. To improve their self-awareness skills, Helen uses another technique from her coaching toolbox. Helen will assign her clients to take a third-person stance on their own lives, to observe what is going on in a nonjudgmental way. If an individual is attuned to when they are about to spiral into an undesirable mood, they can choose to deploy tools like anchors and go in a different direction. At this point in the conversation, Helen pauses and explains that much of her role as a coach is psychological education—she provides clients with tools to become mindful of what is happening to them emotionally, cognitively, socially, and physically and techniques to make better choices. During the first few sessions working with a client, Helen takes the role of the third-party observer, holding up the mirror for her clients, but by the end of her engagement, her clients have the know-how to do this on their own. Helen assigns plenty of homework to her clients along the way, testing their personal commitment to change.

The concepts Helen relies on come from the same toolbox as those used by some of the other psychologists interviewed in this book, but are tailored to meet the specific goals of her clients. For example, Mark uses acceptance and commitment therapy in his work with athletes, while Suzanne uses concepts from cognitive-behavioral therapy to address hoarding behavior. Held in common is the ability to change an individual's "mind talk" to achieve a different version of self that can often feel out of reach. "Letting in the voice of potential, rather than interference, is critical," explains Helen, as clients learn "to quiet their minds." She deploys a range of visioning techniques to get a sense of the possible. For example, she might ask her client to fast-forward to a time when the problem or challenge has been overcome. She will then ask a series of questions like, "What do you see? What is happening? What are you doing, thinking, and feeling? How are others responding to you?" Such questions can help the individual move from "problem talk to solution talk."

Standing in the way between a client's preferred vision of themselves and the current reality are beliefs. Feelings like inadequacy or unworthiness can sabotage confidence and the attainment of goals. Helen's approach is not to judge these beliefs, but to acknowledge and evaluate their influence, before finding a strategy to circumvent. This is where commitment comes in; if an individual wants a life goal enough, Helen will help find a pathway that uses "their existing strengths and strategies that have worked well for them in the past." She will also layer in tools to identify triggers and teach ways to challenge cognitive distortions. For example, she might turn to the quick and powerful question, "If you're feeling in a low mood, how would you be acting if you were in a happier state?," to challenge a person's schema that their mood is appropriate for the present moment.

The situation gets much more complex when a client displays a "secondary disturbance," whereby feelings spiral into themselves and become additive. Using an example from the literature on food, a client might have overconsumed indulgent foods in reaction to feeling stressed and out of control, which then can spiral into self-criticism. To truly be effective, a coach will need to address both how the client reacts to anxiety and their tendencies toward self-criticism. In a similar vein, self-gifts might work to improve mood in the short term or even act as an anchor to reset the narrative, but likely will be inadequate to counteract the underlying causes for bad moods. Helen points out that many of our first reactions to negative stimuli are emotional, "we seek out ways for self-protection," with more cognitive strategies coming second. So, if a person reaches out for that soda or candy bar instinctively, it is better to acknowledge and accept the action without judgment, before attempting to address the cognitive reasons why it was consumed in the first place.

Toward the back of the store at Blue Sun, a wall displays staff picks that encourage customers to branch out and try something new. Yet, the majority of comments overheard by customers are along the lines of, "I have not seen this soda in years—I thought they stopped making it." A big part of the happiness Mark sells is due to nostalgia, as evidenced by another review on the website, "This place makes me feel like a kid again!!" Customers are taken back to their childhood when they come across brands like Dad's Root Beer, Vernors Ginger Ale, or Moxie. For those who have never tasted these brands before, the reason for their appeal can be lost, as it has less to do with the flavor than the memories associated with it. For example, I bought a bottle of Moxie at Blue Sun and although I agree with the tagline of the soda being "distinctively different," I'm not sure I would seek out a Moxie again, as I lack that emotional attachment. Mark retold the story of a particular World War II vet, who routinely came to Blue Sun to buy cases of Grape Nehi, which transported him to his youth and happier times. When I asked Mark about his own nostalgic flavor, he landed on Orange Crush, which brought back memories of taking bike rides to a soda machine at a local horse farm, after a hard day of chores. As in Mark's childhood memory, sodas were often a special treat and intended to be "sipped rather than guzzled, to make the calories worth it." Being mindful of the drink you are enjoying is part of the experience and somehow gets lost in the supersized drinks offered at gas stations and movie theaters.

Nostalgia plays a major role in the consumption of self-gifts like soda and chocolate, acting as a mechanism to transport individuals back in time. To trigger nostalgia, self-gifts tap into memories of similar experiences with people, places, or things that were usually more common in an individual's youth. Implied by this definition is a bittersweet feeling, in that the primary experience has been lost in some way, either because culture has moved on or a particular object or environment is difficult to attain. Morris Holbrook and Robert Schindler differentiate the experience of eating ice cream, which although might have started during childhood can still be experienced today, and eating junket, which is the predecessor of store-bought pudding.[24] No longer regularly experienced and tied into the experience of watching a parent cook it on the stove, junket is easily classified as a nostalgic food.

Nostalgic items are typically experienced at critical periods during an individual's preference formation and follows a similar pattern to imprinting, with enduring effects. For musical preferences, individuals will typically feel nostalgic for songs first heard in their late teens or early 20s. Movie genre and star preferences seem to peak earlier, around the age of 14.[25] Research by Holbrook and Schindler suggests that nostalgia can form across a wide range of topics, but depends on age-related bonding with a particular item or experience.[26] People can be nostalgic due to their sensory experience, reminders of their "homeland," reliving a rite of passage, or a connection with loved ones, among other stimuli. Some individuals seem to be more prone to feelings of nostalgia, attaching heightened emotional significance for the past, than to appreciating the current moment and societal progress. Personal identity may also play into whether feelings of nostalgia arise. To preserve their past and create a sense of life continuity, individuals will turn to nostalgic experiences to reaffirm who they are.[27] Interestingly, consumers don't necessarily require

---

[24] Holbrook, M., and Schindler, R. (2003). Nostalgic bonding: Exploring the role of nostalgia in the consumption experience. Journal of Consumer Behaviour, 3, 107–127.

[25] Schindler, R., and Holbrook, M. (2003). Nostalgia for early experience as a determinant of consumer preferences. Psychology and Marketing, 20, 275–302.

[26] Holbrook, M., and Schindler, R. (2003). Nostalgic bonding: Exploring the role of nostalgia in the consumption experience. Journal of Consumer Behaviour, 3, 107–127.

[27] Sierra, J., and McQuitty, S. (2007). Attitudes and emotions as determinants of nostalgia purchases: An application of social identity theory. Journal of Marketing Theory and Practice, 15, 99–112.

direct experience with an item or experience to feel the tugs of nostalgia; all the item needs to do is elicit feelings of pleasure and longing.

Nostalgia provides a mixture of positive and negative affect at the same time. On the one hand, the nostalgic item is reminiscent of something important and pleasurable. Yet on the other hand, the focal point has been lost in some way, whether it was a personal relationship, a time in life, or simply a sensation that is impossible to replicate. Research conducted by Xuehua Wang, Hean Tat Keh, and Chen-Ho Chao confirmed the role that social relationships play in moderating the influence of nostalgia and consumption when applied to foods like candy, soda, and chocolate.[28] When individuals are reminded of the meaningful social connections underpinning food, like a mother making junket for her family, they will turn to indulgent food to a greater extent. Additionally, consuming nostalgic food with friends or family can affect their enjoyment of indulgent food and can lead to overeating, as conversation can overwhelm self-awareness about how much they are ingesting.

Across the themes outlined by Holbrook and Schindler, food plays most heavily on nostalgia by reminding individuals of similar sensory experiences.[29] The smell and taste of foods can elicit memories of simpler or better times, acting at a basic hedonic level requiring little conscious thought to make the association. Like the Grape Nehi of Blue Sun's World War II vet, taste alone can transport an individual back in time. However, food is also consumed in social settings, where significant events or people are brought back into memory by enjoying similar food in a similar environment. If not raised up automatically, all it takes is a slight nudge to bring nostalgia into consciousness, as demonstrated by research led by Xinyue Zhou.[30] If menus and food labels are written explicitly in a nostalgic way or food items packaged in boxes from the past, consumers tend to buy and eat more.

To gain an appreciation for how food can elicit nostalgia in social settings, I joined a group of seniors on a private tour of the Blue Sun bottling operation. My group of 30 seniors was met at the door by our guide, Neil, the incredibly articulate and friendly store manager at Blue Sun. Like so much at Blue Sun, Neil's own journey into the world of soda was serendipitous. Coming off a successful run as a professional circus clown with Ringling Brothers, Neil was approached by Mark to offer some light entertainment at the shop's

[28] Wang, X., Tat Keh, H., and Chao, C. (2018). Nostalgia and consumer preference for indulgent foods: The role of social connectedness. International Journal of Consumer Studies, 42, 316–326.

[29] Holbrook, M., and Schindler, R. (2003). Nostalgic bonding: Exploring the role of nostalgia in the consumption experience. Journal of Consumer Behaviour, 3, 107–127.

[30] Zhou, X., et al. (2019). Hungering for the past: Nostalgic food labels increase purchase intentions and actual consumption. Appetite, 140, 151–158.

grand opening. Neil had the perfect costume, an old soda jerk outfit, and when he wore it he brought to life the enduring mascot of Billy the Soda Jerk, a character that is dotted around the website and the basis for one of their product lines, called "Billy's Bubble Pop." With five flavors that are deliberately mismatched with the color of the drink, the line is playful and summed up by a picture of Billy on the bottle stating proudly, "I made this." In real life, Neil is nothing like Billy; he is quick at building rapport and makes his group feel at ease, before imparting a wealth of knowledge not only about Blue Sun's operation but also about the history of the soda fountain itself.

Before the tour began, it was easy to notice the instant connections the seniors were making with the shop displays of candy and soda. Mentions of Grape Nehi and Orange Crush were made, as were those about candy buttons and saltwater taffy. Neil corralled the group into the soda fountain section of the store, beginning the tour with a brief history of soda and its transition from medicine to tasty drink and from pharmacy to diner. He pointed out that Blue Sun deliberately reinforces that soda is a joyful product, "It is how we like to think of it—our store is full of nostalgia and bright colors." Neil stressed that how we enjoy soda today has changed dramatically over history, with older brands tasting less sweet and more medicinal, not only because of the ingredients but also due to higher levels of carbonation. Plastic bottles are more porous than their glass equivalents and therefore, large manufacturers have increased the level of carbonization in the drink. This has had a lasting impact on the expectations of consumers and when they taste a product like Whistler, it does not have the same fizz and bubble, due to limits of the original machinery.

We were next encouraged to enter into the bottling area, where we met the vintage 1952 Crown Cork and Seal Dixie Bottler, which itself was an embodiment of nostalgia with its classic turquoise color and rounded corners. Neil fondly referred to the machine as a "diva," as it has a personality of its own and occasionally "eats bottles" when temperamental. Working on one bottle at a time, the Dixie Bottler can produce approximately 3,000 bottles per day, in comparison to the industry giants whose machines can bottle roughly the same amount in 1 minute. To rein in some of the machine's nastier habits, the mastermind of the operation, Tyler, has fabricated guides and safety mechanisms that were never part of its original design and keep the bottles from exploding. Displayed on the wall, pictures of beaches covered with plastic bottles remind staff and visitors that machines like this are doing their part to reduce pollution and environmental harm. Each Whistler bottle can be used around 300 times, through the washing and sanitizing that occurs at the beginning of the bottling line. Beyond waste, glass bottles provide more shelf life to the product, which can last two years with minimal effects on taste or carbonation.

Neil pointed out that at its core, soda only has a handful of ingredients. Sugar, carbonated water, food coloring, flavoring, and preservatives are all that it takes to create the product, yet the balance between flavors and hitting optimal fizz takes years to master. In recent years, Tyler experimented with the formula by creating diet versions or adding caffeine to the drinks, but ultimately could not get the "diva" machine to cooperate and produce a consistent batch. Through trial and error, the team has learned a few lessons about what people enjoy about their sodas. First, local ingredients matter. Everything from the labels to the extracts are sourced from the region, which helps differentiate a craft soda line from the global giants. Knowing that Tyler has crafted each flavor using local ingredients and individually flips each bottle as it comes off the line to prevent separation is part of the consumer experience. Second, the team has learned to offer unique combinations that are playful and delicious. The Blue Sun family is eleven brands strong, each playing on a combination of nostalgia and different taste palettes. Beyond Whistler, brands like Wacky Wizard Brews, State Fair Soda, and Serenity Sodas target different consumer segments.

The experimentation needed to build out these lines resulted in a third lesson, specifically to retire products that do not transition from curiosity into return purchases. For example, Tyler once created a spaghetti flavored soda with highlights of tomato, basil, and garlic. Although interesting to try, customers never transitioned to buying a second bottle and the team shelved the product, alongside a soda based on cheese curds from the State Fair line. Others like Chocolate Chip Cookies and Rocket Bomb Pop made the cut, the latter propelled by its neon blue coloring, which for some reason universally drives higher sales in comparison to other colors. During the tasting session of the tour, Neil emphasized that Blue Sun keeps to the "friendly flavors" and is not tempted to create disgusting flavors that might be bought for novelty, but will never become a personal favorite.

After touring the bottling line, the group returned to the soda fountain to taste four very different sodas. Incredibly, Neil expertly poured tasters for the entire group using only a single bottle of each type of soda. The small cups encouraged us to "sip rather than slam" the soda, to take in the balance of flavors. The first was Root Beer and Vanilla Bean from the Serenity line, which attempts to perfectly balance two complementary flavors. Neil pointed out that among the different categories of soda, root beer has the broadest variation in flavor across dimensions like creaminess and bite. This particular version was a hit among the seniors, with many stating that it reminded them of having a float with a friend. Next up was the Rocket Bomb Pop, which didn't fare as well. Although it tasted exactly like its namesake, the experience reminded me of what happens when you leave your popsicle out for too long on a hot summer day and are left drinking the syrup from the bottom of the wrapper. We finished the tasting with Pineapple Orange and then Strawberry Daiquiri, the latter likewise brought up nostalgic comments among the seniors, but more about its alcoholic cousin.

What was evident to me throughout the tasting was the role that expectation plays into each person's enjoyment of the sodas. As Neil asked the group when talking about sipping instead of slamming, "What do people expect when tasting soda? What should it look and smell like? How much carbonization should it have and what taste should it leave on your tongue?" The expectation of what a grape soda should be is informed by our previous experience and memories, making up the nostalgia we have for our favorite brands. From there, it is up to the soda creators to create a balanced and consistent product that can help deliver on those expectations and if lucky, create a completely new flavor that can be the basis for new memories. I'm not sure that I will ever be nostalgic about pickle or kettle corn, but a flavor like pineapple orange has potential for me if shared with close friends or at a memorable event.

How does soda compare to other sweet things on its potential to improve mood across the spectrum of physical, cognitive, and emotive characteristics? Research by Charles Spence, Arume Corujo, and Josef Youssef would suggest that the top prize should go instead to cotton candy (also known as candy floss or fairy floss depending on the country) if the decision rests entirely on nostalgia.[31] Although earlier ways of making cotton candy date back to the 15th century, the modern version debuted in 1897 with the invention of a mechanical spinner that rotates approximately 3,450 times per minute, while heating sugar to 149 degrees. Creating the sugar version of glass, the treat is said to powerfully elicit memories of childhood and fun fairs to such an extent that it has limited its broader appeal. In the authors' words, "It is, in fact, rare to find a food that has such strong positive associations across cultures and one that is so closely associated with childhood." Another limitation noted by the researchers is cotton candy's strong association with sweetness. Its texture and shape convey so much about sweetness that any expectation about added flavor (for example, purple color means grape) becomes an afterthought for the consumer.

[31] Spence, C., Corujo, A., and Youssef, J. (2019). Cotton candy: A gastrophysical investigation. International Journal of Gastronomy and Food Science, 16, 100146.

If we are instead looking for depth in the taste experience, then there is no better indulgent food than chocolate. Meier, Noll, and Molokwu report that chocolate provides a perfect combination of cues to increase its desirability, with "its good taste, the pleasant physiological effects of the ingredients, the association with childhood experiences, and its consumption in pleasurable situations."[32] Parker, Parker, and Brotchie point out that chocolate's uniqueness as a source of craving is hard to replicate, with its combination of fat, sweet, salt, smell, and texture.[33] Compared with candy or soda that are consumed primarily for mood repair and result from carbohydrate craving, chocolate craving is driven by a more complex version of pleasure seeking involving dopamine centers of the brain. In their words, "When craving chocolate specifically, only chocolate will satisfy that craving." When linked to nostalgia, chocolate is transformed into the ultimate comfort food, reminding of good times with family and friends and rekindling the associated feelings of safety, security, and intimacy.[34]

Chris Huset, owner of Legacy Chocolates, couldn't agree more with these sentiments. He works to deliver on the company promise to "have everyone know about and fall in love with the earth's most perfect food—REAL chocolate."[35] I met up with Chris just after the morning coffee rush at his storefront, which recently celebrated its 20th anniversary. Chris is not the original owner of Legacy Chocolates, but rather bought the business three years ago and with it, an opportunity to transform his life. Like Scott from Chapter 6, Chris is an entrepreneur at heart and is unfazed by the hustle and risk that goes along with running a small business. His strong work ethic developed from the many long and hot days working as a laborer for a landscaping company. It was through this first work experience, under the supervision a great leader, that Chris gained an appreciation for how work culture fosters great customer service, a lesson that he brings to life at his chocolate shop. Chris continued his education and attained a degree in finance and entrepreneurial management, which in turn led to a stable job with a premier accounting firm. Although professionally successful, Chris was increasingly restless in his job and the consulting lifestyle. He missed being on his feet and seeing the tangible outcomes of his work.

[32] Meier, B., Noll, S., and Molokwu, O. (2017). The sweet life: The effect of mindful chocolate consumption on mood. Appetite, 108, 21–27.
[33] Parker, G., Parker, I., and Brotchie, H. (2006). Mood state effects of chocolate. Journal of Affective Disorders, 92, 149–159.
[34] Wang, X., Tat Keh, H., and Chao, C. (2018). Nostalgia and consumer preference for indulgent foods: The role of social connectedness. International Journal of Consumer Studies, 42, 316–326.
[35] Legacy Chocolates. Website. https://legacychocolates.com (accessed May 2, 2023).

Chris's relationship to chocolate is strangely related to soda. As a kid in Oregon, Chris would collect aluminum cans for recycling, pocketing the money to buy a bar of chocolate as his reward. Chris rekindled his love for chocolate later in life by indulging himself with a portion of dark chocolate as a capstone to a good dinner, which eventually turned into a proper craving. The next step along his chocolate journey occurred in 2009, when he was working in London and met a chief chocolatier on a mission to convert the UK palate away from fat and sugar to "seeing chocolate as a food that could be nutritious," a lesson that Chris carries forward today with Legacy Chocolates. Using London as his base, Chris packed his bags and traveled the continent on weekends, making sure to stop into chocolate cafes, soak in their atmospheres, and indulge his cravings for dark chocolate. Like a couple of the other fanatics profiled in this book, Chris loves the outdoors and therefore was pulled toward the Swiss Alps, which coincidentally is the center of the universe for fine chocolate.

Chris came back stateside and moved a few blocks away from his future shop, where he soon became a regular. "I met the owners and after a few years, learned that they were looking to sell the business. One thing led to another and I ended up buying them out," which was the best career decision Chris ever made. Although the days can be long and stressful, he gains a type of pleasure from the job that was missing when he was working as a consultant. Every day, the results of his work are tangible; not only is he selling a great product but he feels that he is building a community. The business sits alongside a florist and wedding shop in a historic apartment building of roughly 250 units, and the business owners keep close, finding ways to mutually support each other. His regulars stop down from their apartments above for a cup of Joe and to share in the daily news. Chris tells the story of one customer who routinely takes part in "Laid Back Fridays" by wearing a t-shirt just like the shop employees. Such connections take effort and Chris reminds his staff that "no matter how long the line is, if you are handing a customer something, make sure they know you care. It is all about how you make them feel." This sentiment extends to the type of culture Chris strives to create for his team, where one of his best moments in the shop was listening to the "heavy and genuine laughing" heard up front. At that moment, he knew he succeeded in creating a vibrant community both inside and outside the shop.

In our interview together, Chris is quick to talk about the health benefits of chocolate and his mission to help people return to real and nutritious food. He insists that "chocolate is a food, rather than candy. Real cocoa has natural minerals, like iron and magnesium, and vitamins that your body needs. It is also packed with antioxidants." On his chocolate blog, Chris lists out the various medical benefits that real chocolate has on health, from acting to prevent serious illness like stroke, to reducing bad cholesterol and lowering blood pressure.[36] The benefits extend to the brain in how it makes you think and feel. Dark chocolate is reported to boost the production of endorphins and serotonin, which marries up to the research discussed earlier in this chapter about how sweet things can improve mood and bust through mental funks. Yet all this depends on consuming real chocolate, which is different from what many of us experience on a typical day. Chris refers to it as "supermarket chocolate," characterized by sugar substitutes, partially hydrogenated oils, and artificial colors and flavorings.[37] He is on a mission to "change people's eating habits from fast chocolate to real chocolate, made with the best ingredients available." Better still, he is looking for ways for source ingredients directly from farmers, going beyond fair trade.

Chris let his love for chocolate transform his professional life, and he hasn't looked back since. His fanaticism for chocolate is not really about the consumption of chocolate, although he continues to enjoy his daily portion of dark chocolate. Rather, chocolate provided him with independence and a means to make a tangible impact on the happiness of customers and the community around him. Chris's fanaticism intersects with his love for the outdoors and wellness, making his relationship to chocolate stickier. Like Scott from Chapter 6, Chris's personality is well suited for being an entrepreneur, with a combination of openness to new experience, resilience, decisiveness, and a low fear of failure, allowing him to take risks and remain committed to the long-term. Like Mark at Blue Sun, Chris's fanaticism is based on building a business that brings happiness to his customers and in the process, he is mastering the craft of chocolate making. He takes joy in his work, as a form of hedonic motivation, but also finds meaning through the impact he has on his employees and community. Toward the end of the interview, I noticed a picture of Chris's children at the shop, sitting on the countertop. When I asked about the picture, it was easy to see the pride and happiness Chris had for creating a place for his family to enjoy too, potentially giving the name "legacy" a new meaning if either of them developed a similar fanaticism for chocolate.

As a means to either maintain or repair a positive mood, individuals often turn to chocolate or other self-gifts for an immediate emotional boost. Their own specific type of fanaticism can play into the choice of self-gift, whether focused on cosmetics, clothes, or indulgent foods, but the latter works particularly well as a result of the physical effects sweet and fatty foods have on

---

[36] Is Chocolate Good for You?, Legacy Chocolates Blog, March 7, 2023.
[37] What Makes "Real" Chocolate Better, Legacy Chocolates Blog, April 7, 2022.

our bodies. Self-gifts can either be deliberate, like a taking a trip to Blue Sun to buy a Grape Nehi, or stopping by Legacy Chocolates for a truffle, or driven by impulse, such as buying candy at the register in a supermarket, with similar effects on mood. Some of the personality differences that we have seen in other chapters appear to play a role in an individual's tendency to buy self-gifts, such as sensation-seeking when discussed in relation to extreme sports. Other traits, like a lack of self-control, have not been encountered in this book before, but play a role in whether individuals give in to temptation.

When repeated, indulgent treats can become an anchor for mood maintenance, which is not necessarily a bad thing. Rather, such behavior can demonstrate that individuals have strong self-awareness of their moods and are taking action to move in a new direction. Eating a bit of chocolate or drinking a soda on a daily basis is the norm, but can tip into overindulgence when individuals struggle with self-control and experience high levels of anxiety. No longer are self-gifts a beneficial means to regain homeostasis, but rather are contributing to wider swings in mood that are further amplified by feelings of guilt about overeating. If self-gifts become part of the problem, other techniques to improve happiness are needed, such as visualization or acceptance and commitment therapy.

There are many roads to happiness. Some of these roads are taken with the companionship of a coach to forge an unbeaten path, while other roads take us back in time to simpler days. Nostalgia plays a critical role in the enjoyment of indulgent treats and is often the basis for the fanaticism shown toward them. We hold expectations about what the treat should smell, taste, and look like, anticipating the power of the treat to bring us back to long-lost relationships or experiences. When combined with a shared experience and identity, like the seniors on the soda bottling tour, nostalgia for an indulgent food or drink makes happiness attainable. Establishments like Blue Sun and Legacy Chocolates are built on selling happiness, offering long-forgotten flavors for rediscovery or a chance to build memories around a new favorite. For Mark and Neil at Blue Sun, their fanaticism is less about soda and more about the reactions they get from their customers. No longer a professional circus clown, Neil takes obvious delight in his animated performances during tours, while Mark takes pride that he pulled off that "soda shop thing," which continues to bring smiles to the faces of his customers as they wander the isles of endless varieties of root beer and cola. Chris at Legacy Chocolates aspires to remind customers about the difference between fast and real chocolate, as well as to provide the opportunity for indulging in cafe culture. Whether consumed or procured for others, there are many ways to be a fanatic about happiness.

9
Action

Revel in Fanaticism

Across the eight chapters in this book, we've met some amazing people. From Ben the ultramarathon runner to Barbara the roller coaster enthusiast and everyone in between, each one of the fanatics I interviewed discovered something they were passionate about and made it part of who they are. Instead of being hung up on the negative connotations of what fanaticism could mean, involving either extreme views[1] or strangeness,[2] I prefer to look at the psychological benefits that fanaticism offers to both the individual and the community around them. In writing this book, I have gained an appreciation for a nearly unlimited range of foods, hobbies, sports, professions, social causes, and other potential areas of focus that could be the stem for a fanaticism, even if the specific topic slides under conscious recognition. Fanaticism provides a sense of purpose, shapes our identity, and directs our behavior. When shared with others, it provides an opportunity for connection and can be the basis for deeper and more intimate relationships, even if the other person is not drawn to the same area of fanaticism.

At its very core, this book is about action and why an individual is drawn toward a particular experience, product, or social cause. Using applied psychology as a guide,[3] we explored motivations across the social, physical, cognitive, and emotive domains both through the available psychological research and in conversation with real-world fanatics. Individuals in each of the areas of fanaticism gravitated toward a predominant driver (for example, fanatics of science fiction conventions were motivated most by the social domain, while thrill-seekers gravitated toward the emotive), but were not constrained to any one domain. Without fail, each of the types of fanaticism discussed played on

---

[1] Merriam-Webster. Fanatic definition. https://www.merriam-webster.com/dictionary/fanatic (accessed April 19, 2023).
[2] Cambridge Dictionary. Fanatic definition. https://dictionary.cambridge.org/dictionary/english/fanatic (accessed April 19, 2023).
[3] Edgerton, N., and Palmer, S. (2005). SPACE: A psychological model for use within cognitive behavioural coaching, therapy and stress management. Coaching Psychologist, 2, 25–31; Weiss, R., Edgerton, N., and Palmer, S. (2017). The SPACE coaching model: An integrative tool for coach therapists. Coaching Today, October, 12–17.

Fanatic. Joe Ungemah, Oxford University Press. © Oxford University Press 2024. DOI: 10.1093/9780197783894.003.0010

a diverse range of drivers that combined to make that pursuit much stickier for the individuals profiled. Moreover, the stories captured demonstrated that these drivers could overlap, for example, with many of the fanatics sharing a love for the outdoors. They can also be useful for either embellishing a positive or alleviating a negative. Carly and Michael, whom we met in Chapter 2, did not choose to be a fanatic around their given social causes, but felt compelled to turn hardship into something better. Such stories were intentionally paired with fanatics who are looking to the future (not the past) for their inspiration, notably Scott introducing the world to the Skyride and Chris bringing real chocolate to the masses.

Each of the individuals I met were relatively easy to spot as fanatics, and only a few opening questions sparked a rich discussion on their area of interest. Luckily, a number of social scientists have provided more grounded guidance on how best to distinguish a true fanatic from a "tourist," as described by our skydiver, Kate. The research team of Ahuvia, Batra, and Bagozzi suggest that love transcends personal relationships and applies to a broad range of contexts that involve the consumption of products, ideas, brands, nature, pets, activities, and more.[4] Reporting that more than 70% of people love at least one thing other than a person, the researchers point out that the love of things is a common feature of the human condition. When an object is loved, it becomes part of your self-identity, as described by one of their study's participants, "When you're talking about what you love . . . you are essentially talking about yourself." Getting to the optimal level of integration is said to be dependent on whether the object can be incorporated cognitively and physically (either literally or metaphorically) with a person's self-concept. In addition, integration is aided by whether the object carries social meaning and allows for self-expression. This last feature is noteworthy, as areas of fanaticism that involve creativity, like Kris's costume-making, already carry significance for individuals and therefore, will contribute to their overall level of fanaticism.

Follow-up research by the same researchers, specifically on the consumer experience, unearthed a set of core features that can objectively determine whether someone is in love.[5] The first group was characterized by the passion exhibited in either attaining or experiencing the object, including their desire to use the object, willingness to invest resources, and past involvement with the object. A second group concerned the level of self-brand integration, including the current and desired self-identity, perceptions of life meaning, and

[4] Ahuvia, A., Batra, R., and Bagozzi, R. (2009). Love, desire, and identity: A conditional integration of the love of things in D. MacInnis, C. Park, and J. Priester (eds.), The Handbook of Brand Relationships (342–357). New York: M E Sharpe.

[5] Batra, R., Ahuvia, A., and Bagozzi, R. (2012). Brand love. Journal of Marketing, 76, 1–16.

frequency of thoughts about the object. The last group involved the positive emotional connections held with the object and the intuitive fit the object had for the self, the person's emotional attachment with the object, and whether it created a positive affect (e.g., feelings of contentment, fun, or excitement). Beyond these elements, the length of relationship with the object, anticipated stress if the object is taken away, and certainty that the feelings of love are real, all played a direct role in determining the strength of brand love.

Alternatively, Vallerand and his colleagues place similar emphasis on the internalization of a love object into self-identify, but diverge on the implications. In their dualistic model of passion, the researchers make the distinction between harmonious and obsessive forms of passion.[6] Harmonious passion can help make a life worth living, whereby internalization of an activity happens autonomously, with individuals feeling good about their choice and willingly investing energy toward it. The activity becomes part of their self-identity and they are free to experience feelings of flow, satisfaction, and accomplishment that come by pursuing it. Over time, they take on labels, like "guitar player," "furry," or "runner," that indicate that the activity has become part of their identity. Although the same could be said for the obsessive form of passion, the difference lies in how forced and controlled the internalization is for the individual. With obsessive passion, feelings of low self-esteem, overexcitement, or anxiety about social acceptance overwhelm the individual and take control of their behavior. The individual has no choice but to engage in the activity, very much like the hoarders encountered by Suzanne or an ultramarathon runner who continues to run with a leg injury. Vallerand points out that obsessive passions build and eventually consume a disproportional amount of a person's identity, in turn creating conflict with personal commitments and taking a toll on personal well-being.[7]

A bottom-up, research-driven model for identifying fanatics is proposed by Plante and colleagues, who meticulously reviewed the psychological literature on a wide range of fans.[8] Their review unearthed a total of 28 separate constructs that all had the potential to affect fan behavior, regardless of activity or interest area, that when empirically tested consolidated into a 4-factor, 18-subscale solution. The resulting CAPE model identified fans on the basis of their Commitment (e.g., investing time and money in following their activity,

[6] Vallerand, R., et al. (2003). Les passions de l'ame: On obsessive and harmonious passion. Journal of Personality and Social Psychology, 85, 756–767.
[7] Vallerand, R. (2012). The role of passion in sustainable psychological well-being. Psychology of Well-Being: Theory, Research, and Practice, 2, 3–21.
[8] Plante, C., et al. (2021). CAPE: A Multidimensional Model of Fan Interest. Commerce, TX: CAPE Model Research Team.

seeing themselves as part of the fan community, and self-reporting high commitment, participation, and loyalty to their interest) and their stating that they gained Assets (e.g., a boost in self-esteem, financial benefits, and feelings of accomplishment, even at the expense of taking part in other activities). Fans also hold feelings of Presence (e.g., experiencing something novel, a distraction from everyday problems, and something exciting) and enjoy the freedom of self-Expression (e.g., finding extra life meaning and experiencing personal growth, uniqueness, and opportunities to demonstrate creativity and appreciate art).

The research discussed helps identify the true fanatics around us. To answer why a person becomes a fanatic in the first place, I suggest a return to the motivations of the fanatics profiled in this book. While the following set of 20 drivers is not exhaustive, it collectively represents each of the social, physical, cognitive, and emotive domains and its parts are sufficiently repeated in various combinations to suggest a level of universality for driving an individual toward becoming a fanatic. For the social domain, the strongest and most consistent motivation was a sense of identity gained from being a fanatic. From Marj's identity as a Trekkie, proudly wearing her communicator badge, to Felix's creation of an unique online persona in *Final Fantasy 14*, all the fanatics took pride in their association with their pursuit and demonstrated great energy when we had the opportunity to discuss it. Beyond identity, other social motivations included a sense of camaraderie, support, and personal growth that result from sharing a pursuit in common with others. Camaraderie (i.e., fanship) provides feelings of belonging and voice, while support (i.e., fandom) involves a deeper level of community, where psychological needs are fulfilled and which sometimes compels fanatics to become better people. As a last motivator in the social domain, the concept of "communitas" was identified as a shorthand for language and behavior that develops within a community and aids in skill development. From bottle collecting to gaming and skydiving, communitas glues a community together, but can also work to isolate novices who are new to the community and their common pursuit.

I was reminded of the strong connection between mind and body when exploring fanaticisms that have a strong physical element. As Ben runs his ultramarathon or Kate completes a skydive, their brains are inundated with neurotransmitters like norepinephrine and epinephrine that help them focus on their goals and maintain the energy needed to complete their tasks. When they cross the finish line or open the canopy, a different set of chemicals is released, notably dopamine and endorphins, resulting in feelings of euphoria and relief that work as a reward for their hard work. Beyond these highly physical types of fanaticism, pursuits like gaming, thrill-seeking, or innovating play on the same reward centers and provide a motivational force to their participants. For example, feelings of relief occur both for a runner after surviving the Zombie Apocalypse and a coaster enthusiast that has just sped through Goliath's double inversion. As a last physical motivator, fanatics often wish to build up their physical or mental strength, which will help them dig deep when times get tough.

On a related note, fanatics might feel compelled to master new skills, as witnessed by collectors like Dave or costume designers like Kris. Complementing this cognitive motivation is discipline, where they thrive in the routine and predictability of their craft. Other cognitive motivations play on time, with fanatics striving for elements of the past in the form of nostalgia or alternatively, by aspiring toward a brighter future. Barbara's connection to roller coasters was rooted in memories from her childhood, similar to Dave's memory of his great aunt's collection of European coins. Carly's and Michael's fanaticism may originate from their past, but is future-focused with the goal of preventing others from experiencing trauma. Entrepreneurs like Scott, Mark, and Chris are fully dedicated to the future, aspiring to build products and companies that people will love. For some of the fanatics profiled, their pursuit allowed a momentary cognitive escape from reality and the ability to gain a new perspective on life, as seen with Felix and his use of virtual reality.

Complementing an aspiration for escape is the motivation for achieving a state of flow, described as a sense of timelessness and full absorption into the task at hand. Four other emotive motivations are characterized by how fanaticism makes a participant feel. Notably, hedonic feelings like satisfaction and pleasure were witnessed for every individual profiled in this book and appear to be a second type of fundamental driver for fanaticism, similar to identity. Other emotive outcomes included eudaimonic feelings (i.e., the attainment of personal meaning) and feelings of achievement when personal goals are met. The most curious motivation across the 20 discovered in this book was that of benign masochism, which was the feeling of intense relief at surviving something difficult or repulsive, as witnessed most by those taking part in extreme sports.

The 20 drivers described across the social, physical, cognitive, and emotive domains apply to a wide range of fanaticisms and take on unique combinations depending on the person. To illustrate how the 20 drivers combine to move an individual toward a passion area, I have borrowed from chemistry and suggest a periodic table of sorts (see Figure 9.1). Just like their atomic equivalents of alkali metals or noble gases, the drivers of fanaticism fall into families according to whether they pull on social, physical, cognitive, or emotive psychological properties. Also like their atomic counterparts, the drivers

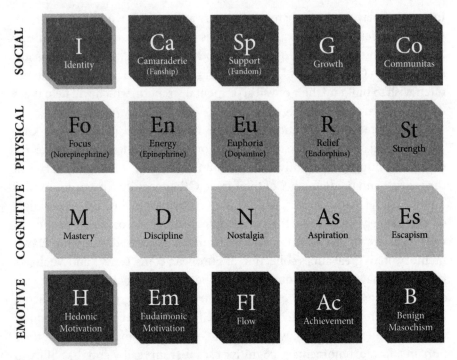

Figure 9.1 The Twenty Fanatic Drivers Across Four Psychological Domains

come together to form molecules that can describe a person's relationship with their specific area of fanaticism.

Among the people profiled in this book, Kate and Ben, the skydiver and ultra-marathoner, demonstrated the most complex molecules, capitalizing on the full range of physical and emotive motivations, as well as a splattering of other drivers. Additionally, Ben's relationship with running overlapped with a fanaticism of the outdoors, binding to form a new compound at the core of his self-concept. With no judgment on the strength of their specific forms of fanaticism, Marj and Barbara had molecules that were composed of relatively few drivers. An example comparison between Ben and Marj, in molecular format, demonstrates the uniqueness and potential complexity of how the drivers for fanaticism come together (see Figure 9.2).

As mentioned briefly, the two drivers of identity and hedonic motivation appeared for everyone profiled in the book and therefore, seem more universal for all fanatics, in line with the research lead by Ahuvia[9] and

[9] Ahuvia, A., Batra, R., and Bagozzi, R. (2009). Love, desire, and identity: A conditional integration of the love of things in D. MacInnis, C. Park, and J. Priester (eds.), The Handbook of Brand Relationships (342–357). New York: M E Sharpe.

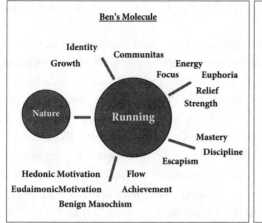
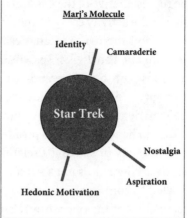

Figure 9.2 A Comparison Between Two Profiled Fanatics

Vallerand.[10] These two drivers have been highlighted in the model and to-gether indicate that a basic foundation for why someone becomes a fanatic is to gain pleasure and a sense of self from the activity. Not only do fanatics enjoy playing guitar or dressing-up as a furry but also the activity becomes integrated into their self-concept and thereby carries social significance. The remaining 18 drivers layer on top of identity and hedonic motivation, making the activity stronger and stickier.

There is subtlety in what I just described about the focal point for any type of fanaticism. While writing this book, I was surprised by the discovery of hidden motivations, whereby fanatics were drawn to their specific pursuit for tangential or indirect reasons. For example, I initially sought out Mark and Chris for their interest in indulgent food, but discovered through interview that the true basis for their fanaticism was not simply in consuming soda or chocolate, but rather was rooted in creating businesses that brought happi-ness to their customers. Similarly, collectors might be intrigued or have a per-sonal association with a specific type of object, but their fanaticism rests in the acquisition, curation, and display of precious items. Alternatively, attendees to science fiction conventions go beyond watching a sci-fi series and into interests like fan fiction or cosplay. Fanaticism is fundamentally about action; what someone does during or around the consumption of a product, service, or experience and the benefits they receive from that activity. The most iden-tifiable feature of a fanaticism, like a bite of chocolate or drink of soda, might

[10] Vallerand, R., et al. (2003). Les passions de l'âme: On obsessive and harmonious passion. Journal of Personality and Social Psychology, 85, 756–767.

be representative of the passion area, but is only the tip of the iceberg for what makes the activity captivating.

Beyond the drivers, fanaticism appears dependent on both context and personality. Fanaticism spawns at critical times in a person's life, when they are most apt to receive and relish the rewards of a new passion. For Mark, he happened to watch a video of Galco's Soda Pop Stop at the same time that he experienced a poor night out at the brew pub and had some extra office space on hand. For others profiled in this book, major life events like moving to a new city or starting a relationship were core components of their origin stories. Whether or not a person takes advantage of a new fanaticism appears related to common personality traits about whether they are first able to effectively spot the opportunity and then whether they are likely to stick with it. Individuals who are open to new experiences, sensation-seeking, have a low fear of failure and, more typically extroverted, are likely to take advantage of a catalyst experience that builds the footholds for a new fanaticism. Kate demonstrated these traits when first accepting the challenge to skydive with her new boyfriend. What kept her attached to the sport was a handful of other personality traits, specifically resilience, decisiveness, persistence, and a need for control. From Carly and Michael to Scott and Chris, the fanatics in this book show great resolve to continue with their fanaticism even when times get tough. In an effort to build out a more complete model (see Figure 9.3), the elements of context and individual differences are added to our periodic table of fanaticism.

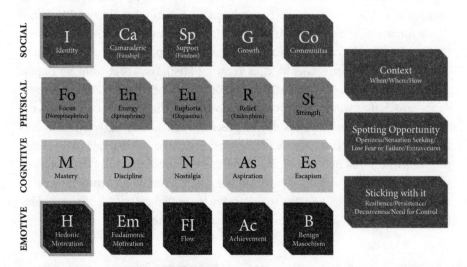

Figure 9.3 A Periodic Table of Fanaticism

For all the benefits that fanaticism may bring, there are limitations and risks to becoming a fanatic. Beyond the self-harm that results from obsessive forms of passion,[11] fanaticism can spill into interpersonal relationships. Connections with loved ones can be squeezed out, as time and energy are redirected to areas of personal interest. Examples from earlier in this book include the hooligans who thrive on intergroup rivalry and societal harm, as well as the hoarders who put the health and safety of their family at risk. To help unpack the line between a healthy version of fanaticism and maladaptive behavior, I interviewed an amazing group of applied psychologists who are committed to making us better versions of ourselves. Suzanne and Renae work with clients to alleviate tendencies toward hoarding and obsessive-compulsive disorder, whereas Zach is dedicated to helping clients through chemical and process addictions. Mark and Richard work closely with professional athletes to improve performance and share many commonalities with Helen, who helps others attain personal goals and reach higher levels of life satisfaction. These practitioners might use different techniques, like exposure and response prevention therapy, acceptance and commitment therapy, or cognitive-behavior therapy, but they all share in the common goal of raising the individual's awareness of problematic behavior, exploring why it has taken hold, and then finding tangible ways to live a better life.

I also encountered a second group of psychologists who use fanaticism in a much more direct and applied way, as means to build connections to their clients, create safe spaces, and provide opportunities to try out something new. Justine talks with her clients about their fanship as a way to externalize problems and explore potential causes on a deeper, more objective level. Anastasia uses fanship as a means to understand trauma and create an opportunity to rewrite the narrative or put painful memories to rest. In a similar vein, Stacy helps guide clients through trauma and grief, with the hope that some individuals can transcend into a state of posttraumatic growth. A more direct application of fanship, in the form of gaming, is performed by Jordan, where he encourages clients to try out a new identity and apply different tactics to resolve relationship issues.

Outside of the world of psychology, I encountered fanatics using technology for social good. Amir advocates for the use of virtual reality to allow participants to experience life from a different vantage point, as a means to build cultural understanding and empathy. Chuck uses 360-degree films to

---

[11] Vallerand, R. (2012). The role of passion in sustainable psychological well-being. Psychology of Well-Being: Theory, Research, and Practice, 2, 3–21.

bring nature and culture back to individuals who are unable to travel to them in person, while Thong focuses on the future, using technology to envision communal spaces that do not yet exist. The excitement and energy of these fanatics, like the others profiled in this book, are contagious and led me to seek out my own experiences to sample a little of their fanaticisms. Some of these experiences tapped already existing interests like running, science fiction, amusement parks, and gaming, while others, notably singing, were new to me and probably will never be repeated. Even if I fail to become a true fanatic of any of these pursuits, I gained an appreciation for the activity that I would not have had without the direct experience.

These personal experiences also allowed me to develop a deeper connection with the fanatics whom I profiled and to have a more robust discussion of the social, cognitive, physical, and emotive motivations behind their passions. This is one of the fundamental lessons I learned from writing this book. Knowing that fanaticism is core to an individual's self-concept and often shared with close friends, identifying and then asking questions about their passion will open a window to a person's core self. I gained a glimpse of their personality traits, motivations, and dreams that guided their behavior, and along the way, I built rapport and trust in the relationship. Yet this only occurred if I practiced appreciative inquiry, by demonstrating genuine interest in their topic even it fell outside of my personal interest, reminiscent of the definition of a fanatic as being "strange" to those who do not share in the same passion. Fanaticism is a two-way street, and being open about my own areas of fascination helped build bridges for others, however I recognized that there was a point of oversharing, like the book collector, quoted in Chapter 5, who routinely lost his audience when reciting all the genres he was interested in.

The fanatics discussed in this book do so much for society, from helping others by establishing or taking part in social causes to creating innovations that revolutionize how we live. On a more a basic level, they might bring a smile to our face with something indulgent or playful. Being a fanatic is not limited to a special group of people, but is within each one of us and is ready to be discovered and shared. I truly believe that we are all fanatic about something or at least have the potential to be. If you are struggling to identify what you are passionate about, take a minute to look back at the times that you were most happy. Helen's visioning techniques might help. For example, envision a time when you felt fulfilled. What were you doing, thinking, and feeling? Where were you, and who were you with? Such questions might tap a long-lost fanaticism with the potential to be rekindled. If nothing meaningful comes to mind, maybe it is time to find a new passion. Look for those catalyst moments, take time to spot opportunities, and when ready, open yourself up to new experiences. Once you find your passion area, embrace it and allow it to redefine who you are. Stick with it. Be prepared to share the joy that your passion brings, and above all, revel in being a fanatic.

Bibliography

Abuhamdeh, S., and Csikszentmihalyi, M. (2015). Enjoying the possibility of defeat: Outcome uncertainty, suspense, and intrinsic motivation. Motivation and Emotion, 39, 1–10.

Ahuvia, A. (2022). The Things We Love. New York: Hachette Book Group.

Ahuvia, A., Batra, R., and Bagozzi, R. (2009). Love, desire, and identity: A conditional integration of the love of things in D. MacInnis, C. Park, and J. Priester (eds.), The Handbook of Brand Relationships (342–357). New York: M E Sharpe.

Allen, B. (2010). Nice children stolen from car. Journal of Geriatric Care Management, 20, 25–27.

American Coaster Enthusiasts. Website. https://www.aceonline.org (accessed December 4, 2022).

Among Fandoms, Marvel May Reign Supreme, Poll Finds, Hollywood Reporter, July 17, 2019.

Amos, C., Holmes, G., and Keneson, W. (2013). A meta-analysis of consumer impulse buying. Journal of Retailing and Consumer Services, 21, 86–97.

Andrus, M. (1997). As Good as It Gets. TriStar Pictures.

Antique Auction Forum. The Current State of the Bottle Hobby. https://antiqueauctionforum.com/blog/guest-blogs/the-current-state-of-the-bottle-hobby (accessed July 9, 2022).

Arnett, J. (1994). Sensation seeking: A new scale and a new conceptualisation. Personality and Individual Differences, 16, 289–296.

As Industry Grows, Percentage of US Sports Fans Steady by Jeffrey Jones, Gallup, June 17, 2015.

Atalay, A., and Meloy, M. (2011). Retail therapy: A strategic effort to improve mood. Psychology and Marketing, 28, 638–660.

Atlas Obscura. Sir John Soane's Museum. https://www.atlasobscura.com/places/sir-john-soanes-museum (accessed September 21, 2021).

Babel, P. (2016). Memory of pain induced by physical exercise. Memory, 24, 548–559.

Back When Chicago Was Fun Town by Darnell Little, Chicago Tribune, June 17, 1997.

Baer, R., Smith, G., Hopkins, J., Krietemeyer, J., and Toney, L. (2006). Using self-report assessment methods to explore facets of mindfulness. Assessment, 13, 27–45.

Batra, R., Ahuvia, A., and Bagozzi, R. (2012). Brand love. Journal of Marketing, 76, 1–16.

Beaton, A., Funk, D., Ridinger, L., and Jordan, J. (2011). Sport involvement: A conceptual and empirical analysis. Sport Management Review, 14, 126–140.

Beck, K., Bilder, M., and McDonald, A. (2002). Collectors on Collecting. Rare book exhibition programs, Boston College of Law School.

Belmont Park. Website. https://www.belmontpark.com (accessed November 22, 2022).

Blading on Thin Ice, Newsweek, December 11, 1994.

Blue Sun Soda Shop. Website. https://www.bluesunsodashop.com (accessed February 4, 2023).

Boecker, H., Sprenger, T., Spilker, M., Henriksen, G., Koppenhoefer, M., Wagner, K., Valet, M., Berthele, A., and Tolle, T. (2008). The runner's high: Opioidergic mechanisms in the human brain. Cerebral Cortex, 18, 2523–2531.

Boldak, A., and Guszkowska, M. (2016). Sensation seeking as one of the motivating factors for performing skydiving. Polish Journal of Sport Tourism, 23, 94–98.

Bonanno, G., Wortman, C., and Nesse, R. (2004). Prospective patterns of resilience and maladjustment during widowhood. Psychology and Aging, 19, 260–271.

Boss, P. (2010). The trauma and complicated grief of ambiguous loss. Pastoral Psychology, 59, 137–145.

Boss, P., and Yeats, J. (2014). Ambiguous loss: A complicated type of grief when loved ones disappear. Cruse Bereavement Care, 33, 63–70.

Bottle Store. The Bottle Blog. https://blog.bottlestore.com (accessed July 9, 2022).

Brown, R. (1990). The construct and concurrent validity of the social dimension of the Brown Locus of Control Scale. Educational and Psychological Measurement, 50, 377–382.

Buck, K., Spittler, J., Reed, A., and Khodaee, M. (2018). Psychological attributes of ultramarathoners. Wilderness and Environmental Medicine, 29, 66–71.

Buckley, R.C. (2018). To analyze thrill, define extreme sports. Frontiers of Psychology, 9, 1216. https://doi.org/10.3389/fpsyg.2018.01216 published under the Creative Commons Attribution License (CC BY), https://creativecommons.org/licenses/by/4.0/.

Bulach, C. (1993). A measure of openness and trust. People and Education, 1, 382–392.

Burton, T., and McDowell, M. (1993). The Nightmare Before Christmas. Touchstone Pictures.

Button, S., Mathieu, J., and Zajac, D. (1996). Goal orientation in organizational research: A conceptual and empirical foundation. Organizational Behavior and Human Decision Processes, 67, 26–48.

Cacciotti, G., Hayton, J., Mitchell, J., and Giazitzoglu, A. (2016). A reconceptualization of fear of failure in entrepreneurship. Journal of Business Venturing, 31, 302–325.

Cambridge Dictionary. Fanatic definition. https://dictionary.cambridge.org/dictionary/english/fanatic (accessed April 19, 2023).

Cardaciotto, L., Herbert, J., Forman, E., Moitra, E., and Farrow, V. (2008). The assessment of present-moment awareness and acceptance: The Philadelphia Mindfulness Scale. Assessment, 15, 204–223.

CareerTrackers. Website. https://www.CareerTrackers.org.au (accessed November 28, 2021).

Carnival. Website. https://www.carnival.com/onboard/skyride (accessed May 22, 2023).

Caves, S. (1990). Hollow Pursuits, episode of Star Trek: The Next Generation. Paramount Domestic Television.

Cedar Fair Parks Take Top Honors in Annual Poll, Cedar Fair Press Release, September 8, 2013.

Celsi, R. (1992). Transcendent benefits of high-risk sports in J. Sherry and B. Sternthal (eds.), Advances in Consumer Research (volume 19, 636–641). Provo, UT: Association for Consumer Research.

Celsi, R., Rose, R., and Leigh, T. (1993). An exploration of high-risk leisure consumption through skydiving. Journal of Consumer Research, 20, 1–23.

Chadborn, D., Edwards, P., and Reysen, S. (2017). Displaying fan identity to make friends. Intensities: The Journal of Cult Media, 9, 87–97.

Cherrier, H., and Ponnor, T. (2010). A study of hoarding behavior and attachment to material possessions. Qualitative Market Research, 13, 8–23.

Cho, H., Pyun, D., and Wang, C. (2019). Leisure nostalgia: Scale development and validation. Journal of Leisure Research, 50, 330–349.

Cline, E. (2011). Ready Player One. New York: Random House.

Coles, M., Frost, R., Heimberg, R., and Rheaume, J. (2002). "Not just right experiences": Perfectionism, obsessive-compulsive features and general psychopathology. Behaviour Research and Therapy, 41, 681–700.

Collett, J. (2019). Unpacking hoarding disorder. InPsych, 41, 5, 1–14.

Collins Dictionary. Fanatic definition. https://www.collinsdictionary.com/us/dictionary/english/fanatic (accessed April 19, 2023).

Conroy, D., Kaye, M., and Fifer, A. (2007). Cognitive links between fear of failure and perfectionism. Journal of Rational-Emotive and Cognitive-Behavior Therapy, 25, 237–253.

Conroy, D., Willow, J., and Metzler, J. (2002). Multidimensional fear of failure measurement: The Performance Failure Appraisal Inventory. Journal of Applied Sport Psychology, 14, 76–90.

Constantin, T., Holman, A., and Hojbotă, A. (2011). Development and validation of a motivational persistence scale. Psihologija, 45, 99–120.

Costrel, F. (2020). High Score, Netflix documentary mini-series. Great Big Story.

Cross, S., Leizerovici, G., and Pirouz, D. (2018). Hoarding: Understanding divergent acquisition, consumption, and disposal. Journal of the Association for Consumer Research, 3, 81–96.

Csikszentmihalyi, M. (1975). Beyond Boredom and Anxiety. San Francisco: Jossey-Bass Publishers.

Csikszentmihalyi, M., and Csikszentmihalyi, I. (1988). Optimal Experience. Cambridge: Cambridge University Press.

Curl, J., and Wilson, S. (2015). The Oxford Dictionary of Architecture. Oxford: Oxford University Press.

DeWine, S. (1987). Evaluation of organizational communication competency: The development of the Communication Training Impact Questionnaire. Journal of Applied Communication Research, 15, 113–127.

Dickman, S. (1990). Functional and dysfunctional impulsivity: Personality and cognitive correlates. Journal of Personality and Social Psychology, 58, 95–102.

Dingemans, A., Martijn, C., van Furth, E., and Jansen, A. (2009). Expectations, mood, and eating behavior in binge eating disorder: Beware of the bright side. Appetite, 53, 166–173.

Disneyland's Record-Breaking Regular Shares His Wisdom from Nearly 3,000 Park Visits in a Row by A.J. Willingham, CNN, April 10, 2023.

Doosje, B., Ellemers, N., and Spears, R. (1995). Perceived intragroup variability as a function of group status and identification. Journal of Experimental Social Psychology, 31, 410–436.

Douglas, R., Alvis, L., Rooney, E., and Busby, D. (2021). Racial, ethnic, and neighborhood income disparities in childhood posttraumatic stress and grief: Exploring indirect effects through trauma exposure and bereavement. Journal of Trauma Stress, 34, 1–14.

Duckworth, A., and Quinn, P. (2009). Development and validation of the Short Grit Scale (GritS). Journal of Personality Assessment, 91, 166–174.

Dumitru, D., Dumitru, T., and Maher, A. (2018). A systematic review of exercise addiction: Examining gender differences. Journal of Physical Education and Sport, 18, 1738–1747.

Dunning, E. (2000). Towards a sociological understanding of football hooliganism as a world phenomenon. European Journal on Criminal Policy and Research, 8, 141–162.

Duyff, R., Birch, L., Byrd-Bredbenner, C., Johnson, S., Mattes, R., Murphy, M., Nicklas, T., Rollins, B., and Wansink, B. (2015). Candy consumption patterns, effects on health, and behavioral strategies to promote moderation: Summary report on a round table discussion. Advanced Nutrition, 6, 139–146.

Edgerton, N., and Palmer, S. (2005). SPACE: A psychological model for use within cognitive behavioural coaching, therapy and stress management. Coaching Psychologist, 2, 25–31.

Edmondson, A. (1999). Psychological safety and learning behavior in work teams. Administrative Science Quarterly, 44, 350–383.

Elliot, A., and Harackiewitz, J. (1996). Approach and avoidance achievement goals and intrinsic motivation: A meditational analysis. Journal of Personality and Social Psychology, 70, 968–980.

Ersche, K., Lim, T., Ward, L., and Robbins, T. (2017). Creature of habit: A self-report measure of habitual routines and automatic tendencies in everyday life. Personality and Individual Differences, 116, 73–85.

Fan Favorite: The Global Popularity of Football Is Rising, Nielsen, June 2018.

501st Legion. Website. https://www.501st.com (accessed May 18, 2023).

Fordyce, M. (1988). A review of research on The Happiness Measures: A sixty second index of happiness and mental health. Social Indicators Research, 20, 355–381.

For Riot-Damaged Twin Cities Businesses, Rebuilding Begins with Donations, Pressure on Government by Jeffrey Meitrodt, Star Tribune, June 14, 2020.

Foschi, A., and Ortolani, F. (2007). Is it more thrilling to ride at the front or back of a roller coaster? Physics Teacher, 45, 536–541.

Freimuth, M., Moniz, S., and Kim, S. (2011). Clarifying exercise addiction: Differential diagnosis, co-occurring disorders, and phases of addiction. International Journal of Environmental Research and Public Health, 8, 4069–4081.

Freud, W., Faust, S., Birklein, F., Gaser, C., Wunderlich, A., Muller, M., Billich, C., Juchems, M., Schmitz, B., Gron, G., and Schutz, U. (2012). Substantial and reversible brain gray matter reduction but no acute brain lesions in ultramarathon runners: Experience from the TransEurope-FootRace project. BMC Medicine, 10, 170.

Freud, W., Faust, S., Gaser, C., Gron, G., Birklein, F., Wunderlich, A., Muller, M., Billich, C., and Schutz, U. (2014). Regionally accentuated reversible brain grey matter reduction in ultramarathon runners detected by vowel-based morphometry. BMC Sports Science, Medicine and Rehabilitation, 6, 4.

Fullerton, C., Lane, A., Nevill, A., and Devonport, T. (2018). Does the brief self-control scale assess relatively stable individual differences in self-control among endurance athletes? Journal of Sport Behavior, 41, 27–39.

Funk, D., Ridinger, L., and Moorman, A. (2004). Exploring origins of involvement: Understanding the relationship between consumer motives and involvement with professional sport teams. Leisure Sciences, 26, 35–61.

Fuss, J., Steinle, J., Bindila, L., Auer, M., Kirchherr, H., Lutz, B., and Gass, P. (2015). A runner's high depends on cannabinoid receptors in mice. PNAS, 112, 13105–13108.

GalaxyCon Minneapolis Program, November 8, 2019.

The Game that Took Jack's Life: Boy's "Hypoxic Blackout" Death by Angela Thompson, Sydney Morning Herald, February 15, 2013.

Gardner, M., Wansink, B., Kim, J., and Park, S. (2014). Better moods for better eating? How mood influences food choice. Journal of Consumer Psychology, 24, 320–335.

George, L., Schkade, J., and Ishee, J. (2004). Content validity of the relative mastery measurement scale: A measure of occupational adaptation. Occupational Therapy Journal of Research, 24, 92–102.

Giasullo, Gia, and Freeman, Peter. (2014). The Soda Fountain. Berkeley: Ten Speed Press.

Gibson, W. (1984). Neuromancer. New York: The Berkeley Publishing Group.

Gillies, J., and Niemeyer, R. (2006). Loss, grief, and the search for significance: Toward a model of meaning reconstruction in bereavement. Journal of Constructivist Psychology, 19, 31–65.

Gineikiene, J. (2013). Consumer nostalgia literature review and an alternative measurement perspective. Organizations and Markets in Emerging Economies, 4, 112–149.

Gomez, A., Brooks, M., Buhrmester, M., Vazquez, A., Jetten, J., and Swann, W. (2011). On the nature of identity fusion: Insights into the construct and a new measure. Journal of Personality and Social Psychology, 100, 918–933.

Gordon, S., Yuzna, B., and Naha, E. (1989). Honey, I Shrunk the Kids. Walt Disney Pictures.

Goulet-Pelletier, J., Gaudreau, P., and Cousineau, D. (2021). Is perfectionism a killer of creative thinking? A test of the model of excellencism and perfectionism. British Journal of Psychology, 113, 176–207.

The Great 1980s Dungeons & Dragons Panic by Peter Allison, BBC Magazine, April 11, 2014.

Hartl, E., and Berger, B. (2017). Escaping reality: Examining the role of presence and escapism in user adoption of virtual reality glasses. Conference: European Conference of Information Systems. Proceedings of the Association of Information Systems 2017.

Hausenblas, H., and Downs, D. (2002). Exercise dependence: A systematic review. Psychology of Sport Exercise, 3, 89–123.

Heavy Drinking Among US Adults, NCHS Data Brief No. 374, CDC, August 2020.

Hepper, E., Ritchie, T., Sedikides, C., and Wildschut, T. (2012). Odyssey's end: Lay conceptions of nostalgia reflect its original Homeric meaning. Emotion, 12, 102–119.

Hermans, H. (1970). A questionnaire measure of achievement motivation. Journal of Applied Psychology, 54, 353–363.

Hess, J., Kacen, J., and Kim, J. (2006). Mood-management dynamics: The interrelationship between moods and behaviours. British Journal of Mathematical and Statistical Psychology, 59, 347–378.

Hetland, A., and Vitterso, J. (2012). The feelings of extreme risk: Exploring quality and variability in skydiving and BASE jumping. Journal of Sport Behavior, 35, 154–180.

Heyman, I., Mataix-Cols, D., and Fineberg, N. (2006). Obsessive-compulsive disorder. BMJ, 333, 424–429.

Highfield, T., Harrington, S., and Bruns, A. (2013). Twitter as a technology for audiencing and fandom: The #Eurovision phenomenon. Information, Communication and Society, 16, 315–339.

Hills, P., and Argyle, M. (2002). The Oxford Happiness Questionnaire: A compact scale for the measurement of psychological well-being. Personality and Individual Differences, 33, 1073–1082.

Holbrook, M., and Schindler, R. (2003). Nostalgic bonding: Exploring the role of nostalgia in the consumption experience. Journal of Consumer Behaviour, 3, 107–127.

Hollenbeck, J., Klein, H., O'Leary, A., and Wright, P. (1989). Investigation of the construct validity of a self-report measure of goal commitment. Journal of Applied Psychology, 74, 951–956.

A Horse Race Without a Horse: How Modern Trail Ultramarathoning Was Invented by Karen Given, Only a Game, June 28, 2019.

Hotel Scents. Website. https://www.hotelscents.com (accessed May 21, 2023).

Howarth, R. (2011). Concepts and controversies in grief and loss. Journal of Mental Health Counseling, 33, 4–10.

How Gaming Became a Form of Meditation by Kate Spicer, BBC Culture, April 13, 2020.

Hurt, H., Joseph, K., and Cook, C. (1977). Scales for the measurement of innovativeness. Human Communication Research, 4, 58–65.

Hurt, H., and Teigen, C. (1977). The development of a measure of perceived organizational innovativeness in B. Ruben (ed.), Communication Yearbook I (377–385). New Brunswick, NJ: Transaction Books.

Huta, V., and Ryan, R. (2010). Pursuing pleasure or virtue: The differential and overlapping well-being benefits of hedonic and eudaimonic motives. Journal of Happiness Studies, 11, 735–762.

INROADS. Website. https://www.inroads.org (accessed November 25, 2021).

International Association of Amusement Parks and Attractions North America Fixed-Site Amusement Ride Injury Survey, National Safety Council, August 2022.

Is Chocolate Good for You?, Legacy Chocolates Blog, March 7, 2023.

I Was Addicted to Drugs, Now I'm Addicted to Running by Hannah Price and Sophie Haydock, BBC Three, June 17, 2019.

Iyer, G., Blut, M., Xiao, S., and Grewal, D. (2020). Impulse buying: A meta-analytic review. Journal of the Academy of Marketing Science, 48, 384–404.

Jackson, S., and Marsh, H. (1996). Development and validation of a scale to measure optimal experience: The flow state scale. Journal of Sport and Exercise Psychology, 18, 17–35.

Jindra, M. (1994). Star Trek fandom as a religious phenomenon. Sociology of Religion, 55, 27–51.

John, O., and Srivastava, S. (1999). The big five trait taxonomy: History, measurement, and theoretical perspectives in L. Pervin and O. John (eds.), Handbook of Personality: Theory and Research (2nd ed., 102–138). New York: Guilford Press.

Johnson, J., Keiser, H., Skarin, E., and Ross, S. (2014). The dispositional flow scale-2 as a measure of autotelic personality: An examination of criterion-related validity. Journal of Personality Assessment, 96, 1–6.

Jones, A., and Crandall, R. (1986). Validation of a short index of self-actualization. Personality and Social Psychology Bulletin, 12, 63–73.

Kanarek, R., D'Anci, K., Jurdak, N., and Mathes, W. (2009). Running and addiction: Precipitated withdrawal in a rat model of activity-based anorexia. Behavioral Neuroscience, 123, 905.

Kardefelt-Winther, D. (2014). The moderating role of psychological well-being on the relationship between escapism and excessive online gaming. Computers in Human Behavior, 38, 68–74.

Kashdan, T., Gallagher, M., Silvia, P., Winterstein, B., Breen, W., Terhar, D., and Steger, M. (2009). The Curiosity and Exploration Inventory-II: Development, factor structure, and psychometrics. Journal of Research in Personality, 43, 987–998.

Kashdan, T., Rose, P., and Fincham, F. (2004). Curiosity and exploration: Facilitating positive subjective experiences and personal growth opportunities. Journal of Personality Assessment, 82, 291–305.

Kasser, T., and Ryan, R. (1993). A dark side of the American dream: Correlates of financial success as a central life aspiration. Journal of Personality and Social Psychology, 65, 410–422.

Kilroy-Marac, K. (2018). An order of distinction (or, how to tell a collection from a hoard). Journal of Material Culture, 23, 20–38.

Knechtle, B., and Nikolaidis, P. (2018). Physiology and pathophysiology in ultramarathon running. Frontiers in Physiology, 9, 634.

Knijnik, J., and Newson, M. (2021). "Tribalism" identity fusion and football fandom in Australia: The case of Western Sydney. Soccer and Society, 22, 248–265.

Kochen, E., Jenken, F., Boelen, P., Deben, L., Fahner, J., van den Hoogen, A., Teunissen, S., Geleijns, K., and Kars, M. (2020). When a child dies: A systematic review of well-defined parent-focused bereavement interventions and their alignment with grief and loss theories. BMC Palliative Care, 19, 1–22.

Kouali, D., Hall, C., and Pope, P. (2020). Measuring eudaimonic wellbeing in sport: Validation of the Eudaimonic Wellbeing in Sport Scale. International Journal of Wellbeing, 10, 93–106.

Kuo, C., Wu, L., Ye, P., Laksari, K., Camarillo, D., and Kuhl, E. (2017). Pilot findings on brain displacements and deformations during roller coaster rides. Journal of Neurotrauma, 34, 3198–3205.

Kyle, G., Absher, J., Norman, W., Hammitt, W., and Jodice, L. (2007). A modified involvement scale. Leisure Studies, 26, 399–427.

Labrecque, L., Krishen, A., and Grzeskowiak, S. (2011). Exploring social motivations for brand loyalty: Conformity versus escapism. Journal of Brand Management, 18, 457–472.

Lalli, M. (1992). Urban-related identity: Theory, measurement, and empirical findings. Journal of Environmental Psychology, 12, 285–303.

Leach, C., Van Zomeren, M., Zebel, S., Vliek, M., Pennekamp, S., Doosje, B., Ouwerkerk, J., and Spears, R. (2008). Group-level self-definition and self-investment: A hierarchical (multicomponent) model of in-group identification. Journal of Personality and Social Psychology, 95, 144–165.

Leadville Trail 100 Run. Athlete Guide. https://www.leadvilleraceseries.com/wp-content/uploads/2019/08/Leadville-Athlete-Guide-100-RUN-Read-Only.pdf (accessed August 17, 2019).

Legacy Chocolates. Website. https://legacychocolates.com (accessed May 2, 2023).

Lengieza, M., Hunt, C., and Swim, J. (2019). Measuring eudaimonic travel experiences. Annals of Tourism Research, 74, 195–197.

Lloyd, S., Schmidt, U., Khondoker, M., and Tchanturia, K. (2015). Can psychological interventions reduce perfectionism? A systematic review and meta-analysis. Behavioural and Cognitive Psychotherapy, 43, 705–731.

Lox, C., Jackson, S., Tuholski, S., Wasley, D., and Treasure, D. (2000). Revisiting the measurement of exercise-induced feeling states: The physical activity affect scales (PAAS).
Measurement in Physical Education and Exercise Science, 4, 79–95.

Luhtanen, R., and Crocker, J. (1992). A collective self-esteem scale: Self-evaluation of one's social identity. Personality and Social Psychology Bulletin, 18, 302–318.

Lukas, A., Sasvari, P., Varga, B., and Mayer, K. (2019). Exercise addiction and its related factors
in amateur runners. Journal of Behavioral Addictions, 8, 343–349.

Luomala, H., and Laaksonen, M. (1999). A qualitative exploration of mood-regulatory self-gift
behaviors. Journal of Economic Psychology, 20, 147–182.

Lyubomirsky, S., and Lepper, H. (1999). A measure of subjective happiness: Preliminary reliability and construct validation. Social Indicators Research, 46, 137–155.

Mackenzie, S. (2013). Beyond thrill-seeking: Exploring multiple motives for adventure participation. Journal of Outdoor Recreation, Education, and Leadership, 5, 136–139.

Maltby, J., Giles, D., Barber, L., and McCutcheon, L. (2005). Intense-personal celebrity worship and body image: Evidence of a link among female adolescents. British Journal of Health
Psychology, 10, 17–32.

Manea, M., Milea, B., and Campean, A. (2018). Problematic exercise: A new behavioral addiction. Civilization and Sport, 19, 37–44.

Marawa the Amazing: How One Woman with 200 Hula Hoops Became a Teen Girl Guru by
Jane Howard, Guardian, February 21, 2019.

Markstrom, C., Sabino, V., Turner, B., and Berman, R. (1997). The Psychosocial Inventory of
Ego Strengths: Development and assessment of a new Eriksonian measure. Journal of Youth
and Adolescence, 26, 705–762.

Martin, A., and Marsh, H. (2003). Fear of failure: Friend or foe? Australian Psychologist,
38, 31–38.

Martinelli, M., Chasson, G., Wetterneck, C., and Hart, J. (2014). Perfectionism dimensions
as predictors of symptom dimensions of obsessive-compulsive disorder. Bulletin of the
Menninger Clinic, 78, 140–159.

Mataix-Cols, D., Billotti, D., de la Cruz, L., and Nordsletten, A. (2013). The London field trial
for hoarding disorder. Psychological Medicine, 43, 837–847.

Mattie, P., and Monroe-Chandler, K. (2012). Examining the relationship between mental
toughness and imagery use. Journal of Applied Sport Psychology, 24, 144–156.

McCutcheon, L., Lange, R., and Houran, J. (2002). Conceptualization and measurement of celebrity worship. British Journal of Psychology, 93, 67–87.

McDougall, C. (2009). Born to Run. New York: Vintage Books.

McGregor, H., and Elliot, A. (2005). The shame of failure: Examining the link between fear of
failure and shame. Personality and Social Psychology Bulletin, 31, 218–231.

McKenzie, S., McMahon, B., Verlaat, I., and Snow, S. (2015). Collecting in an urban context: Relationships between collections and space in the home. Australian Journal of Popular
Culture, 4, 15–27.

McMillan, D., and Chablis, D. (1986). Sense of community: A definition and theory. Journal of
Community Psychology, 14, 6–23.

Meier, B., Noll, S., and Molokwu, O. (2017). The sweet life: The effect of mindful chocolate consumption on mood. Appetite, 108, 21–27.

Merchant, A., LaTour, K., Ford, J., and Latour, M. (2013). How strong is the pull of the past?
Measuring personal nostalgia evoked by advertising. Journal of Advertising Research, 53,
150–165.

Merriam-Webster. Fanatic definition. https://www.merriam-webster.com/dictionary/fanatic
(accessed April 19, 2023).

Minds Run Free by Christian Jarrett and Ella Rhodes, Psychologist, May 2017.

Minnesota Force. Website. https://www.minnesotaforce.wordpress.com (accessed May 18, 2023).

Mountaineer Viridiana Alvarez Chavez of Mexico Snags Guinness World Records Title by Stacey Lastoe, CNN, August 25, 2020.

Mroczek, D., and Kolarz, C. (1998). The effect of age on positive and negative affect: A developmental perspective on happiness. Journal of Personality and Social Psychology, 75, 1333–1349.

Mulvihill, A. (2020). Action Park. New York: Penguin Books.

Mutterlein, J. (2018). The three pillars of virtual reality? Investigating the roles of immersion, presence, and interactivity. Conference: 51st Hawaii International Conference on System Sciences. Proceedings of the University of Hawaii at Manoa 2018.

My Disabled Son's Amazing Gaming Life in the World of Warcraft by Vicky Schaubert, BBC News, February 7, 2019.

Neria, Y., and Litz, B. (2004). Bereavement by traumatic means: The complex synergy of trauma and grief. Journal of Loss Trauma, 9, 73–87.

Newman, D., Sachs, M., Stone, A., and Schwarz, N. (2020). Nostalgia and well-being in daily life: An ecological validity perspective. Journal of Personality and Social Psychology, 188, 325–347.

Norbury, A., and Husain, M. (2015). Sensation-seeking: Dopaminergic modulation and risk for psychopathology. Behavioral Brain Research, 288, 79–93.

Nordsletten, A., and Mataix-Cols, D. (2012). Hoarding versus collecting: Where does pathology diverge from play? Clinical Psychology Review, 32, 165–176.

Nørfelt, A., Kock, F., Karpen, I., and Josiassen, A. (2023). Pleasure through pain: An empirical examination of benign masochism in tourism. Journal of Travel Research, 62, 448–468.

Novack, M. (2010). Rooms of shame: Senior move manager's perspective on hoarding. Journal of Geriatric Care Management, 20, 21–24.

Obst, P., and White, K. (2005). Three-dimensional strength of identification across group memberships: A confirmatory factor analysis. Self and Identity, 4, 69–80.

Obst, P., Zinkiewicz, L., and Smith, S. (2002a). Sense of community in science fiction fandom, part 1: Understanding sense of community in an international community of interest. Journal of Community Psychology, 30, 87–103.

Obst, P., Zinkiewicz, L., and Smith, S. (2002b). Sense of community in science fiction fandom, part 2: Comparing neighborhood and interest group sense of community. Journal of Community Psychology, 30, 105–117.

Oliver, M., and Bartsch, A. (2010). Appreciation as audience response: Exploring entertainment gratifications beyond hedonism. Human Communication Research, 36, 53–81.

Orazi, D., Mah, K., Derksen, T., and Murray, K. (2023). Consumer escapism: Scale development, validation, and physiological associations. Journal of Business Research, 160, 1–13.

Oreg, S. (2003). Resistance to change: Developing an individual differences measure. Journal of Applied Psychology, 88, 680–693.

Parker, G., Parker, I., and Brotchie, H. (2006). Mood state effects of chocolate. Journal of Affective Disorders, 92, 149–159.

Perugini, M., Gallucci, M., Presaghi, F., and Ercolani, A. (2003). The personal norm of reciprocity. European Journal of Personality, 17, 251–283.

Pierce, G., Sarason, I., and Sarason, B. (1991). General and relationship-based perceptions of social support: Are two constructs better than one? Journal of Personality and Social Psychology, 61, 1028–1039.

Pinna, F., Dell'Osso, B., Nicola, M., Janiri, L., Altamura, A., Carpiniello, B., and Hollander, E. (2015). Behavioural addictions and the transition from DSM-IV-TR to DSM-5. Journal of Psychopathology, 21, 380–389.

Plante, C., Reysen, S., Brooks, T., and Chadborn, D. (2021). CAPE: A multidimensional model of fan interest. Commerce, TX: CAPE Model Research Team.

Postmes, T., Haslam, S., and Jans, L. (2013). A single-item measure of social identification: Reliability, validity, and utility. British Journal of Social Psychology, 52, 597–617.

Prati, G., and Pietrantoni, L. (2009). Optimism, social support, and coping strategies as factors contributing to posttraumatic growth: A meta-analysis. Journal of Loss and Trauma, 14, 364–388.

Raichlen, D., Bharadwaj, P., Fitzhugh, M., Haws, K., Torre, G., Trouard, T., and Alexander, G. (2016). Differences in resting state functional connectivity between young adult endurance athletes and healthy controls. Frontiers in Human Neuroscience, 10, 610.

Raichlen, D., Foster, A., Gerdeman, G., and Seillier, A. (2012). Wired to run: Exercise-induced endocannabinoid signaling in humans and cursorial mammals with implications for the "runner's high." Journal of Experimental Biology, 215, 1331–1336.

Ramakrishnan, S., Robbins, T., and Zmigrod, L. (2022). The Habitual Tendencies Questionnaire: A tool for psychometric individual differences research. Personal Mental Health, 16, 30–46.

Ray, A., Plante, C., Reysen, S., Roberts, S., and Gerbasi, K. (2017). Psychological needs predict fanship and fandom in anime fans. Phoenix Papers, 3, 56–68.

Redaelli, C., and Riva, G. (2011). Flow for presence questionnaire in L. Canetta, C. Redaelli, and M. Flores (eds.), Digital Factory for Human-oriented Production Systems (3–22). London: Springer.

Remke, Stacy. (2013). Insider's Guide to Grief. St. Paul: Lowertown Press.

Reysen, S., and Branscombe, N. (2010). Fanship and fandom: Comparisons between sport fans and non-sport fans. Journal of Sport Behavior, 33, 176–193.

Reysen, S., Plante, C., Roberts, S., and Gerbasi, K. (2015). A social identity perspective of personality differences between fan and non-fan identifies. World Journal of Social Science Research, 2, 91–103.

Rheinberg, F., Vollmeyer, R., and Engeser, S. (2002). The acquisition of the flow experience in J. Stiensmeier-Pelster and F. Rheinberg (eds.), Diagnostics of Motivation and Self-concept (261–279). Göttingen: Hogrefe.

Rimm, S. (2007). What's wrong with perfect? Clinical perspectives on perfectionism and underachievement. Gifted Education International, 23, 246–253.

The Rise and Fall of Rollerblading by Sport History Weekly, August 21, 2022.

The Rise of Anorexia Athletica: I Ran Until I Was Sick and Swam Until I Fainted by India Sturgis, Telegraph, August 15, 2016.

Robitschek, C. (1998). Personal growth initiative: The construct and its measure. Measurement and Evaluation in Counseling and Development, 30, 183–198.

Robitschek, C., Ashton, M., Spering, C., Geiger, N., Byers, D., Schotts, C., and Thoen, M. (2012). Development and psychometric evaluation of the Personal Growth Initiative Scale–II. Journal of Counseling Psychology, 59, 274–278.

Roebuck, G., Fitzgerald, P., Urquhart, D., and Ng, S. (2018). The psychology of ultramarathon runners: A systemic review. Psychology of Sport and Exercise, 37, 43–58.

Roller Skating Museum. The History of Inline Skating. https://www.rollerskatingmuseum.org (accessed February 10, 2022).

Routledge, C., Arndt, J., Sedikides, C., and Wildschut, T. (2008). A blast from the past: The terror management function of nostalgia. Journal of Experimental Social Psychology, 44, 132–140.

Rozin, P., Guillot, L., Fincher, K., and Rozin, A. (2013). Glad to be sad, and other examples of benign masochism. Judgment and Decision Making, 8, 439–447.

Ryff, C. (1989). Happiness is everything, or is it? Explorations on the meaning of psychological well-being. Journal of Personality and Social Psychology, 57, 1069–1081.

Saltz, E. (2010). Hoarding and elders: Current trends, dilemmas, and solutions. Journal of Geriatric Care Management, 20, 4–9.

Schindler, R., and Holbrook, M. (2003). Nostalgia for early experience as a determinant of consumer preferences. Psychology and Marketing, 20, 275–302.

Schroder, K., Ollis, C., and Davies, S. (2013). Habitual self-control: A brief measure of persistent goal pursuit. European Journal of Personality, 27, 82–95.

Schroy, C. (2016). Different motivations as predictors of psychological connection to fan interest and fan groups in anime, furry, and fantasy sport fandoms. Phoenix Papers, 2, 148–167.

Scott Olson Interview: Skyride, Rollerblade, Shark Tank, More by Lauren Ashburn, Daily Beast, July 13, 2017.

Seligman, M., Steen, T., Park, N., and Peterson, C. (2005). Positive psychology progress: Empirical validation of interventions. American Psychologist, 60, 410–421.

Shallow Water Blackout Prevention. Website. https://www.shallowwaterblackoutprevention. org (accessed January 6, 2022).

Shelley, M. (1818). Frankenstein. London: Lackington, Hughes, Harding, Major and Jones.

Shoham, A., Rose, G., and Kahle, L. (1999). Practitioners of risky sports: A quantitative study. Journal of Business Research, 47, 237–251.

Sierra, J., and McQuitty, S. (2007). Attitudes and emotions as determinants of nostalgia purchases: An application of social identity theory. Journal of Marketing Theory and Practice, 15, 99–112.

Siricharoen, W. (2019). The effect of virtual reality as a form of escapism. Conference: International Conference on Information Resources Management. Proceedings of the Association for Information Systems 2019.

Six Flags. Website. https://www.sixflags.com/greatamerica/attractions/Goliath (accessed October 5, 2022).

Slochower, J., Kaplan, S., and Mann, L. (1981). The effects of life stress and weight on mood and eating. Appetite, 2, 115–125.

Smith, B., Dalen, J., Wiggins, K., Tooley, E., Christopher, P., and Bernard, J. (2008). The Brief Resilience Scale: Assessing the ability to bounce back. International Journal of Behavioral Medicine, 15, 194–200.

Smith, D., and Meaney, D. (2002). Roller coasters, G forces, and brain trauma: On the wrong track? Journal of Neurotrauma, 19, 1117–1120.

Smith, R., Karaman, M., Balkin, R., and Talwar, S. (2019). Psychometric properties and factor analyses of the achievement motivation measure. British Journal of Guidance and Counselling, 48, 1–13.

Soane. Our History. https://www.Soane.org (accessed September 21, 2021).

Soda Pop Stop. Website. https://www.sodapopstop.com (accessed February 5, 2023).

Spaaij, R. (2008). Men like us, boys like them: Violence, masculinity, and collective identity in football hooliganism. Journal of Sport and Social Issues, 32, 369–392.

Spence, C., Corujo, A., and Youssef, J. (2019). Cotton candy: A gastrophysical investigation. International Journal of Gastronomy and Food Science, 16, 100146.

Sri Chinmoy Self-Transcendence: The 3,100-mile Race around New York by Justin Goulding, BBC Sport, June 21, 2019.

Stavropoulos, V. (2019). My avatar, my self: Exploring the world of online gaming and avatar-related wellbeing. InPsych, 41, 43–48.

Steger, M., Frazier, P., Oishi, S., and Kaler, M. (2006). The meaning in life questionnaire: Assessing the presence of and search for meaning in life. Journal of Counseling Psychology, 53, 80–93.

Stenseng, F., Falch-Madsen, J., and Hygen, B. (2021). Are there two types of escapism? Exploring a dualistic model of escapism in digital gaming and online streaming. Psychology of Popular Media, 10, 319–329.

Stenseng, F., Rise, J., and Kraft, P. (2012). Activity engagement as escape from self: The role of self-suppression and self-expansion. Leisure Science, 34, 19–38.

Stephenson, N. (1992). Snow Crash. New York: Bantam Books.

Stoeber, J., and Otto, K. (2006). Positive conceptions of perfectionism: Approaches, evidence, challenges. Personality and Social Psychology Review, 10, 295–319.

Stoll, O. (2019). Peak performance, the runner's high, and flow in M. H. Anshel (ed.), APA Handbook of Sport and Exercise Psychology, vol 2: Exercise Psychology.

Stroebe, M., and Schut, H. (1999). The dual process model of coping with bereavement: Rationale and description. Death Studies, 23, 197–224.

Szabo, A., Mesko, A., Caputo, A., and Gill, E. (1998). Examination of exercise-induced feeling states in four modes of exercise. International Journal of Sport Psychology, 29, 376–390.

Take Note: Dr. Tashel Bordere on Suffocated Grief by Lindsey Whissel Fenton, WPSU, July 17, 2020.

Tedeschi, R., and Calhoun, L. (2004). Posttraumatic growth: A new perspective on psychotraumatology. Psychiatric Times, 21, 58–60.

Thayer, R. (1989). The Biopschology of Mood and Arousal. New York: Oxford University Press.

Tolstikova, K., Fleming, S., and Chartier, B. (2005). Grief, complicated grief, and trauma: The role of the search for meaning, impaired self-reference, and death anxiety. Illness, Crisis and Loss, 13, 293–313.

Traveling While Black: Behind the Eye-Opening VR Documentary on Racism in America by Dream McClinton, Guardian, September 3, 2019.

Ultimate Limit of Human Endurance Found by James Gallagher, BBC News, June 6, 2019.

Vallerand, R. (2012). The role of passion in sustainable psychological well-being. Psychology of Well-Being: Theory, Research, and Practice, 2, 3–21.

Vallerand, R., Blanchard, C., Mageau, G., Koestner, R., Ratelle, C., Gangné, M., and Marsolais, J. (2003). Les passions de l'âme: On obsessive and harmonious passion. Journal of Personality and Social Psychology, 85, 756–767.

VandeWalle, D., Cron, W., and Slocum, J., Jr. (2001). The role of goal orientation following performance feedback. Journal of Applied Psychology, 86, 629–640.

Verplanken, B., and Sato, A. (2011). The psychology of impulse buying: An integrative self-regulation approach. Journal of Consumer Policy, 34, 197–210.

Vignoles, V., Regalia, C., Manzi, C., Golledge, J., and Scabini, E. (2006). Beyond self-esteem: Influence of multiple motives on identity construction. Journal of Personality and Social Psychology, 90, 308–333.

Vinney, C., Dill-Shackleford, K., Plante, C., and Bartsch, A. (2019). Development and validation of a measure of popular media fan identity and its relationship to well-being. Psychology of Popular Media Culture, 8, 296–307.

Virtual Reality Society. Virtuality—A New Reality of Promise, Two Decades Too Soon. https://www.vrs.org.uk/dr-jonathan-walden-virtuality-new-reality-promise-two-decades-soon (accessed January 8, 2021).

Visual, WellnessVR Evaluation Study, 2018.

Vohs, K., and Faber, R. (2007). Spent resources: Self-regulatory resource availability affects impulse buying. Journal of Consumer Research, 23, 537–547.

Vuorre, M., Johannes, N., Magnusson, K., and Przybylski, A. (2022). Time spent playing video games is unlikely to impact well-being. Royal Society Open Science, 9 (7).

Walach, H., Buchheld, N., Buttenmüller, V., Kleinknecht, N., and Schmidt, S. (2006). Measuring mindfulness: The Freiburg Mindfulness Inventory (FMI). Journal of Personality and Individual Differences, 40, 1543–1555.

Wan, D., Hackathorn, J., and Sherman, M. (2017). Testing the team identification-social psychological health model: Mediational relationships among team identification, sport fandom, sense of belonging, and meaning in life. Group Dynamics: Theory, Research, and Practice, 21, 94–107.

Wang, X., Tat Keh, H., and Chao, C. (2018). Nostalgia and consumer preference for indulgent foods: The role of social connectedness. International Journal of Consumer Studies, 42, 316–326.

Warmelink, H., Harteveld, C., and Mayer, I. (2009). Press enter or escape to play: Deconstructing escapism in multiplayer gaming. Conference: Breaking New Ground: Innovation in Games, Play, Practice and Theory. Proceedings of DiGRA 2009.

Waterman, A. (2003). Predicting the subjective experience of intrinsic motivation: The roles of self-determination, the balance of challenges and skills, and self-realization values. Personality and Social Psychology Bulletin, 29, 1447–1458.

Waterman, A., Schwartz, S., Zamboanga, B., Ravert, R., Williams, M., Agocha, V., Kim, S., and Donnellan, M. (2010). The questionnaire for eudaimonic well-being: Psychometric properties, demographic comparisons, and evidence of validity. Journal of Positive Psychology, 5, 41–61.

Watson, D., and Clark, L. (1988). Development and validation of brief measures of positive and negative affect: The PANAS scales. Journal of Personality and Social Psychology, 54, 1063–1070.

Watson, D., and Clark, L. (1994). The PANAS-X: Manual for the positive and negative affect schedule (expanded form). Iowa Research Online.

Weiss, R., Edgerton, N., and Palmer, S. (2017). The SPACE coaching model: An integrative tool for coach therapists. Coaching Today, October, 12–17.

Weissinger, E., and Bandalos, D. (1995). Development, reliability and validity of a scale to measure intrinsic motivation in leisure. Journal of Leisure Research, 27, 379–400.

What Makes "Real" Chocolate Better, Legacy Chocolates Blog, April 7, 2022.

When She Was Down, "The Next Gen" Beamed Her Up by Ian Spelling, Chicago Tribune, July 30, 1993.

White, S., Lee, Y., Phan, J., Moody, S., and Shirtcliff, E. (2019). Putting the flight in "fight-or-flight": Testosterone reactivity to skydiving is modulated by autonomic activation. Biological Psychology, 143, 93–102.

Why Computer Games Are More Than a Lockdown Distraction by Chris Baraniuk, BBC News, April 12, 2020.

Why You Need to See This VR Documentary "Traveling While Black" by Jennifer Kite-Powell, Forbes, February 25, 2019.

Williams, H., and Palmer, S. (2010). CLARITY: A cognitive behavioural coaching model. Coaching Psychology International, 3, 5–7.

Williams, H., Palmer, S., and O'Connell, B. (2011). Introducing SOLUTION and FOCUS: Two solution focused coaching models. Coaching Psychology International, 4, 6–9.

Wisconsin Man Celebrates Scarfing Down Big Macs Almost Every Day for 50 Years by Antonio Planas, NBC, May 20, 2022.

Xu, Y., Hamid, N., Shepherd, D., Kantono, K., and Spence, C. (2019). Changes in flavour, emotion, and electrophysiological measurements when consuming chocolate ice cream in different eating environments. Food Quality and Preference, 77, 191–205.

Yee, N. (2007). Motivations of play in online games. CyberPsychology and Behavior, 9, 772–775.

Yigit, M. (2020). Consumer mindfulness and impulse buying behavior: Testing moderator effects of hedonic shopping value and mood. Innovative Marketing, 16, 24–36.

Zemeckis, R., and Gale, B. (1985). Back to the Future. Universal Pictures.

Zhang, H., Chen, F., Chen, C., and Schlegel, R. (2018). Personal aspirations, person-environment fit, meaning in work, and meaning in life: A moderated mediation model. Journal of Happiness Studies, 20, 1–17.

Zhou, X., van Tilburg, W., Mei, D., Wildschut, T., and Sedikides, C. (2019). Hungering for the past: Nostalgic food labels increase purchase intentions and actual consumption. Appetite, 140, 151–158.

Index

For the benefit of digital users, indexed terms that span two pages (e.g., 52–53) may, on occasion, appear on only one of those pages.

Figures are indicated by an italic f following the page number.

Robin (hoarder), 126–27
Rocket Bomb Pop soda, 193–94
role-playing
 cosplay, 9–10, 24
 stigma, 26–27
 See also virtual reality gaming
Rollerblade, 134–37
roller coasters and roller coaster enthusiasts,
  160–66
 adrenaline, 162
 Barbara, 160–62, 176–77
 The Beast, 162–63
 Busch Gardens, 161
 Cedar Point, 161
 Elitch Gardens, 161–62
 Giant Dipper, 162–63
 Goliath, 162–66
 Hersheypark, 161
 Himalayan Express, 162
 King's Island, 161
 Mean Streak, 162–63
 Millennium Force, 162
 sense of community, 161–62
 Six Flags, 161
 Superman: Ultimate Flight, 163
 Top Thrill Dragster, 162
 See also amusement parks
Root Beer and Vanilla Bean soda, 193–94
Rose, Randall, 166–67, 170, 172, 173
RowBike, 136–37, 138, 141
Rozin, Paul, 157–58
Running People (Tarahumara tribe), 58

Saltz, Emily, 124
Sato, Ayana, 184–85
Saturday Night Live (SNL), 14
Schaubert, Vicky, 84–85
Schindler, Robert, 190–91
Schut, H., 36–37
sci-fi conventions. *See* fandom and
  conventions
scuba diving, 167
self-awareness, 187
self-compassion
 coping with grief and trauma, 42
 OCD treatment, 151
self-gifts
 alternative psychological anchors, 187–89
 chocolate, 195–98
 instinct for, 189
 nostalgia and, 189–98

retail therapy, 181–85
 soda, 178–81, 191–94
sensation-seeking
 Action Park, 155–57
 benign masochism, 158–59, 176, 203
 cortisol, 159
 dopamine, 158–59
 hedonic stimuli, 158–59, 176
 roller coasters, 157–58, 160–66
 sense of community and, 161–62, 167–68,
  176–77
 testosterone, 159
 See also high-risk sports
sense-making of loss and trauma. *See*
  posttraumatic growth
shallow water (hypoxic) blackout, 37–38, 39
Shatner, WIlliam, 9, 10–11, 14
Shirk, Ken (Cowman), 59–60
Shoham, Aviv, 170
Simon, Kai, 85
Sir John Soane Museum, 114–16, 118–19
skydiving, 159–60, 166–67, 168–72
Skyride, 137–38, 141, 144
Slochower, Joyce, 183
SNL (Saturday Night Live), 14
Snow Crash (game), 89–91
Soane, John, 118
social domain of fanaticism, 202, 204f
 See also fandom and conventions;
  posttraumatic growth
soda
 Coca- Cola, 178
 Dr. Pepper, 178
 Grape Nehi, 189–90
 Moxie, 178, 189–90
 Orange Crush, 189–90
 Pepsin Punch, 178
 Pineapple Orange, 193–94
 Rocket Bomb Pop, 193–94
 Root Beer and Vanilla Bean, 193–94
 Strawberry Daiquiri, 193–94
 See also Blue Sun Soda Shop
SOLUTION coaching model, 187
Spaaij, Ramon, 20
SPACE coaching model, 3nn.8–9
Space Invaders (game), 82–83
Spence, Charles, 194
sports fans, 7, 19–21
Sri Chinmoy Self- Transcendence, 60
StarCon, 8–9
Star Fox (game), 82–83